Islamic Diplomacy in Post-Revolution Iran

Hayat Parviz

CONTENT

CHAPTER I
Introduction

Introduction

Today, the progress of new ideas in international relations -such as critical, normal and developing theories and post-modern viewpoints- emphasize on cultural elements in forming political relationships, the effect of religion component on international relations directions In line with human's happiness. New thinkers and theorists of international relations have focused much on norms, thus we have observed the effect of religion components in some of international relations areas, with rise of religious and spiritual movements in some of regions of the world along with more needs for establishment of peace, justice the importance of religion has been increased, so that today utilizing the religion element and spirituality and understanding political and international changes are more consistent with reality.

In this respect of religion on social movements in the third world, globalization, as well as the effect on international disputes and international cooperation's and its positions in establishment of the world security and peace challenging the current order by religion teaching, standing against totalitarianism and dominance of western civilization and its effect on international policy, necessitate the implementation of theology in current international relation policy.

Considering current in international relations theories especially after the cold war, it needs that the role and position of religion in international relations direction need to be studied. With Westefalia's hypothesis in international relations and ignoring to the role of religion and philosophy, same western theorists neglected religion interference on international relations.

Islamic Revolution established at 1979 on the basis of Islam and framed as social movement, with emphasis on Islamic value seeking for new version of relation between nations. This revolution is not only considered as great point of Iran's transformations but also in the world. Revival of Islam is the most important result of Islamic Revolution. By this great movement, Islamic world got new dynamic which effect of that could be felt for some years in other Islamic countries.

Returning to purified Islam considers as core thought of all these movement. In fact this revolution rose in time of secularism discussions.

Though from the theoretical point of view returning to religion and its importance in international regime posed at 1990 but Islamic republic took benefit of that in practice as main changeable in domestic and international and foreign policy orientation. Islamic republic of Iran is the first or might said the only religious revolution in modern international regime, thus in addition to imposing the result of one revolution to current international order, added the requirements of religion to international regime.

Nevertheless Islamic republic of Iran considered as a pattern and pioneer in adding Islam to international regime and this issue follows some results that should pay attention to foreign policy of Iran doesn't known only as foreign policy of this country but considered beside that foreign policy of Islamic government. This investigation function of Islam in the sphere of international relations theorists will be explained. As well as the role of Islam as a key variable in the Islamic Republic of Iran after the Islamic Revolution of Iran's foreign policy and in the creation international relations will be study based on the role of Islamic doctrines.

Selection of an approach and theory for foreign policy analysis is considered as one of the important issues. There is also a need for the analysis of foreign policy of the Islamic Republic of Iran. Therefore, the study will try to analyze the foreign policy of the Islamic Republic of Iran using the dominant theories in international relations. Although it cannot ignore the ideas of international relations to analyze the foreign policy of the Islamic Republic of Iran, one can state that neither of the theories can independently analyze the foreign policy of the Republic Islamic Iran. The reason for this is that, firstly, all theories and discourses of the formulation are based on the understanding of the societies and realities of the countries, and therefore they cannot be ignored. Secondly, the nature of the Iranian revolution is due to Islamism, and any theory cannot be accepted without consideration of Islamic principles and be under the burden of it.

Religion is one of the important factors in Iran, which has the potential to control political authority, the governing system, and even daily life of the public unlike other countries in today's world. In order to understand what is going on in Iran requires knowing how the state perceives and interprets religion. In other words, it does not mean there is one Islamic religion and each Muslim country applies it, of course there is one Islam, but each state interprets it differently, just as Judaism is interpreted differently by the state of Israel in the West Asian region. To stand far from oriental perspective Iran interprets Islam from its own point of view; Iran's aspect does not resemble any other Muslim country in the region. It has idiosyncratic state behaviour patterns both in domestic and foreign affairs. Although, the Islamic Republic of Iran has a rooted past, the clergy does not like West backed *Shah* (Muhammad Reza Pahlavi) and the Iran Islamic Revolution occurred in 1979. The 1979 revolution brought a new vision, new understanding about religion and differentiation in both domestic and foreign politics. The 1979 Iran Islamic Revolution sharpened the state foreign policy and brought a totally different governing elite, regime, and governing system, which is beyond comparison with other states in the region and even in the world. Khomeini was the leader and prime mover of the 1979 Islamic Revolution, who brought a system which is called *velayat-e faqih* (Guardianship of Islamic Jurists), based on Islamic law

Despite the numerous views on international relations theory, there is no general and universal theory that can analyze foreign policy of countries. The foreign policy of the Islamic Republic of Iran is based on some principles based on religious teachings and therefore, for the analysis of the foreign policy of the Islamic Republic of Iran based on the views of international relations, it is not absolute rejection nor absolute acceptance, but the choice of a third way different from the politics of all systems, revolutions and governments. Understanding the foreign policy of the Islamic Republic of Iran is crucial for understanding its nature and ontology. It is very important to understand the nature of the actor, the central scholar, the orbital task of collecting between dignity and wisdom in making decisions, as well as paying attention to immaterial matters in the analysis and understanding of Iran's foreign policy.

Religion is expressed as a set of rules, regulations, and laws; these rules are sent by God himself to place a set of rules, which people need to obey. Islam is an option, and a choice of life style and side. Islam is directly related to life and politics; they both nest with one another since the birth of Islam. Islam is closely related to the complete life of Muslims. Religious authority is an important figure for political life as well. Islam offers a life style, which Muslims need to live by, by adhering to the law of God (*Sharia*). People need to desire and make effort to live under certain rules.

Within this context, political Islam became a strong and effective phenomenon throughout the world. Although, Islam has been universally accepted as the faith of the Muslims, nevertheless as in any other religion or way of life, there are numerous understandings and interpretations. There is not one common legitimate understanding of the given set of rules; everyone may understand these written rules or recommendations from their own point of views. Religion has been understood and interpreted in myriad forms throughout history. Textual meaning is interpreted in different ways by different communities. This has caused the differentiation of individual faith, which has later divided people into separated communities according to beliefs. Communities formed their identities, and as a natural result of the developments, state systems were created, and religion played a preliminary role for the politics of the states. States are governed under the strong effect of religion; religion and particularly Islam shaped the politics of states throughout history. Although some theories of international relations may have the ability to analyze some of the foreign policy issues in the periods of the history of foreign policy of the Islamic Republic of Iran after the revolution, but there is no possibility for complete analysis because of the foreign policy difference of the Islamic Republic of Iran. Therefore, in order to analyze the foreign policy of the Islamic Republic of Iran, it is necessary to state that it is to answer all the issues of foreign policy of the Islamic Republic of Iran.

Concepts of Islamic Republic:

The Islamic Republic is composed of two words of the republic and of Islam. In other words, the system of the Islamic Republic of Iran is the name of the Iranian government, which is based on Republican rule and Islamism in accordance with its constitution.[1] Republican is the people's vote and will in the administration of

---

[1] Arasta, Mohammad Javad, "*A look at the analytical foundations of the Islamic Republic of Iran*" *reflections on political jurisprudence and jurisprudential principles of the constitution of the Islamic Republic of Iran*, Qom, Bostan-e ketab Publishing, 2012, p. 84.

the affairs of the country, and Islamism means conforming to the laws of Islam.[2] In other words, the republic means that the sovereignty is in the hands of the people. The word Republic defines the form of government and the Islamic word defines the content of the rule. From the content of conforming to laws and decisions based on the religion of religious teachings,[3] The Islamic Republic's thought with the efforts and initiative of Imam Khomeini, after the victory of the Islamic Revolution, was institutionalized during the referendum on July 12, 1979, with 98.2 percent of the votes cast in Iran's political life and political life, and the Iranian regime's model of Islamic Republic changed its form and content.

The Islamic Republic, as a new concept of the Islamic state, which was pursued by Imam Khomeini, was not only a completely new and unknown western state but also an inseparable, specific, and indivisible concept from the angle of the Islamic tradition. In this regard, when Imam Khomeini is asked to compare the concept of "Islamic Republic" with other existing governments in today and in the past, they emphasize, without mentioning the similarity, that "the Islamic Republic ... when it comes to acting, The world will know what it is.[4]

The concept of revolution

The term "revolution" was originally from the terminology of the science of astronomy, which means the rotation of the planet and the return of the planets to the first place, but today it is used in various issues such as industrial revolution, social, intellectual, and so on.[5] In the definition of the revolution, the martyr Motahhari stated that the revolution is the upheaval and rebellion that people make against the existing ruling system to create a desirable state of affairs.[6] There is

[2] Seyyed Mohammad, Hashemi, *"Basic Law of the Islamic Republic of Iran,"* Tehran, Mizan Publishing, 2008, p. 35.

[3] "http://rc.majlis.ir/fa/content/iran_constitution

[4] Mohsen Askarian, "*Examining the Concept of the Islamic Republic*" in the words of Imam Khomeini, Tabnak site, (http://www.tabnak.ir/fa/news/235259)

[5] Hannah Arendt, *"Revolution"*, Translated by Ezatollah Fouladvand, Tehran, Kharazmi publishing, 1982, p. 36.

[6] Motahari, Morteza, *"Future of the Islamic Revolution"*, Tehran, Sadra Publication, 2008, p. 59.

another definition of the revolution, and that the revolution of fundamental change in all social, moral, economic, legal and, in particular, political, areas, has remained firmly established before the revolution, and these changes are always suppressed by the overthrow of the ruling political system It comes with less calm and often synchronizes with violent, and destructive work.[7]

The word "revolution" in the field of human and social sciences has also been used in two other ways: one means the rapid, intense and radical transformation that occurs as a result of the uprising of the public in the political situation of society and as a result of a political, legal and economic system. It gives itself another system, and the other means a radical and non-political transformation that takes place slowly and without violence. Like the scientific, industrial, Cultural Revolution... The common denominators the two meanings of the term revolution are the same as a fundamental, general change.[8]

The Islamic Revolution of Iran is considered one of the great revolutions, in addition to having the basic characteristics of a revolution such as being popular, deep dissatisfaction with the status quo and the development of a revolutionary spirit among the masses of the people, has caused a change in the basis and type of government, as well as Led to a change in decision making in the political and social arena. The Islamic revolution of Iran is a product of political Islam; it is the significant manifestation against a Eurocentric world order. Islam challenges the theory of nationalism with the concept of the *ummah*. Islam attempts to go beyond ethnicity because a major tenant in Islam is that establishing a good government or making successful politics cannot be achieved healthily via the idea of tribalism and blood ties. Islam has an institutional identity in the international arena, and it is beyond the policies and actions of individual states, leaders, and movements. Islam tries to go beyond ethnicity through the idea of universal equality of Muslims. This vision is called the conscience of the *"ummah"*. Thereby, the ideal of the *ummah* exceeds the ideal of the nation state, and spiritual unity is a fixed goal. The *ummah*

---

[7] Abdulhamid Abolmohammad, *"the Principles of Politics,"* Tehran, Toos Publishing, 1997, p. 364.

[8] Giddens, Anthony, *"Sociology,"* Translated by Manouchehr Saboori, Tehran, Nashr-e-Ney Publishing, 2000, p. 660.

is blessed by God but a national state is a human creation; it has no such kind of spiritual value. In today's world, Islamists try to spread and enlarge the orbit of consciousness of the *ummah* through international communication channels and electronic networks (*virtual ummah*).

The word revolution in this research, given its unique characteristics, is one of the most distinct revolutions in the world and gives rise to a new concept of revolution. Some of these qualities include: enjoying the Islamic nature, based on culture and belief, and the rule of monotheistic culture rather than ontological and authoritarian culture.[9] Therefore, this revolution has the following characteristics: (a) Resistance to Western domination, (b) Promoting freedom, independence, anti-tyranny and colonialism, and reviving the spirit of struggle and striving for a better future,(c) reviving the political culture based on the Quran, and the need for a return to pure Islam (peace is upon him), (d) The reconstruction of Islamic civilization.

The Basics of Islam

The basics mean the foundation and whatever it takes on it and relying on it. The foundations are those elements and religious guidelines that are in the form of principles and affairs in one field, and have the following aspects for the rest of the elements, and they explain them in a way. These elements, such as the "must" cases, have a credible aspect and, in fact, are the results of the Islamic worldview.[10]

It is always a major determinant of decision-making, the foundations and intellectual structure, and the beliefs of the government of men and politicians.[11] The types of governments and the bases of their legitimacy differentiate the basis and manner of their foreign policy behaviour, as their domestic politics. . There are different views on legitimacy in the Islamic state (such as the Islamic Republic of

---

[9] Mozaffari, Ayat, "*Political Thought of the Supreme Leader (Ayatollah Khamenei),*" Tehran, Zamzam Hedayat Publishing, 2008, p. 222.

[10] Hussein ibn Muhammad, Raghib Isfahani, "*Mofradat al-Alfaze al-Quran,*" Beirut, Dar al-Shamieh publishing, 2004, P. 147.

[11] Qavam, Seyyed Abdolali, Anatomy of the Interactions of the Political System and National Interest, Tehran, Foreign Policy Magazine, Eighth, 1994, P. 3.

Iran). As it affects domestic decision-making, it can also form the basis of separate theories in foreign policy.[12]

In general, Islamic foundations can be divided into three categories. First: Principles such as monotheism, prophecy and justice. Second: the prophecy of religion, like the religious duties like prayer, fasting, Hajj, third: ethics: like mutual respect to each other.

Foreign Policy Indications of Pre-Revolutionary Period

The Muhammad Reza Shah period is important in understanding the causes of the revolution. The last *Shah* of the monarchical rule was Muhammad Reza who took the throne after the abdication of his father Reza *Shah*. Muhammad Reza continued the policy of authoritarian modernization while being pro-Western as his father. The last *Shah* had problems with his Prime Minister Mohammad Mossaddeqh who was a very nationalist person and attempted to nationalize Iran's oil industry. Mossaddeqh and general protests about the oil nationalization forced the *Shah* to leave the country and with the help of British and U.S. intelligence services, he overthrew the Mossadeq and the *shah* returned to power in 1953. The sudden increase on the oil revenue of Iran in 1974 paved the way for transformation, and the Iranian economy transformed from being an agricultural and commerce based economy to a one-product oil based one. Hence the rentier (deriving substantial portion of its national revenues from the oil rent) nature of the Iranian economy easily erased the bonds linking the state to civil society. The state viewed itself as independent so the demands of the public were undermined.

Mohammad Reza Shah's policies did not satisfy the people of Iran. There were promises but Reza *Shah* did not keep to his word. Political and economic decentralization failed. Despotism, corruption, imprisonment, terrorization and repression increased. Moreover, Iran's oil revenue increased because of the Arab-Israeli wars. Iran had a very good economy in 1975, and the *Shah* had the largest navy in the Persian Gulf, the largest air force in Western Asia, and one of the largest armies in the world. However, besides the economic well-being of the country, there was injustice and a large gap between the rich and poor.

---

[12] Haghighat , Seyyed Sadegh, *"Principles and Objectives of Foreign Policy of the Islamic State,"* Qom, Islamic Center of Science and Culture press ,2006, P. 27.

Government strategy was to give welfare to the elites who wanted to build companies, factories and businesses. Iran had one of the most unequal income distributions of the time. The wealth of the state may be best explained in that there was no public transportation service, but only private cars; there was no emphasis on public health and public goods in general. Injustice became the main issue for the public.

The concept of foreign policy in Islam

The political relationships between governments have long existed between societies, although the terminology used today is not classical in the classical vocabulary, but in practice, as it was stated, and within the framework of a series of established principles And predetermined relations, to achieve the goals of foreign policy with far-flung countries. If the use of the tool of war or colonialism and the seizure of a land of interest to countries was used nowadays, countries now use the diplomacy tool to communicate with others, and they will benefit from it.[13]

Today, although the geographical boundaries are separating societies, they are, at the same time, linked to a larger society called the international community. This larger community resembles a home that has about **185 rooms**, each of which, under the name of a country, forms international relations and is known as "political units" in the political science literature.[14] Each of these units organized their political affairs in a category called "foreign policy", which was transferred to an organization called the Foreign Ministry.

Foreign policy is primarily about the activities of a country in a foreign environment.[15] In this regard, foreign policy can be defined as a strategy or plan of action that is carried out by decision makers of a country against other countries or

---

[13] Behzadi, Hamid , *"Principles of International Relations and Foreign Policy,"* Tehran, Dehkhoda Publishing, 1994 , p. 9.

[14] Velayati, Aliakbar and others; *"issues in foreign policy"* Tehran, Office of Political and International Studies publishing, 1985, p. 19.

[15] Holsti, K. J, *International Politics: A Framework for Analysis*; New Jersey: Prentice-Hall International, 1982, p. 54.

international organizations to achieve goals that are called national interests of that country. Foreign policy is also a process including specific goals, certain foreign factors depending on the above objectives, and the ability of the country to achieve the desired results, develop a useful strategy, implement the strategy, evaluate and control it.[16]

The term "diplomacy" has a Greek root, which means scrolling. Later this term was referred to the Charter or official document of the ambassadors and envoys of states to other governments. Despite the relative consensus on the notion of diplomacy, several definitions have been proposed, some of which refer to the nature of diplomacy and others to its special function.[17] What is clear from the definition of diplomacy is that diplomacy is of a peaceful nature, and dialogue and dialogue are the hallmark of this, so that establishing peace and peaceful life are the main agenda of this activity and all these activities are in the field of Known as foreign policy. On this basis, diplomacy has been defined and described as a forum for foreign policy management or for the regulation of international relations as well as the resolution of international disputes through peaceful means.[18] In other words, it can be said: "Diplomacy is a means by which foreign policy, by exploiting it, instead of war, reaches its goals through compromise"[19]

One of the most important tools in achieving the goals of foreign policy of countries in various world scenes is the use of diplomacy, which its significance in Islam from the beginning of the mission of the Prophet (PBUH) has been seriously addressed by him. Sending the Ambassador and Representative to the great powers of that time, sending the ambassadors of Islam to promote the people of the land of Hejaz and other areas to the religion of Islam, and various talks and treaties with their tribes and their leaders, all indicate the importance and attention to peaceful

---

[16] Jack C. Plano & Roy Olton, "*the International Relations Dictionary*," Forth Edition, New York: Longman, 1988, p. 78.

[17] Aladpush, Ali and Toutunchian, Alireza, "*Diplomat and Diplomacy* ," Tehran, Office of Political and International Studies publishing, 1993, p. 6.

[18] Qavam, Abdolali, "*Principles of Foreign Policy and International Politics*", Tehran, Samt publishing, 2005, p. 207.

[19] Ashoury, Dariush, *Political Encyclopedia: Dictionary of political terminology and schools*, Tehran, Nashr- e Morvarid Publishing, 2002, P. 270.

diplomacy in Islam and the holy shrine of the Prophet.[20] Therefore, it is necessary to understand the managerial dimensions and political behavior of the Prophet and his secret of success in the Islamic State's foreign relations, In particular, the magnanimous, in spite of many problems, was able to spread Islam beyond the boundaries of the Islamic state through the use of appropriate diplomacy.[21]

It describe diplomacy as the art of negotiation or describe it as an instrumental tool for achieving goals, this definition will be true for the active diplomacy of the Prophet Muhammad (peace is upon him). The privilege of the diplomacy of the Prophet of Islam is that he relies on social laws and realistic worldviews, and human values and principles, and is based on the principles and rules that come from the revelation and the well-known principles of reason.[22]

Islamic diplomacy is based on the principles that govern Islamic State foreign policy. And the Prophet (peace be upon him) as the head of government at the dawn of Islam and his deputies and ambassadors to achieve the basic goals based on Islam, obeyed those principles. The prophet of Islam (PBUH), in his relations with tribes, relatives, nations and heads of states, considers the people the main owners of the right to establish diplomatic relations. He sees these relationships not in the sense of compromise, but as a means of reaching constructive agreements, and absolutely does not replace any diplomacy or war.[23] Referring to the verses of the Qur'an and the Sunnah of the Prophet, one can infer the principles and general lines of diplomacy in Islam.

- The principle of monotheism and the principle of divine sovereignty.
- The principle of the rejection of mustache and Islamic dignity.
- Use of peaceful means to resolve disputes.
- Respecting Mutual Respect and International Decency.

---

[20] Nasser Hozy nia, "Principles of Peaceful Diplomacy of the Prophet Muhammad (peace is upon him and his family)" *Islamic Republic Newsletter (Iran)*, Vol. 17 ,No. 68, 2014.

[21] Amid Zanjani, Abbasali, *"Political Jurisprudence (The Rights of International Commitments and Diplomacy in Islam)"*, Tehran, Samt publishing, 1979, p.134.

[22] Ibid

[23] Montazeri, Hossein Ali, *"Islamic jurisprudential principles,"* translated by Mahmoud Salavati, Tehran, Tafakkor Publishing , 1995, p. 89.

• Principle of worship and respect for contracts and treaties.

Based on these principles, there are strategies such as an invitation strategy, a strategy for peace and a strategy for jihad.

Islamic diplomacy is based on the five principles of human relations in diplomatic relations, freedom, discretion, mutual respect, goodwill and honesty that the Prophet of Islam (PBUH) was in dealing with tribes, representatives of tribes and rulers who had some kind of diplomatic connection with them.

Following the principles of diplomacy in Islam, there are some goals that are:
• to bring justice in the world and prosperity and human perfection.

• Oppression and the establishment of a lasting global peace.

• The formation of a monotheistic government in the world.

Quranic verses about foreign policy;

In general, if we are to provide a comprehensive definition of foreign policy, these are government policies that focus on international affairs (not internal affairs), and the way in which the government deals with matters outside the country takes its own interests for the preservation of sovereignty and the defence of existence and [pursuit of education].[24] In this regard, the occurrence of the Islamic Revolution in Iran is considered a turning point in the study of foreign policy of Iran, because it has changed the essence of Iran's foreign policy.

Given that the nature of the foreign policy of the Republic of Iran is Islamic, it is based on the principles that are the source of the Holy Quran and the Prophet of Islam and the Imams (as). Below is a reference to the verses of the Holy Qur'an, which can be used to understand the concepts of the Islamic Republic of Iran.

---

[24] Mansoori, Javad, "*A Review of Foreign Policy of the Islamic Republic of Iran*," Tehran, Amir Kabir Publishing, 1986, p. 11.

Around the concept of foreign policy in the Quran verses that guide the regulation of relations between two or more countries, a verse has been revealed by God which is referred to below.

1. The negation of the domination of the unbelievers by believers;

«﴿ وَلَن يَجْعَلَ اللّهُ لِلْكَافِرِينَ عَلَى الْمُؤْمِنِينَ سَبِيلاً[25]﴾».

And Allah will not give the disbelievers any way (of success) against the believers.

2. Use good wisdom and controversy in political bargaining between the two countries;

«﴿ ادْعُ إِلَى سَبِيلِ رَبِّكَ بِالْحِكْمَةِ وَالْمَوْعِظَةِ الْحَسَنَةِ وَجَادِلْهُم بِالَّتِي هِيَ أَحْسَنُ إِنَّ رَبَّكَ هُوَ أَعْلَمُ بِمَن ضَلَّ عَن سَبِيلِهِ وَهُوَ أَعْلَمُ بِالْمُهْتَدِينَ[26]﴾».

Call unto the way of thy Lord with wisdom and fair exhortation, and reason with them in the better way. Lo! Thy Lord is Best Aware of him who strayed from His way, and He is Best Aware of those who go aright.

3. Lack of friendship with the enemies of Islam;

«﴿ يَا أَيُّهَا الَّذِينَ آمَنُوا لَا تَتَّخِذُوا عَدُوِّي وَعَدُوَّكُمْ أَوْلِيَاء تُلْقُونَ إِلَيْهِم بِالْمَوَدَّةِ وَقَدْ كَفَرُوا بِمَا جَاءكُم مِّنَ الْحَقِّ يُخْرِجُونَ الرَّسُولَ وَإِيَّاكُمْ أَن تُؤْمِنُوا بِاللَّهِ رَبِّكُمْ إِن كُنتُمْ خَرَجْتُمْ جِهَادًا فِي سَبِيلِي وَابْتِغَاء مَرْضَاتِي تُسِرُّونَ إِلَيْهِم بِالْمَوَدَّةِ وَأَنَا أَعْلَمُ بِمَا أَخْفَيْتُمْ وَمَا أَعْلَنتُمْ وَمَن يَفْعَلْهُ مِنكُمْ فَقَدْ ضَلَّ سَوَاء السَّبِيلِ[27]﴾».

O ye who believe! Choose not my enemy and your enemy for allies. Do ye give them friendship when they disbelieve in that truth which hath come unto you, driving out the messenger and you because ye believe in Allah, your Lord? If ye have come forth to strive in My way and seeking My good pleasure,(show them not friendship). Do ye show friendship unto them in secret, when I am Best Aware

---

[25] Surah Nisa, verse 141.
[26] Surah Nahl, verse 125.
[27] Sura Mumtahaneh, verse 1.

of what ye hide and what ye proclaim? And whosoever doeth it among you, he verily hath strayed from the right way.

4. The first principle is the uncertainty of the opponents of Islam;

«يا أَيُّهَا الَّذِينَ آمَنُوا لا تَتَّخِذُوا بِطانَةً مِنْ دُونِكُمْ لا يَأْلُونَكُمْ خَبالاً وَدُّوا ما عَنِتُّمْ قَدْ بَدَتِ الْبَغْضاءُ مِنْ أَفْواهِهِمْ وَ ما تُخْفي صُدُورُهُمْ أَكْبَرُ قَدْ بَيَّنَّا لَكُمُ الْآياتِ إِنْ كُنْتُمْ تَعْقِلُونَ[28]».

O ye who believe! Take not for intimates others than your own folk, who would spare no pains to ruin you; they love to hamper you. Hatred is revealed by (the utterance of) their mouths, but that which their breasts hide is greater. We have made plain for you the revelations if ye will understand.

5. Not accepting the province and guardianship of foreigners, infidels and oppressors in establishing foreign relations;

«لا يَتَّخِذِ الْمُؤْمِنُونَ الْكافِرِينَ أَوْلِياءَ مِنْ دُونِ الْمُؤْمِنِينَ وَ مَنْ يَفْعَلْ ذلِكَ فَلَيْسَ مِنَ اللهِ في شَيْءٍ إِلاَّ أَنْ تَتَّقُوا مِنْهُمْ تُقاةً وَ يُحَذِّرُكُمُ اللهُ نَفْسَهُ وَ إِلَى اللهِ الْمَصِيرُ[29]».

Let not the believers take disbelievers for their friends in preference to believers. Whoso doeth that hath no connection with Allah unless (it be) that ye but guard yourselves against them, taking (as it were) security. Allah bids you beware (only) of Himself. Unto Allah is the journeying.

6. The need to accompany the oppressed and the oppressed and their efforts to free them;

«وَ ما لَكُمْ لا تُقاتِلُونَ في سَبِيلِ اللهِ وَ الْمُسْتَضْعَفِينَ مِنَ الرِّجالِ وَ النِّساءِ وَ الْوِلْدانِ الَّذِينَ يَقُولُونَ رَبَّنا أَخْرِجْنا مِنْ هذِهِ الْقَرْيَةِ الظَّالِمِ أَهْلُها وَ اجْعَلْ لَنا مِنْ لَدُنْكَ وَلِيًّا وَ اجْعَلْ لَنا مِنْ لَدُنْكَ نَصِيراً[30]».

---

[28] Surah al-Imran, verse 118.
[29] Surah al-Imran, verse 28.
[30] Sura Nisa, Verse 75.

How should ye not fight for the cause of Allah and of the feeble among men and of
the women and the children who are crying: Our Lord! Bring us forth from out this
town of which the people are oppressors! Oh, give us from thy presence some
protecting friend! Oh, give us from Thy presence some defender!

7. The need to provide the necessary military equipment and equipment for the
Islamic government to defend position of Islam;

«وَ أَعِدُّوا لَهُمْ مَا اسْتَطَعْتُمْ مِنْ قُوَّةٍ وَ مِنْ رِباطِ الْخَيْلِ تُرْهِبُونَ بِهِ عَدُوَّ اللَّهِ وَ عَدُوَّكُمْ وَ آخَرينَ مِنْ دُونِهِمْ لا
تَعْلَمُونَهُمُ اللَّهُ يَعْلَمُهُمْ وَ ما تُنْفِقُوا مِنْ شَيْءٍ في سَبيلِ اللَّهِ يُوَفَّ إِلَيْكُمْ وَ أَنْتُمْ لا تُظْلَمُونَ[31]».

Make ready for them all thou canst of(armed)force and of horses tethered, that
thereby ye may dismay the enemy of Allah and your enemy, and others beside
them whom ye know not. Allah knows them. Whatsoever ye spend in the way of
Allah it will be repaid to you in full, and ye will not be wronged

8. Avoiding compromise with the enemy on the principles of religion;

«فَلا تُطِعِ الْمُكَذِّبينَ . وَدُّوا لَوْ تُدْهِنُ فَيُدْهِنُونَ[32]».

Therefore obey not thou the rejecters - who would have had the compromise, that
they may compromise

9. Realization of social justice on a global level for all human beings, which is the
purpose of the prophets (peace be upon him).

«لَقَدْ أَرْسَلْنَا رُسُلَنَا بِالْبَيِّنَاتِ وَأَنزَلْنَا مَعَهُمُ الْكِتَابَ وَالْمِيزَانَ لِيَقُومَ النَّاسُ بِالْقِسْطِ وَأَنزَلْنَا الْحَدِيدَ فِيهِ بَأْسٌ شَدِيدٌ
وَمَنَافِعُ لِلنَّاسِ وَلِيَعْلَمَ اللَّهُ مَن يَنصُرُهُ وَرُسُلَهُ بِالْغَيْبِ إِنَّ اللَّهَ قَوِيٌّ عَزِيزٌ[33]».

---

[31] Surah Anfal, verse 60.
[32] Surah al-Qalam, Verses 8 -9.
[33] Surah Hadid, Verse 25.

We verily sent Our messengers with clear proofs, and revealed with them the Scripture and the Balance, that mankind may observe right measure; and He revealed iron, wherein is mighty power and(many)uses for mankind, and that Allah may know him who helped Him and His messengers, though unseen. Lo! Allah is Strong, Almighty.

10. Obedience to the divine leaders (chapter of the judgment of the divine leaders in the creation and dissolution of the contract or relations with other states);

«﴿ يَا أَيُّهَا الَّذِينَ آمَنُواْ أَطِيعُواْ اللّهَ وَأَطِيعُواْ الرَّسُولَ وَأُوْلِي الأَمْرِ مِنكُمْ فَإِن تَنَازَعْتُمْ فِي شَيْءٍ فَرُدُّوهُ إِلَى اللّهِ وَالرَّسُولِ إِن كُنتُمْ تُؤْمِنُونَ بِاللّهِ وَالْيَوْمِ الآخِرِ ذَلِكَ خَيْرٌ وَأَحْسَنُ تَأْوِيلاً[34]﴾».

O ye who believe! Obey Allah, and obey the messenger and those of you who are in authority; and if ye have a dispute concerning any matter, refer it to Allah and the messenger if ye are (in truth) believers in Allah and the Last Day. That is better and more seemly in the end.

11. Verses related to jihad, defense, dealing with captives and opponents are also verses that can illustrate relations between countries.

«﴿ وَقَاتِلُواْ فِي سَبِيلِ اللّهِ الَّذِينَ يُقَاتِلُونَكُمْ وَلاَ تَعْتَدُواْ إِنَّ اللّهَ لاَ يُحِبِّ الْمُعْتَدِينَ[35]﴾».

Fight in the way of Allah against those who fight against you, but begin not hostilities. Lo! Allah loves not aggressors.

«﴿ وَجَاهِدُوا فِي اللَّهِ حَقَّ جِهَادِهِ هُوَ اجْتَبَاكُمْ وَمَا جَعَلَ عَلَيْكُمْ فِي الدِّينِ مِنْ حَرَجٍ مِّلَّةَ أَبِيكُمْ إِبْرَاهِيمَ هُوَ سَمَّاكُمُ الْمُسْلِمِينَ مِن قَبْلُ وَفِي هَذَا لِيَكُونَ الرَّسُولُ شَهِيدًا عَلَيْكُمْ وَتَكُونُوا شُهَدَاء عَلَى النَّاسِ فَأَقِيمُوا الصَّلَاةَ وَآتُوا الزَّكَاةَ وَاعْتَصِمُوا بِاللَّهِ هُوَ مَوْلَاكُمْ فَنِعْمَ الْمَوْلَى وَنِعْمَ النَّصِيرُ[36]﴾».

And strive in His cause as ye ought to strive, (with sincerity and under discipline). He has chosen you, and has imposed no difficulties on you in religion; it is the

---

[34] Sura Nisa, Verse 59.
[35] Baqara Sura, verse 190.
[36] Hajj surah, verse 78.

religion of your father Abraham. It is He Who has named you Muslims, both before and in this (Revelation); that the Messenger may be a witness for you, and ye be witnesses for mankind! So establish regular prayer, give Zakat, and hold fast to Allah. He is your Protector - the Best to protect and the Best to help!

12. Necessary to fulfill that promise;

« يَا أَيُّهَا الَّذِينَ آمَنُواْ أَوْفُواْ بِالْعُقُودِ[37]».

O ye who believe! Fulfill your indentures.

---

[37] Surah Ma'edeh, verse 1.

Theoretical framework

At the beginning, it is necessary to clarify a problem and what is the relation between the theory of international relations and foreign policy? Is it possible to use the International Relations Theories as a universal and comprehensive version for foreign policy analysis? Given that theories of international relations have been set in line with the analysis and explanation of international relations, there is a controversy in using these theories and theories in analyzing foreign policy of countries. Some, like Kenneth Waltz, believe that international relations theories cannot be used for foreign policy processing and analysis, so they distinguish between two areas of foreign policy and international relations.[38] In contrast to another group of theorists, the field of foreign relations and politics externally, two domains are interdependent and complementary. In other words, although the scope and subject areas of these two disciplines are different, one can use theories of international relations to analyze the foreign policy of the countries.[39]

The use of international relations theories for analyzing foreign policy of countries in terms of persistence and discontinuity in the external behaviour of countries can indicate that theories of international relations, the ability to explain and provide the general principles of analysis have foreign policy. Hence, there is a constructive interactive between them. Although it may not be possible to obtain a general and universal version of international relations theory for analyzing foreign policy, international relations theories can be used to analyze foreign policy.

Foreign policy is a kind of scrutiny of the external behaviour of states that arises from the interaction between their internal and international variables, and the foreign policy of each country is influenced by its internal and external spiritual and material policies and the requirements of the international system.[40]

---

[38] Dehghani Firoozabadi, Seyyed Jalal, *"Foreign Policy of the Islamic Republic of Iran,"* Tehran , Samt publishing, 2016, p. 13.

[39] Ibid, p. 3.

[40] Qavam, Abdolali, Javdani, Mehdi, "Structural Analysis of Foreign Policy Foundations of the Islamic Republic of Iran", *Quarterly Foreign Policy Journal (Iran)*, Vol.9, No3, 2005, p. 92.

Since the continuation of the life of nations due to the extraordinary importance of the political and social life of countries to foreign policy, it is important to recognize and explore the nature of the political approach of a country in the external dimension. Usually, countries try to determine and direct their foreign policy orientation using a particular logic and theory that is accepted by the international system. Although this decision logic is usually accepted, there are exceptions. For example, the Iranian people's revolution in 1979 was based on a particular ideology and goals. But despite the help of some theories governing international relations theories such as realism and idealism, but in terms of the Islamic nature of the Iranian revolution, one cannot use a particular theory to analyze the foreign policy of the Islamic Republic of Iran. Therefore, it is necessary to design foreign policy of the Islamic Republic of Iran on the basis of principles and principles that could respond to the demands of the revolution and the people of Iran.

Before expressing the dominant analyzes in the foreign policy analysis of the Islamic Republic of Iran, it is necessary to point out that many scholars have tried to compile articles and scientific books by analyzing and theorizing themselves by taking into account objective observations of policy orientations The foreign policy of the Islamic Republic of Iran provides a variety of analyzes. For example, professors such as Ahmad Bakhsheezi Ardestani, Manouchehr Mohammadi, Mohammad Javad Larijani, Bijan Izadi have tried to base their idealistic approach on analyzing the foreign policy of the Islamic Republic of Iran. Professors such as Mohammad Reza Dehshiri, in their books and articles, are useful in analyzing the realistic idealism for analyzing the foreign policy of the Islamic Republic of Iran. Others, such as Hossein Seifzadeh, believe that foreign policy of the Islamic Republic of Iran is neither idealistic nor perfect, but the realistic idealism can be a good basis for analyzing the foreign policy of the Islamic Republic of Iran. Amir Mohammad Haji Yousefi considers the theory of neo-reality as a good basis for analyzing foreign policy. Some, like Alireza Azghandi, in their recent papers consider constructivist theory as the correct basis for analyzing the foreign policy approach of the Islamic Republic of Iran.[41]

---

[41] Alireza, Rezaei , Foreign Policy Analysis of the Islamic Republic of Iran in the light of International Relations Theories, Strategy Quarterly(Iran), Vol.5, No.17 , 2009, p. 264.

Therefore, in order to analyze the foreign policy of the Islamic Republic of Iran, many theoretical approaches such as idealism, liberalism, realistic idealism, institutionalism of neo-liberalism, the theory of discourse, constructivism, geopolitical theory and so on, and for each of the There are also advocates, but there are a number of popular approaches to the analysis of foreign policy of the Islamic Republic of Iran, including the realism, idealism and constructivism that are referred to below.

The theory of realism

Although the roots of classical realism have been visible in Thucydides for twenty-seven centuries, it has entered the field of international relations as a theoretical approach since the late 1930s. Realism emphasizes the three pillars of statehood, survival and self-esteem.[42] Ontology in realism is based on two principles: first based on pessimism to human beings. Philosophically, realism is rooted in theology of Christianity, and it gives man a guilty look, a worker and driven from heaven, which is due to the sin of Adam who has fallen from heaven to earth. The result of this is the wickedness of knowledge and the power of mankind, and this is reflected in governments, and consequently the scene of international relations becomes a force for governments and in this anarchical system, governments seek to maximize their profits. Governments are constantly in constant conflict to survive.[43] So that the root of war is in their essence, and this has made human security more secure.[44]

The second basis on the ontology of realism is that there is no real and objective universe of our minds (whether we know it or not). The ontology of realism resists the scepticism and ontological ideology that denies the existence of external facts.

---

[42] Schmidt, B.C., *"On the History and Historiography of International Relations, in W. Carlsnaes,"* T. Risse and B.A. Simmons (eds), Handbook of International Relations. London: Sage, 2002, pp .3-22.

[43] Buzan, Barry, *"From International to World Ssociety? English School Theory and the Social Structur of Globalization,"* Cambridge, uk: Cambridge University Press, 2008, p .84.

[44] Ibid, p. 85.

[45]Therefore, in this approach, immaterial matters are not taken into consideration. Considering the security-cantered view of realism, things like religion are seen as a security threat, and a positive attitude toward religion is important as long as it leads to advancement of material goals and interests. But from the standpoint of the viewpoint of Islamic philosophers, the existence of the outside world is innate and obvious, and is more certain to us than anything else.[46]

Comprehensive measure in the pillars and basic components of realism, such as central government, power, survival and security, can be put forward in the concept of national interests as a key concept in the analysis of foreign policy of countries. Many believe that the concept of national interest can be used to analyze the foreign policy of the Islamic Republic of Iran. Although some scholars have spoken against this belief, realism cannot explain and analyze all aspects of the foreign policy of the Islamic Republic of Iran.[47] There seems to be a lack of analysis, because the circle of defining national interests in the Islamic Republic of Iran is much broader than what realists believe. National interest is not only material and tangible, but the Islamic Republic of Iran has interests that have an ideological aspect, hence its benefits include immaterial affairs. Ideological influence, software power, conquering the hearts of believers and liberators are among the immaterial things that realism has not paid attention to, but these components are very important in foreign policy of the Islamic Republic of Iran.

Neo-realism is one of the important issues within the paradigm in the theory of realism. The belief in anarchism as the most important concept in neo-realism was raised by Kenneth Waltz. And in that human war in the field of international relations, human beings are fully inclined to believe that the law can only be applied within countries and outside it there is no coercive force to enforce the law.

---

[45] Fathali, Mahmoud and others, *"An Introduction to the Basics of Islamic Thought,"* Qom, Imam Khomeini Institute of Educational and Research press, 2002, p. 24.

[46] Tabatabai, Mohammad Hussein, *"Principles of Philosophy and the Method of Realism,"* Tehran, Sadra Publication, 1985, p. 92.

[47] Dehghani Firoozabadi, Seyyed Jalal, *"Foreign Policy of the Islamic Republic of Iran,"* Tehran , Samt publishing, 2016, p. 31.

Therefore, the environ end of the international environmental is anarchy, and this state There are many who can benefit from this environment.[48]

It also believes that the foreign policy of countries is in an anarchic structure, and this structure shows how the distribution of power and the orientation of foreign policy of countries are. Undoubtedly, in anarchic space, governments are looking for the greatest benefit that determines the totality of these foreign policy affairs. Despite Waltz's theory of how neo-realism (structural realism) is considered a theory of international politics, one can, based on its principles and assumptions, draw an intellectual and analytical framework for foreign policy of the Islamic Republic of Iran. Based on this theory, the structure of the international system can be considered as a major variable in Islamic foreign policy of Iran and can also be effective in determining its goals and motivations.[49]

According to what has been said, this analysis, not in general, but in detail, cannot be correct, since the nature of the Islamic Revolution of Iran is in such a way as to have an impact on the structure of the international system (not its impact). The nature of the Islamic Revolution of Iran has the principles and foundations that are in keeping with the national interests, interests and benefits of an Islamic system (Islamic Republic of Iran).

With the exact knowledge of the root of anarchism, which means state of affairs and the lack of government,[50] it can be understood that anarchism means the absence of any class structure or government and the hierarchy of power and considers human prosperity in destroying the state and its laws,[51] and he believes that the existence of government and religion is harmful to the progress of the

---

[48] Rahim Bayazidi, "Paradigms of International Relations: A Survey on the Paradigm of Theoretical Approaches of International Relations in Theoretical, Methodological, and Epistemological Dimensions," *International Journal of Political Studies, Islamic Azad University – Iran-(Shahreza Branch)*, Vol. 6, No. 18, 2014, p. 228.

[49] Dehghani Firoozabadi, Seyyed Jalal, *"Foreign Policy of the Islamic Republic of Iran,"* Tehran , Samt publishing, 2016, p.37.

[50] Ali Agha Bahkshi, *"Political Science Culture,"* Tehran, Thunder Publishing, 1984, p.22.

[51] Hyundai, Andrew , *"Key Concepts in Political Science,"* Translated by Hasan Saeed Kolahi and Abbas Kardan, Tehran, Scientific and Cultural Press, 2006, p. 57.

human community.[52] Therefore, by eliminating the rule of law, and establishing an "arbitrary and free agreement" between the people, there can be real access to "equality" and "justice". Although some Islamic anarchism may be used to propagate the authoritarian thinking among Muslims, this vision is based on the premise of surrender to God and the rejection of any human domination, not what theorists of anarchism express.

By studying Islamic doctrines, there is no belief in the anarchy of the political system at international level. Indeed, Islamic teachings have sought to push political systems towards the establishment of a universal, universal justice and coherence with the establishment of mechanisms that are in line with the mechanism the universe is for observance of the rights of all human beings.[53] This is while neo-realists who believe in international political anarchism believe. Thus neo-realism, which has a particular look at the structure of the international system, has a special emphasis on international anarchism; hence the foreign policy analysis of an Islamic state (Islamic Republic of Iran) with this approach is absent.

Theory of liberalism

The idea of liberalism in international relations was formed within the framework of idealism between the First World War and the Second World War, and its theoretical foundations are based on cooperation, interaction and reduction of differences in the pursuit of global peace. Liberalism, with all the paradigmatic differences, emphasizes democratic peace and institutionalism.[54] It was philosophically and anthropologically borrowed from the philosophical ideas of the Stoics and the teachings of Christianity, and in the 18th century Kant gave it a philosophical colour. While the Stoic Religious emphasized the good nature of man and promising peace, Kant introduced the wisdom as the light of the future of mankind. Kant believes that rational thinking in humans leads him to a free society in which peace dominates. If in the attitude of realism, central government, pivotal

---

[52] B, N, Ahoja, *"the political science,"* Delhi, culture of the Indiana Academy of Publication, 1997, p. 13.

[53] Journal of Porseman Online, Iran , No. 16, 2003.

[54] Moshirzadeh, Homeira , *"The Transformation in Theories of International Relations,"* Tehran: Samt publishing, 2007, p. 27.

power, and war dominate international relations, then idealist ideology attempted to eliminate the elements of the permanent conflict, which included the centrality of power and state, and instead of the state, man and Instead of power, it governs all kinds of relationships, economic and cultural affairs.[55]

Rationalism, idealism and optimism to the international system are based on the beliefs of liberalism and emphasize ethical principles and international law for the establishment and management of peace, as well as collective security and disarmament, and warfare and anarchy, in the nature of the state Rejects host.[56]

The liberals, with an emphasis on peace through understanding and rights, norms and international organizations, used prescriptive methods in their work and, in fact, based on the ideals and beliefs they believed to be thinking. . The liberalism approach, with all the paradigmatic differences for religion, does not play an independent role in directing international relations.

Unlike the Realists, the idealists, in contrast to the Realists, believe that we must emphasize the dues and emphasize and interpret the world as it should be, not as it is. Therefore, idealism theory includes ethical and normative principles that are the basis of foreign policy analysis and has a prescriptive and policy orientation. The prescription is based on the replacement of the world-wide peace-centered anarchic world, the replacement of unity, cooperation, and the emphasis on values and morals with conflict, conflict and the replacement of software power instead of physical and hardware power.[57]

With regard to what you have said, the analysis of the foreign policy behavior of the Islamic Republic of Iran based on idealistic theory can be used at some points in Iranian political history and can be used. For example, the discourse governing foreign policy in the governments of Hassan Rouhani and Seyyed Mohammad

---

[55] Schmidt, B.C, *"On the History and Historiography of International Relations"*, in W. Carlsnaes, T. Risse and B.A. Simmons (eds), Handbook of International Relations. London: Sage, 2002, p. 154-198.

[56] Rahim Bayazidi, "Paradigms of International Relations: A Survey on the Paradigm of Theoretical Approaches of International Relations in Theoretical, Methodological, and Epistemological Dimensions," *International Journal of Political Studies, Islamic Azad University- Iran- (Shahreza Branch),* Vol. 6, No. 18, 2014, p. 229.

[57] Dehghani Firoozabadi, Seyyed Jalal, *"Foreign Policy of the Islamic Republic of Iran,"* Tehran, Samt publishing , 2016 , p. 20.

Khatami, with a view to solving the problems, can be seen as peaceful, negotiating, negotiating and building bilateral and multilateral coalitions, both with the moral and value of idealism more consistent.

Of course, there is a fundamental point that reflects the fact that although idealistic theory can be used for periods of time. But the general foreign policy of the Islamic Republic of Iran, which has been emphasized in the constitution, cannot be ignored by the rule of law governing all international rules, coalitions and international obligations, for example, if actors in the Islamic state (Islamic Republic of Iran) can conclude that a coalition, peace or any law and order, contrary to the interests of the Islamic state and also opposed to the Islamic law, can refrain from the rule of law on other matters. Therefore, in practice, this ruling discourse based on Islamic principles precedes any other matter. Therefore, foreign policy of the Islamic Republic of Iran cannot be analyzed with idealistic theory.

Constructivism Theory

Constructivism as a dominant paradigm of international relations has been considered in the field of Meta theory in the last two decades. This approach has an ontological nature and takes into account the role of government in the international system, and it can be said that there is ontology between realism and liberalism. In constructivism, culture, beliefs, concepts and meanings are of great importance and are made and presented in the context of events and events. Structuralism addresses how people's social identities and norms can be expanded with their institutional relationships, and relations between states are based on the meaning they hold for each other.

Constructors believe that the imagination of countries from the power of others enables a nation and government to interact with their environment. Conceived by the constructivists of the world, they are made of valuable implications that shape their actions. Governments that are also socially based participate in this collective mentality and understand the world in that framework. And government actors seek to change or maintain the existing order because of these perceptions and draw their foreign policy to unite, collaborate and not cooperate with other states.

Constructors, as one of the post-proof-minded intellectuals, believe that understanding how actors develop their interests can explain or understand the rationale of a wide range of international cases that rationalists have neglected. It is very vital.[58]

From the two directions, we can use constructive theory in analyzing the foreign policy of the Islamic Republic of Iran. First, considering the ontology and epistemology of this theory and its difference with the rationalist views, it is possible to analyze the ideals of national interests based on immaterial power. Secondly, it can be used because it can be behaved in accordance with norms and notions of subjectivity, and these norms mean the expectations of values based on the values of behaviour, conduct and conduct of the foreign policy of the Islamic Republic of Iran. The outcome of internalized internal norms and transnational norms determine the common identity and interests of Iran, which in turn prompts its external behaviour. Through the process of socialization, we can examine social norms within and through the interethnic expectations based on the common values of transnational norms that affect foreign policy.[59]

The theory of constructivism, with the importance of identity and the foundation of subjectivist notions as the consistency of the wisdom, enables the acquisition of the theory of foreign policy. It is the identity that defines norms and directs the actions of governments. Identity allows nations to see the world meaningful and define their limits. This, while identifying the friend and the enemy, also guides the interests[60] the constructivist theory looks positively in terms of semantic identity and semantics that determines its interests and directional decision making, and considers it appropriate for an analysis of foreign policy. But he acknowledges that actors and decision makers are acting in a dialectic manner in dealing with others. This means that foreign policy of the Islamic Republic of Iran, although pursuing its own interests and trying to establish a constructive relationship with all states, but drawing on the principles that are based on the principles and identity of Islam, is never from what as an identity Islamic determines it does not abandon.

---

[58] Mohammad Mahdi Yaghooti, "Identity Analysis of Foreign Policy of the Islamic Republic of Iran," *Foreign Policy Quarterly* (Iran) , 2011, Vol. 25, No. 1, 2011, p .2.

[59] Dehghani Firoozabadi, Seyyed Jalal, *"Foreign Policy of the Islamic Republic of Iran"*, Tehran , Samt publishing, 2016, pp. 47-50.

[60] Mohammad Mahdi Yaghooti, "Identity Analysis of Foreign Policy of the Islamic Republic of Iran," *Foreign Policy Quarterly (Iran)*, 2011, Vol. 25, No. 1, 2011, p. 8.

The foreign policy orientation of the Islamic Republic of Iran depends on several factors, such as religious teachings, national interests, historical look and idealistic, mental factors and meanings. The Iranian political culture has three layers of religion, modernity and tradition, each of which has a great impact on foreign policy. The religious layer has had the most significant impact on the identity of the Islamic Republic of Iran and has been emphasized and given at the beginning of the constitution. "The fundamental feature of this revolution is the Islamic and religious Islam of the other centuries in recent centuries."[61] The Islamic and religious layer was dominated by other layers as a common approach to Iran's political and social culture, on other matters.

Constructivism analysis always perceives the influence of decisions, norms and mental imagery in the internal environment on external decisions and does not consider the effects of the international environment and other policies of the casters as effective in making decisions. Constructivism theory, because it considers internal factors as an effective factor in foreign policy, can be used in foreign policy analysis of the Islamic Republic of Iran. Based on this analysis, there is an adaptation in Iran's foreign policy decisions of the actors within the system, the general principles of the constitution that are consistent with Islam, are considered to be effective in the foreign policy of the Islamic Republic of Iran. To analyze and adapt the constructivist theory to the foreign policy of the Islamic Republic of Iran, Islamic norms allow the Islamic Republic of Iran to support Muslims as long as this country continues its Islamic practices and practices.[62]

In the intellectual system of constructivists, whose norms, norms and norms have a special place, the element of religion is also an important component of this theory. Although the closest theory to explain the position of religion is between theories of international relations is the constructivist approach, this theory cannot, for a number of reasons, consider and apply issues such as religion in its conceptual framework, which is stated below:

1. The sovereignty of the purely secular mainstream rationalism in the theorizing of international relations, including the constructivist theory, has prevented their attention to the religious component and thus neglected.

---

[61] Ibid, p. 3.

[62] Dehghani Firoozabadi, Seyyed Jalal, *"Foreign Policy of the Islamic Republic of Iran"*, Tehran, Samt publishing, 2019, p. 46.

Theorists of international relations believe in non-rationality in religion, therefore, they consider the issues related to religion to be hard and difficult within their conceptual framework.[63]

2. The theory of constructivism, due to its commitment to the evolving role of values, ideas and ideas in the form of immaterial structures, although it is possible to theoretically explain the role of religion in international relations, but due to the emphasis on constructed social and nonmaterial constructivism The human hand and the human community are not capable of explaining transcendental and divine structures and institutions.[64]

3. Constructivism, despite the emphasis on the independent role of cultural and religious ideas and beliefs, regards religion as a factor in conflict and conflict in international relations, and according to Kubalka, it is possible to explain the interrelationship between religion and international relations in the theory there is no mainstream or even conventional constitution. Although there is no coherent and unique work from the structural point of view that can be considered as the only one that describes this school of thought, Alexander Vent's book "The Social Theory of International Politics" is an important and remarkable work in which this theory Expanded Explained.[65]

4. Vent's main focus is on the units that make this international level of "anarchy cultures" as a result of interacting with each other. Therefore, his social and constructivist theory cannot be very religious and alike. Even though his broad and broad classification makes it possible to have the role of religion in international culture possible.[66]

Structuralism is appropriate for emphasizing the role of religion, culture, and ideas, and it can be used to analyze the structure of religious discourse but

---

[63] Moshirzadeh, Homeira, *"The Transformation in Theories of International Relations,"* Tehran, Samt publishing , 2007, pp. 230-265.

[64] Wendt, Alexander, *"Social Theory of International Politics,"* Translated by: Moshirzadeh, Tehran, H, Ministry of Foreign Affairs Press, 2006, P. 24.

[65] Ibid, p. 54.

[66] Rahim Bayazidi, "Paradigms of International Relations: A Survey on the Paradigm of Theoretical Approaches of International Relations in Theoretical, Methodological, and Epistemological Dimensions," *International Journal of Political Studies, Islamic Azad University- Iran- (Shahreza Branch),* Vol. 6, No .18, 2014, p. 233.

denies it because it denies the constructive and independent role of religion. It's true. This is if the position that a religious government (Islamic Republic of Iran) places on religion is above its parallel role with other affairs. Religious affairs are always governed by all the issues and are the main driver of the discourse.[67]

Finally, to summarize this section, the capacity and ability of a constructive approach to analyze foreign policy of the Islamic Republic of Iran, it is necessary to refer to two points.

First: Among the ideas of international relations, perhaps the closest theory for analyzing the foreign policy of the Islamic Republic of Iran is constructivism. Because in the ontology of this theory, the notions and meanings of the mind, culture, religion, and norms are of particular importance. According to this theory, the Islamic Republic of Iran considers helping other Muslims promote Islamic teachings and support Islamic movements as part of its foreign policy.[68]

Second, despite the beliefs of the constructivists about the component of religion and the emphasis on its importance, but because of the secular nature and excessive rationalism in this theory, they do not place an independent role in creating change. If the Islamic government, one of the examples of which is the Islamic Republic of Iran, does not accept such an argument and argument from the constructivists, because religion forms the basis of all decisions and orientations of the foreign and domestic policy of the Islamic Republic of Iran, and the teachings Islam is at the forefront of all matters and can create an independent role in the creation of any kind of transformation. Consequently, the constructive approach cannot be used to analyze the foreign policy of the Islamic Republic of Iran, although, as stated above, some of the foreign policy of the Islamic Republic of Iran can be assessed and analyzed on this basis.

---

[67] Haghighat , Seyyed Sadegh, *"Principles and Objectives of Foreign Policy of the Islamic State,"* Qom, Islamic Center of Science and Culture press, 2006 , p. 75.

[68] Dehghani Firoozabadi, Seyyed Jalal, *"Foreign Policy of the Islamic Republic of Iran,"* Tehran , Samt publishing, 2016 ,pp. 46-51.

CHAPTER II:

Islamic Approach to Foreign Policy

Islamic Approach to Foreign Policy

The previous chapter examined the theoretical framework of foreign policy of the Islamic Republic of Iran. It has been substantiated that the best way to analyze foreign policy of countries is to use the ideas of international relations. In the following chapter, three important theories of international relations, namely, constructivism, realism and realism, were expressed and the foreign policy of the Islamic Republic was analyzed on the basis of these three theories and concluded that none of these theories could be foreign policy analysis Islamic Republic of Iran. It has been argued that rationalist, secular, and materialist theories cannot help analyzing the realities of foreign policy of the Islamic Republic of Iran because Iran's foreign policy is based on a set of values, norms, concepts, principles, and principles that exist. Theology and epistemology are different from other theories. And this requires the need for a different theoretical paradigm from the theory of formatting on international relations that can be used to analyze Iran's foreign policy. Finally, we concluded that for the analysis of the foreign policy of the Islamic Republic of Iran, we should choose a third approach (new approach). This requires understanding the principles and principles of foreign policy of Islam. This will be dealt with in this chapter. Only a full understanding of the principles of foreign policy of Islam can provide a true analysis of the foreign policy orientations of the Islamic Republic of Iran.

The verses of the Holy Qur'an, while emphasizing the necessity of interactions and cooperation, emphasize issues that can be used to translate these verses into the internationalization of human society and the regulation of relations between states.[1] Allah Almighty has emphasized in the Holy Quran principles such as the denial of invasion of other countries, the rejection of the infidel domination, the help of the Muslims, unity, the principle of mutual respect, the emphasis on commonalities, peace, vindication, intercourse and cooperation, all of which guide And defines the principles of Islamic State foreign policy. In this chapter, while attempting to explain the authenticity of the relationship between governments and the role of the Qur'an in internationalizing the human society, the form of international relations from the Quran point of view is also to be considered.

---

[1] Davood Feirhi, "*Power, Knowledge and Legitimacy in Islam*", Tehran, Ney Publication, 2009, p. 55.

The issues and principles of foreign policy of the Islamic Republic of Iran are based on religious and Islamic principles and we will examine it in the next chapter. If it is possible to accurately explain the principles of foreign policy of Islam, the third chapter of the article analyzes the issues of foreign policy of the Islamic Republic of Iran.

The principles of foreign policy of Islam from the point of view of the Holy Quran are based on three fundamental assumptions that, regardless of them, the discussion of Islamic foreign policy seems unfinished.

1. The relationship between religion and politics is considered as a major assumption, since without considering such a problem, the design of the principles of foreign policy of Islam is useless.

2. Islamic teachings and principles always emphasize the necessity of communication and interaction with others, and always seek to explain the general framework of the behaviour and orientation of the two Islamic states to other states.

3. Islam has two fixed and variable parts: its constituents are based on the principles and principles of the behaviour of the religionists, and during the time of survival and survival, but its changing aspect is influenced by the customs and necessities of the time.[2] The variable part of foreign policy refers to this aspect, as it changes in the circumstances and circumstances of the time; therefore, religious thought is limited in terms of general concepts and principles to political issues and social management.

According to the assumptions mentioned, two main topics in this chapter can be investigated: a. The Need for Cooperation and Relationship between Governments in Islamic teachings b. explaining the Fundamentals of Islamic State Foreign Policy.

A: The Necessity of Relationships between Governments in Islamic teachings;

One of the key issues facing governments and nations is the political relationship between countries, which has been complicated for ages. Today, there are widespread developments and deep complexities in relations between

---

[2] http://www.al-falah.ir/portal/?pageID=1356.

countries. The existence of interests, opportunities and threats between countries has made it necessary to research and study in this field as an undeniable necessity. Any country that has accepted isolationism as a principle in its foreign policy will undoubtedly face many problems. Hence, countries will try to have their political, cultural and economic ties to the highest degree with other countries, and this will ensure their interests. And countries need to expand their relations with other countries for development and development. Islamic teachings and at their head, the Holy Qur'an as a comprehensive and comprehensive book that has been revealed to God's servants for guidance from mankind to be a way for the whole of humanity. Given the comprehensiveness of this book, it has undoubtedly expressed issues in all areas, including about relations between states.

One of the main reasons for the discussion of the necessity of the relationship between governments is that the religion of Islam is an incitement and concern for government issues, including government formation, governance, communication and cooperation with other states.[3] Islam is not a religion of isolation and deprivation, but a complete and comprehensive religion that rules for all its affairs and cases. Therefore, the affairs of the world, politics, society, economy, etc. are all that are mentioned in the teachings of Islam, Has been eaten. The main philosophy of Islam is the formation of a universal government based on justice and equality, except through the formation of government, the pursuit of social life, interaction and communication with others. Islam as a religion that meets the essential spiritual and physical needs of humans in all ages and places not only focuses on constructive social relations, but also emphasizes the importance of society in establishing some principles in social relations.

It is natural that each community wants to communicate with other communities in order to meet its needs. In the Holy Qur'an, the necessity of the peaceful association and cooperation between Muslim and non-Muslim nations and governments is emphasized and it is possible to use the Qur'anic verses of the

---

[3] Amini, Abraham, *"Introduction to General Issues of Islam,"* Qom, Ansariyan Publications, 1995, p. 45.

Quran that the social existence of man is established in the context of his creation and creation.[4]

In the Sura of Mobarakeh, the Hujurat of verse 13 says:

"يَا أَيُّهَا النَّاسُ إِنَّا خَلَقْنَاكُم مِّن ذَكَرٍ وَأُنثَى وَجَعَلْنَاكُمْ شُعُوبًا وَقَبَائِلَ لِتَعَارَفُوا إِنَّ أَكْرَمَكُمْ عِندَ اللَّهِ أَتْقَاكُمْ إِنَّ اللَّهَ عَلِيمٌ خَبِيرٌ"

"[O Messenger!] We did not send you But as a guide to all mankind in order to give glad tidings to the believers and to warn those who have gone astray; But the majority of people are Ignorant {so the Messenger will encounter problems along the way of his mission}

Today, the world as a global village and each country as a community, and the expansion of the communications and needs of nations and governments have doubled the need for cooperation. And on the other hand, Islam is a virtue and is equal to the real needs and responses of human needs and has a global challenge.

وَ ما أَرْسَلْناكَ إِلاَّ كَافَّةً لِلنَّاسِ بَشيراً وَ نَذيراً وَ لكِنَّ أَكْثَرَ النَّاسِ لايَعْلَمُونَ؛[5]

O, mankind! Verily, We created you all From a male and female[`Adam and Eve]and appointed for you tribes and Nations to be known to each other[by Specified characteristics]Verily, in Allah's Sight the most honorable of you Is the most pious of you; and Allah is The Informed Owner of Knowledge.

And he considers his plan to be blissful for all nations, groups, races and ... and believes that the message of the Qur'an should be learned throughout the world.

In order to explain the discussion, the question arises as to whether the Quran considers the principle of establishing communication, cooperation and interaction between governments or, on the contrary, emphasizes conflict and contradiction. In answering this question, the study of Qur'anic verses related to this subject shows that communicating with other states is a necessity. The reason for this is that the existential philosophy of the divine prophets, especially the great Prophet

---

[4] Mortaza Motahhari, Society and History, Sadra Publications, Tehran, 2005, pp. 24-21.
[5] Saba , verse 28.

Muhammad, has been the guidance of human societies. Conducting and influencing others when it comes to time, the person who is the owner of the message can communicate with his audience to influence them, and the meaning of this relationship is not limited to relations between the two, but the purpose of the relationship between the states.

God in the Holy Quran calls all human beings into monotheism, and this is impossible without communion with other nations and followers of other religions, which means that the invitation to monotheism without relations is impossible. Therefore, it is necessary for the public invitation to accept Islam and to present the Quranic facts to the people, to establish relations with all races, groups, and nations at the international level and that is why the Prophet of Islam (PBUH) is a letter to The leaders of the empire sent Iran and Rome to invite Islam.

The establishment of a political relationship between governments in Islamic teachings has a specific mechanism that can be called the principles of the Islamic State's foreign policy that defines the orientation of the Islamic state with other states. Therefore, the framework for decision-making in foreign policy of the Islamic State should not be contrary to Islamic principles. Because if the result of establishing the relationship is humiliation and degeneracy and dignity is eliminated in such a way that the oppressor is allowed to interfere in the affairs of the Muslims, it is discredited and explicitly contradictory to the teachings of the verses of the Holy Qur'an; God Almighty states:

يا أَيُّهَا النَّبِيُّ اتَّقِ اللَّهَ وَ لا تُطِعِ الْكافِرِينَ وَ الْمُنافِقِينَ إِنَّ اللَّهَ كانَ عَلِيماً حَكِيماً[6]؛

O, Messenger! Fear from The disobedience of Allah and do not conform to the devilish suggestions Offered by the disbelievers and the hypocrites; verily, Allah is The Absolute Knowing Decrier;

This verse observes obedience to the infidels as contradictory to God's observance, or in another verse, emphasizing that if the relationship is such that it leads to the domination of the unbelievers against the Muslims, it lacks credibility.

---

[6] Surah Ahzab , verse 1.

« وَلَن يَجْعَلَ اللّهُ لِلْكَافِرِينَ عَلَى الْمُؤْمِنِينَ سَبِيلاً[7] ».

And Allah will not give the disbelievers any way (of success) against the believers.

The principle of devotion necessitates the durability of contracts, but if the contract leads to the infidelity, the principle of Nafye Sabil (the negation of the infidels against the Muslims) is abolished.

Allameh Tabatabai, following the interpretation of verse 1 of Surah al-Ahzab, states:

" يا أَيُّهَا النَّبِيُّ اتَّقِ اللَّهَ وَ لا تُطِعِ الْكافِرِينَ وَ الْمُنافِقِينَ إِنَّ اللَّهَ كانَ عَلِيماً حَكِيماً "

O, Messenger! Fear from The disobedience of Allah and do not conform to the devilish suggestions Offered by the disbelievers and the hypocrites; verily, Allah is The Absolute Knowing Decrier;

God has gathered between the unbelievers and the hypocrites and has forbidden both obedience, it is understood in this sense that the unbelievers have asked the Prophet (peace be upon him) against something that was not pleasing to Allah, the hypocrites who are in the queue they were Muslims, they approved the unbelievers, and urged them to insist on accepting the offer of the infidels, and that suggestion was a matter which Allah has given to his science and wisdom against it, and the divine revelation also applies to The contrary was revealed. It is also discovered that this was an important matter that it was feared that the apparent weapon would not contradict it and, on the contrary, would help it, unless God intended to prevent it, so the Prophet The Prophet (peace be upon him) warns the clerk not to obey the unbelievers' request for help, and obey what he has been inspired, and turn away from anyone and trust in God.[8]

But if, at a particular place, the relations or the conclusion of a contract leads to the infidelity of the infidels, and failure to comply with the treaty causes more

---

[7] Surah Nisa , verse 141.
[8] Tabatabaei, Mohammad Hussein, *"the translation of Al-Mizan,"* vol. 16, Islamic Qom Publication, Tehran, 1996, pp. 409-408.

damage to the Islamic state, the Holy Quran, as an exception, has left the way to accept it in an emergency.[9]

(B) The principles of foreign policy of the Islamic State:

1. The principle of expediency (Maslehat)

Expedited in the word means good and benevolent,[10] in the meaning of the term, it means achieving the purpose of the sacred saint (god).[11] Some people believe that expediency does not mean gaining interest and dispossessing it because it is for the benefit and dispossess of the interests of the people, but it is in the interest of protecting the purposes of sharia in protecting creatures.[12]

According to the definition of expediency, "national interests" will be the result of national interests and transnational responsibilities. Imam Ghazzali has expedited interest in the interest or disposal of the sacred purpose of protecting the religion, life, intellect, generation and property, and whatever is in support of these five things, it is called "expediency."[13]

Contrary to national governments that seek to achieve "national interests" in foreign policy, the Islamic state considers "national interests" as a criterion and direction for its foreign policy. The need to respect and adhere to many principles, objectives and policies of politics, the foreign policy of the Islamic state is shaped by the consideration of this principle. Undoubtedly, this expediency, apart from the primary expediency, is based on which the worshiper has made rulings on his servants.

---

[9] Makarem Shirazi, Nasser (in collaboration with a group of scholars), *"Sample Interpretation,"* Daralktb al-Islami, Publications, Tehran , 2005, p. 337.

[10] Fakhr al-Din bin Muhammad al-Tariyah, *"Majma Al Bahrain,"* Volume 3, Beirut, Al-Wafa Institute of Publications, 1986, p. 117.

[11] Seyyed Mohammad Taghi al-Hakim, *"Al-Hussein Al-Mu'min,"* Volume 1, the World Assembly of Ahl al-Bayt Publication, Qom, 1998, p. 381.

[12] Isfahani, Ragheb, *"Mofradat al-al-aq al-Quran,"* vol. 2, Zoya al-Qarbi Publications, Qom, 2001, p. 284.

[13] Seyyed Sadegh Haghighat, *"the Foundations of Political Thought in Islam,"* Qom, Mofid University Press, 2013, p. 86.

Making decisions based on the interests of foreign policy of each country is considered as one of the most important principles of foreign policy of each state and country. This concept has a special place in Islamic teachings. The Islamic State considers material as the criterion and direction of its foreign policy. According to the definition of expediency, national interests will be of interest to national interests and responsibilities. The goals and strategy of foreign policy are shaped by this principle. [14]

The principle of expediency is one of the most fundamental policies of the Islamic State in the domestic and foreign arena, which seeks to achieve national interests with the consideration of the principle of national interests. The Islamic State always considers national interests to be a criterion of foreign policy.[15] If the concept of expediency can be conveyed correctly, many doubts, ambiguities and questions about the orientations and stances of an Islamic state will be resolved. If the Islamic ruler takes different decisions in different places and times, despite the fact that the divine rules are constant.

For example, in a place of peace and engagement with a country, it chooses a policy of isolation and, in another place, chooses a policy of non-engagement, all of which are based on the principle of interest in foreign policy of Islam. Exemplification of other principles of foreign policy is much more important and more applicable.

In other words, it may be in the minds of many thinkers about the foreign policy of the Islamic State (Islamic Republic of Iran) that foreign policy has fixed and irreplaceable principles such as negation of the domination and the province of Kafrn, the principle of cooperation, vindication, And with these assumptions an unconnected and non-flexible foreign policy for an Islamic state. Therefore, the Islamic ruler must always have a consistent orientation in foreign policy. Therefore, the Islamic ruler must always have a consistent orientation in foreign policy. At first glance, this seems to be correct, and the principle is the same, that is, the Islamic state has fixed decisions according to the principles of Islamic teachings.

---

[14] Haghighat, Seyyed Sadegh, *"Principles and Objectives of Foreign Policy of the Islamic State,"* Qom, Islamic Center of Science and Culture press, 2006, P. 75.
[15] Ibid,

The existence of complexities in the foreign policy of each country, along with the numerous national interests of the Islamic state, which is based on national interests, is the driving force behind foreign policy. In other words, despite the acceptance and assumption of Islamic principles in foreign policy, if the Islamic state decides to oppose it at some other time, it will decide whether to cooperate or remain silent. All of these decisions are reflections of the Islamic ruling elucidation on the basis of the best interests and highest benefits within the framework of Islamic law and Islamic law. This shows that the principle of expediency is more important than other principles of foreign policy.

In all Islamic issues and judgments cannot be ruled out on the basis of expediency; some divine orders such as prayer and fasting are based on a religious order, which in these cases is not a place for expediency. But there are some issues that are not part of the affairs of Islam, and there is no reason to deduce it in Islamic sources and holy sharia. Such as war, peace, cooperation and communication with non-Muslims, In this affair, the prophet of Islam, the Prophet (peace be upon him), and the sign of the implication of the necessity of the executors to have an interest in the matter, therefore, the Islamic ruler can deal with such matters on the basis of the interests of the Muslims.[16]

In general, foreign policy is a set of political issues related to the foreign sphere and has two relatively stable and variable parts. The steady part of it expresses the general framework of foreign policy that foreign policy strategies and strategies are regulated within; it is based largely on theoretical doctrines and the value system and ruling ideology. Variable elements of foreign policy are subject to policies that are tailored to the circumstances and conditions, and the principle of expediency is one of these variables.

2.   The principle of interaction and cooperation

Interaction and cooperation for human beings are of great importance and the reason for this is the necessity of the sociality of human life, discussed in the preceding discussion (the necessity of the relationship between states in Islamic teachings). No country in the world can live without interacting with other communities. So interaction is a necessity that people and governments have to choose in relation to others.

---

[16] Ibid , P. 82.

In the contemporary world, given the close linkage between the very close relationships of human societies, the various vital factors of nations are called for peaceful co-operation and coexistence, making it difficult to isolate life, explaining the place of religion, Special Islam is critical in the development of international law, and any ambiguity and ambiguity in this regard can be misleading and problematic, as some have experienced such mistakes.

Some believe that securing world peace and security in a peaceful way is a product of the West's civilization, and believes that it is not possible to realize it except on the basis of the value of Western schools, and it poses the question that the role of religion in the structure of the rules of law Where is the international peace and cooperation platform? Of course, in the area of doubt, ambiguity and denial, some tend to disprove or weaken the role of religion in this regard; as in other areas, this libel is closed to religion and only conscience and reason are considered sources of law and law.[17] This is while God in the verses of the Holy Quran guides humans to co-operation.

»وَ تَعاوَنُوا عَلَى الْبِرِّ وَ التَّقْوى وَ لا تَعاوَنُوا عَلَى الْإِثْمِ وَ الْعُدْوانِ؛[18]

You should help one another in Righteousness and piety, but do not Help one another in sin and Transgression.

It can be deduced from the verses of the Holy Quran that the divine prophets were called to resolve disputes, resolve contradictions and the proximity of hearts by establishing peaceful relations between individuals, tribes and nations of the world. And verse 213 of the Surat al-Baqara refers to the point.

"كانَ النَّاسُ أُمَّةً واحِدَةً فَبَعَثَ اللَّهُ النَّبِيِّينَ مُبَشِّرِينَ وَ مُنْذِرِينَ وَ أَنْزَلَ مَعَهُمُ الْكِتابَ بِالْحَقِّ لِيَحْكُمَ بَيْنَ النَّاسِ فِيمَا اخْتَلَفُوا فِيهِ وَ مَا اخْتَلَفَ فِيهِ إِلاَّ الَّذِينَ أُوتُوهُ مِنْ بَعْدِ ما جاءَتْهُمُ الْبَيِّناتُ بَغْياً بَيْنَهُمْ فَهَدَى اللَّهُ الَّذِينَ آمَنُوا لِمَا اخْتَلَفُوا فِيهِ مِنَ الْحَقِّ بِإِذْنِهِ وَ اللَّهُ يَهْدِي مَنْ يَشاءُ إِلى صِراطٍ مُسْتَقِيمٍ"

At the beginning, people were one Nation; then Allah sent Messengers As Givers of glad-tidings and Warmers ; And sent down[with them]the Book With the Truth to judge between men In whatever they differed. But Those to whom the Scripture was Given, after clear proofs had come to Them, they differed, out of envy and Aggression among themselves. Then Allah by His Will guided those

---

[17] Khademi, Majid, *"War and Peace in the Law of Islam,"* translated by Gholam Reza Saeedi, Bide Publication , 1976, p. 407.
[18] Surah Ma'edeh, verse 2.

who believed the Truth about which there was dispute. And Allah does guide those whom He wills, to the Straight Path.

By studying the history of Islam, it can be concluded that the Prophet (SAW) has always sought to establish a peaceful relationship with others and encourage them to establish a peaceful relationship. The invitation of the Prophet to resolve the disagreement and encouragement of communicating between the two tribes of Ows and Khazraj at the height of Islam is an example of this.[19] In narration, emphasis has been placed on tolerance and coexistence with the people, and the Prophet of Islam (peace be upon him) in this regard states:

"مدارات الناس راس العقل"[20]

(Means kindness and symbiosis with the people of the climax)

Or else in another hadith:

"ان الله تبارک و تعالی امرنی بمداراه الناس کما امرنی باقامه الفرائض"[21]

(Allah Almighty, as he set me up for duty, he also ordered the tolerance with the people.)

There was a peaceful coexistence as an indescribable principle in the regime and the Prophet of Islam.[22] And he refers to two basic points in order to realize this important principle. 1. Necessity of realizing communities and communicating 2. Inviting and delivering the divine message which was one of the most important existential philosophies of the mission of the Prophet of Islam. That realization of these matters can only be realized in a safe and peaceful environment based on peaceful coexistence.

The Prophet tried to regulate the orientation of tolerance and coexistence between them, in order to function as a problematic coexistence with tribes and governments. At the same time, while taking individual allegiance for intercourse and co-operation, he concluded security agreements with the Arab tribes, the

---

[19] Tabari, Mohammad ibn Jabir, Tabari History, Beirut, Dar al-Kotb al-Olamyyah Publications , 1998, p. 558.

[20] Abdurrahman al-Saywati, Jalal al-Din, al-Juma al-Saghir fi al-Ahadis al-Bashir al-Nazir, Volume 2, Beirut, Dar al-Fakr Publications, 1980, p. 3.

[21] Ibid,, p. 359.

[22] Haghighat, Seyyed Sadegh, Principles and Objectives of Foreign Policy of the Islamic State, Qom, Islamic Center of Science and Culture press, 2006. P. 132.

people of the Book and others, and in the framework of these communications and interactions, they institutionalized their mission and invitation.[23]

3.   The principle of defending Muslims and oppressed people:

Defending the identity, territory and interests of the Islamic state is religiously and religiously, and also because of the interests of the Islamic state. Undoubtedly, the weakening of a component of the Islamic society would lead to deterioration in the damage to other components, and this is not consistent with the material, religious, and religious interests of an Islamic state.[24]

Although the defense of an Islamic land and the interests of all Muslims in the world may not be possible for an Islamic state, it is the responsibility of the Islamic State to provide the conditions and facilities for this task. As an example, the Islamic state, which itself has a government, sovereignty, population and independent land, has the duty to help where aid is possible. But if assistance helps weaken the government and its benefits, status and governance weaken, such a duty will be removed from the rule of Tazahom.[25]

The rule of Tazahom is a jurisprudential principle, which means that it is the incompatibility and obstruction of the two judgments, which are due to the power not having to be obliged to do so. In the place where the obligation to perform the assignment cannot be summed up between the two judgments, here the task of performing one's own will be eliminated, in the event of the inability of the void. Therefore, the defense of the Muslims of the world is not definite for the Islamic state and the need for planning and decision-making and positioning is required for the Islamic State to act at its proper time.[26]

Islamic teachings, along with the defense of the Islamic society, consider the defense of the oppressed of the world as a human and moral duty, and, if it is available, it does not consider the assistance limited to Muslims to Muslims. The oppressed are those who are not willing to oppress, but because of the weakness of

[23] Ibid ,P. 131.

[24] Mansouri, Javad, a Commentary on Foreign Policy of the Islamic Republic of Iran, Tehran, Sepehr Publication, 1986, p 28.

[25] Haghighat, Seyyed Sadegh, *"Principles and Objectives of Foreign Policy of the Islamic State,"* Qom, Islamic Center of Science and Culture press, 2006, P. 93.

[26] Ibid ,P. 91

the power of defense, oppression has been imposed upon them. Prophet Muhammad (peace is upon him) says:

من سمع رجلاً ينادى يا للمسلمين فلم يجبه فليس بمسلم.²⁷

He who is hearing a personal voice that asks for the cry of the Muslims to meet the demands of the Muslims and does not answer him is not Muslim.

The school of life of Islam considers human prosperity as one of its goals in the whole of human society. Independence, freedom and social justice are the right of all human beings. Accordingly, a Muslim or Islamic government cannot and should not be indifferent to the oppression of oppressors and oppressors, as well as to the violation of the rights of the deprived and oppressed people, God says in the Quran:

»وَ ما لَكُمْ لا تُقاتِلُونَ فِي سَبِيلِ اللهِ وَ الْمُسْتَضْعَفِينَ مِنَ الرِّجالِ وَ النِّساءِ وَ الْوِلْدانِ الَّذِينَ يَقُولُونَ رَبَّنا أَخْرِجْنا مِنْ هذِهِ الْقَرْيةِ الظَّالِمِ أَهْلُها؛«²⁸

And what is it with you that you do not fight in the Path of Allah? And for those who being weak and oppressed among men, women and children who Cry:" O, our Creator and Nurturer! Rescue us from this town (Makkah City) whose people are Evildoers and oppressors; and appoint for us from Your Presence, a guardian and a protector."

In this verse, the Almighty God invites Jihad, based on the stimulation of human emotions, and states whether your human emotions allow you to be silent and watch these perverse scenes of oppression? Then, in order to ignite the human emotions of the believers, these believers are those who are caught up in shocked environments, and their hope has been cut off everywhere.

According to the meaning of the verse, the defense of the oppressed and the oppressed is in any part of the world, close and far, inside and outside the country is not different. The support of the oppressed in Islam is a principle to be respected, even if it leads to jihad. This command is one of the most valuable

---

[27] Colyni, Aby Ja'far Mohammed ibn Ya'qub, "*Osul kafi*," Volume 2, Beirut, Darolazva Publishing , 1995, p. 164.

[28] Nissaa Sura, Verse 75.

Islamic commands to Muslims, which proclaims the validity of this ritual.[29] However, this is a definite duty for all Muslims to prevent the conflict between the Muslims and to take responsibility for them in this regard, and as an observer, they will not be indifferent to this matter.[30]

4.   The principle of Nafye Sabil[31] (principle of dignity)

One of the most important issues in the foreign policy of the Islamic state is the negation of the non-Muslim provinces towards Muslims. The rule of Nafye Sabil (principle of dignity) as a jurisprudential principle has a lasting role and influences the behaviour, decisions and policies of the Islamic system. This principle is very important in the foreign relations of the Islamic State with foreigners. Independence in decision making, inhibition of the influence of foreigners and preservation of Islamic identity and dignity depends on adherence to this principle.[32] The principle of dignity in the Islamic State's foreign relations reflects the superiority of Islamic teachings and, above all, the superiority of Islamic societies. The verses reflect the dignity of the believers and the Muslims as well as the famous hadiths of "Etela"[33]

"الاسلام يعلو و لايعلى عليه"[34]

(Islam is superior to its dignity and does not equal it.)

This jurisprudential document is considered the principle.[35]

The principle of Islamic dignity in foreign relations is based on the comprehensiveness, perfection and acceptability of religion and the basis of

---

[29] Makarem Shirazi, Nasser (in collaboration with a group of scholars and scholars), "*Sample Interpretation*," Tehran, Volume 2, Daralktb al-Islami , Publication , 2005, pp. 33-337.

[30] Ibid, pp. 33-167.

[31] The meaning of the "Nafye Sabil" is the lack of supremacy of the infidels against the Muslims

[32] Seyyed Sadegh Haghighat, "*the Foundations of Political Thought in Islam*", Qom: Mofid University Press, 2013, p. 95.

[33] The meaning of the "Etela" is superiority

[34] Bojnourdi, Mohammad, "*Al-Qawad al-Fiqahiyah*", Daralfkar Publications, Tehran, 2011, pp. 157-161.

[35] Surah Nisaa, Verse 138 - The New Testament, verse 8

foreign policy of Islam, which God considers this heavenly religion to be the most complete and the highest religion, and expressly emphasizes the lack of acceptance of other religions.[36] In the orientation and behavior of foreign policy, it is necessary to mix the need and the unnecessary and link between good socialization and softness in speech with religious dignity.[37]

Therefore, in its foreign relations, the Islamic state should be politically motivated and behaved so that their dignity is not distorted or diminished. Some verses of the Holy Qur'an have counted the reliance of Muslims on the unbelievers and non-Islamic governments in order to achieve the ugly worldly dignity and dignity, and recalling that all dignity is God and the Prophet and the believers, and Allah has spoken about it:

بَشِّرِ الْمُنافِقِينَ بِأَنَّ لَهُمْ عَذاباً أَلِيماً ـ الَّذِينَ يَتَّخِذُونَ الْكافِرِينَ أَوْلِياءَ مِنْ دُونِ الْمُؤْمِنِينَ أَ يَبْتَغُونَ عِنْدَهُمُ الْعِزَّةَ فَإِنَّ الْعِزَّةَ لِلَّهِ جَمِيعاً [38]

[O, Messenger!]Give glad-tidings to the hypocrites that for them there shall be a Painful Torment; -Those [hypocrites] who take Disbelievers for friends instead of Believers, do they seek honour (Power or glory) with them? Whereas indeed, to Allah Belongs all the Honour.

Thus, the principle of Islamic dignity, like the principle Nafye Sabil (The lack of supremacy of the infidels against the Muslims), governs the treaties and conduct of the Islamic State of the Islamic Republic, so that if the conduct of the foreign policy of the Islamic State leads to the dignity of the infidels and the decline of the Islamic society, it is unlawful and prohibited.

One of the most important verses about the negation of the domination of the unbelievers is that of the Qur'an:

"« وَلَن يَجْعَلَ اللّهُ لِلْكَافِرِينَ عَلَى الْمُؤْمِنِينَ سَبِيلاً[39] »".

---

[36]. "ان الدين عندالله الاسلام " و "و لن يقبل غير الاسلام دينا"
The only religion accepted in Islamic teachings is that it is the religion of Islam.
[37] Mohammad Mohammadi Rey Shahri, *"Musawat al-Amam Ali (as)"*, Dar al-Hadith publications, 2000, p. 337
[38] Surah Nissaa, verse 138-139
[39] Surah Nissaa , verse 141.

And Allah will not give the disbelievers any way (of success) against the believers.

God has not set the path to domination for the unbelievers against the believers. Salam commentators have spoken differently in the interpretation of this verse, some "Nafye Sabil" in the sense of proof and reason, and they have interpreted the verse as follows: God did not put the disbelievers in a superior position against the believers. Some have said that "Nafye Sabil" is to deny the infidel domination of believers at the Day of Resurrection. Meanwhile, Ibn Arabi, with the weakness of both of these possibilities, says there are three possibilities in the "Nafye Sabil" the verse:[40]

1. The unbelievers will never be able to eliminate the Islamic state and eliminate Islam;

2. God has not provided the field for the believers to dominate the disbelievers, these are the Muslims themselves, who provide such a thing by departing from the Islamic teachings;

3. The Lord has not given the believers the right path for the infidels. That is, the lack of permission of the infidels' guardianship over Muslims.

« يَا أَيُّهَا الَّذِينَ آمَنُوا لَا تَتَّخِذُوا عَدُوِّي وَعَدُوَّكُمْ أَوْلِيَاء تُلْقُونَ إِلَيْهِم بِالْمَوَدَّةِ وَقَدْ كَفَرُوا بِمَا جَاءكُم مِّنَ الْحَقِّ يُخْرِجُونَ الرَّسُولَ وَإِيَّاكُمْ أَن تُؤْمِنُوا بِاللَّهِ رَبِّكُمْ إِن كُنتُمْ خَرَجْتُمْ جِهَادًا فِي سَبِيلِي وَابْتِغَاء مَرْضَاتِي تُسِرُّونَ إِلَيْهِم بِالْمَوَدَّةِ وَأَنَا أَعْلَمُ بِمَا أَخْفَيْتُمْ وَمَا أَعْلَنتُمْ وَمَن يَفْعَلْهُ مِنكُمْ فَقَدْ ضَلَّ سَوَاء السَّبِيلِ[41] ».

O ye who believe! Choose not my enemy and your enemy for allies. Do ye give them friendship when they disbelieve in that truth which hath come unto you, driving out the messenger and you because ye believe in Allah, your Lord? If ye have come forth to strive in my way and seeking my good pleasure, (show them not friendship). Do ye show friendship unto them in secret, when I am Best Aware of what ye hide and what ye proclaim? And whosoever doeth it among you, he verily hath strayed from the right way.

«لا يَتَّخِذِ الْمُؤْمِنُونَ الْكَافِرِينَ أَوْلِيَاء مِنْ دُونِ الْمُؤْمِنِينَ وَ مَنْ يَفْعَلْ ذلِكَ فَلَيْسَ مِنَ اللهِ فِي شَيْءٍ إِلاَّ أَنْ تَتَّقُوا مِنْهُمْ تُقَاةً وَ يُحَذِّرُكُمُ اللهُ نَفْسَهُ وَ إِلَى اللهِ الْمَصِيرُ[42]».

Let not the believers take disbelievers for their friends in preference to believers. Whoso doeth that hath no connection with Allah unless (it be) that ye but guard

---

[40] Ibn al-Arabi, "*Ahkamol al-Quran*," Beirut, Dar al-Kitab al-Arabi publications , 1997, p. 554.

[41] Sura Mumtahaneh , verse 1.

[42] Surah al-Imran , verse 28.

yourselves against them, taking (as it were) security. Allah bids you beware (only) of Himself. Unto Allah is the journeying.

The principle of the" Nafye Sabil", in addition to being considered in political discussions and foreign relations, has been accompanied by certain manifestations in the realm of action; Mirza Shirazi's historic fatwa in tobacco sanctions and the fatwa of Imam Khomeini on the capitulation agreement are examples of "Nafye Sabil" in contemporary history.

Imam Khomeini, with serious concern with this principle, discriminates any kind of international relations that violate this principle " Nafye Sabil" and ignore it, and prohibits the conclusion of such treaties; therefore, beyond the political theory, the principle of the " Nafye Sabil" It assumes the implication in foreign relations and gives it fatwa.[43]

5. The principle of mutual respect

In the political manifestation of Islam, disagreements are disproportionate (forbidden). In the Qur'an and the practice of the Holy Prophet of Islam, against the use of common points in diplomacy (relations with other governments), in terms of customs, customs, politics and history, and examples such as that which can be used as a common measure of use It is very visible. For example, God says in the Qur'an:

«قُلْ يا أَهْلَ الْكِتابِ تَعالَوْا إِلى كَلِمَةٍ سَواءٍ بَيْنَنا وَ بَيْنَكُمْ أَلاَّ نَعْبُدَ إِلاَّ اللهَ وَ لا نُشْرِكَ بِهِ شَيْئاً وَ لا يَتَّخِذَ بَعْضُنا بَعْضاً أَرْباباً مِنْ دُونِ اللهِ فَإِنْ تَوَلَّوْا فَقُولُوا اشْهَدُوا بِأَنَّا مُسْلِمُونَ؛[44]

Say [O, Messenger!]:" O, people of The Book! Come to the Word of [Monotheism] which is common between us and you: That we worship none but Allah and that we shall not associate anything with Him and do not some of us take others as the god other than Allah." And if they Turn their backs, then you [Muslims] Say:" Bear witness that we are Muslims And surrender ourselves to Allah's Will."

---

[43] Rohullah (Imam) Khomeini, *"Tahrir al-Wasila,"* Tahra, Muoassese Nashr Va Tanzim Asare Imam Khomeini Publication, 2013, p. 485.
[44] Sura Al-e-Imran , verse. 64.

What is mentioned in this verse is the invitation to common points between Islam and the traditions of" the people of the book[45]". And the verse has directed the Prophet of Islam to invite the people of the book to the monotheism, and this is the true interpretation of the word " كَّلِمَةٍ سَواءٍ". Therefore, the common ground between Jews, Christians and Muslims is their belief in the only God[46] .

Relationship between governments will be tense and will have the necessary strength to enable communication providers to communicate their behavior in a manner that does not offend other parties' values and beliefs, and to persuade the audience to use logical reasoning. Otherwise, it would not be possible to establish a relationship, and the consequences of insulting the values of the opposite side would be nothing but disrespect for each other's beliefs.

«وَلَا تَسُبُّواْ ٱلَّذِينَ يدْعُونَ مِن دُونِ ٱللَّهِ فَيسُبُّواْ ٱللَّهَ عَدْوَا بِغَيرِ عِلْمٍ..»[47]؛

And do not abuse their false gods those they (The polytheists) invoke besides Allah, lest they May abuse Allah in revenge and out Of ignorance…

Given the disparities between governments that are due to their interests and to some extent natural, today, however, paying attention and pushing nations and governments to cultural, political, and international commonalities is one of the basic necessities and necessities in relations between countries. In Qur'anic verses, in the framework of friendly relations and mutual respect, this emphasis has been emphasized and encourages Muslims to engage in cultural and intellectual dialogue and dialogue and the book's calling for convergence based on the principle of unity of monotheism, Can be done. Contrary to the diplomatic relations based on ethnic, racial or territorial affiliation in some states, the Quran has been the centerpiece of international relations as a unity among divine religions.[48]

---

[45] People of the Book: is an Islamic term referring to Jews, Christians, and Sabians and sometimes applied to members of other religions such as Zoroastrians.

[46] Tabatabai, Seyyed Mohammad Hussein, *"Teshir al-Mizan,"* Tehran, Islami Islamic Republic of Qom Publishers, 1996, p. 389.

[47] An'am Sura , verse. 108.

[48] Makarem Shirazi, Nasser (in collaboration with a group of scholars and scholars), *"Sample Interpretation, "* Tehran, Daralktb al-Islami , Publication, 2005, pp. 33-49.

The Holy Quran says that even in order to communicate and negotiate with others in order to prove their beliefs and beliefs, they must come up with arguments, logic and controversy and deny any disrespect to others.

«اُدْعُ إِلَى سَبِيلِ رَبِّكَ بِالْحِكْمَةِ وَالْمَوْعِظَةِ الْحَسَنَةِ وَجادِلْهُمْ بِالَّتِي هِي أَحْسَنُ» [49]

[O, Messenger!] Invite mankind to The Way of your Creator and Nurturer with Divine Reasoning and fair Preaching and argue with them in the best manner.

Because the preacher prefers what is right for the audience. What is important in Islamic diplomacy is reasoning based on wisdom and preaching good and good and good debates.

«وَ لاَ تُجادِلُوا أَهْلَ الكِتابِ إِلّا بِالَّتِي هِي أَحْسَن» [50]

([O, Muslims!]Do not dispute with the people of the Book, except the wrongdoers of them,)

Contrary to diplomacy relations between non-Muslims, today we are very nectarous and contend with deception.[51]

One of the basic necessities and needs in the relations between the governments from the point of view of the Qur'anic verses is mutual respect for other countries and governments. The foreign policy orientation of the Islamic system with other states, as well as mutual respect to them, can be formulated in the following ways:

A: The relationship of Islamic governments with each other;

B) The Islamic State's relationship with monotheistic governments;

C: Relations with non-monotheistic governments;

D: Relations with the arrogant government and the domination system;

1-5. the relationship of Islamic governments with each other;

In many verses, Allah has emphasized the good relations and mutual respect between the governments, especially the Islamic states, and regards the property and the dignity of all Muslims and preserves it as obligatory. The Quran says

---

[49] Nahl Sura, verse 125.

[50] Surah Ankabut , verse 46.

[51] Tabatabaei, Mohammad Hussein, *the translation of Al-Mizan,*" Tehran, Islamic Qom Publication , 1996, p .99.

about the peaceful relationship based on the mutual respect of Islamic governments:

«يَا أَيُّهَا الَّذِينَ آمَنُوا ادْخُلُوا فِي السِّلْمِ كَافَّةً وَ لاتَتَّبِعُوا خُطُواتِ الشَّيْطانِ إِنَّهُ لَكُمْ عَدُوٌّ مُبِينٌ 52

O, you who believe! Enter you all into Submission to Allah [in peace and without dispute] and do not follow the footsteps of Satan; for verily, he is to you an evident enemy;

And in another verse he says:

«إِنَّمَا الْمُؤْمِنُونَ إِخْوَةٌ فَأَصْلِحُوا بَيْنَ أَخَوَيْكُمْ وَ اتَّقُوا اللَّهَ لَعَلَّكُمْ تُرْحَمُونَ 53

The Muslims are considered brothers, so Make peace and agreement between your brothers; and fear from the disobedience of Allah's Commands that you may receive Mercy.

The Islamic State's relationship with monotheistic governments;

Before speaking, monotheistic governments are referred to the followers of the religions that according to Islam, their Prophet had a divine book to direct human beings. Jews and Christians have been examples of this term in Islamic culture. Followers of the Zoroastrian religion and the Sabians have also been named among the scholars of the Islamic scholars.

"إِنَّ الَّذِينَ آمَنُوا وَالَّذِينَ هَادُوا وَالصَّابِئِينَ وَالنَّصَارَى وَالْمَجُوسَ وَالَّذِينَ أَشْرَكُوا إِنَّ اللَّهَ يَفْصِلُ بَيْنَهُمْ يَوْمَ الْقِيَامَةِ إِنَّ اللَّهَ عَلَى كُلِّ شَيْءٍ شَهِيدٌ"54

Those who believe in Islam and those Who follow the Jewish Law and the Sabians, and the Christians and the Magians and the polytheists, they all will Be judged and decided for, by Allah on The Day of Resurrection. Verily, Allah is The Supreme Witness over all things.

---

52 Sura Baqarah , verse 208.

53 Surah Hujurat , Verse 10.

54 Hajj Sura , verse 17.

As the relationship between an Islamic country and another Islamic country is expressed, the principle of the relationship is mutual respect, cooperation, brotherhood and trust. The verses of the Holy Qur'an in relation to the monotheistic governments have emphasized the principle of convergence and the emphasis given to the existence of commonalities to them and avoid disputes. Therefore, when the Lord confesses about the establishment of good relations based on mutual respect between Muslims and others, he says to the Prophet (peace is upon him):

«قُلْ يا أَهْلَ الْكِتابِ تَعالَوْا إِلى كَلِمَةٍ سَواءٍ بَيْنَنا وَ بَيْنَكُمْ أَلاَّ نَعْبُدَ إِلاَّ اللَّهَ وَ لا نُشْرِكَ بِهِ شَيْئاً وَ لا يَتَّخِذَ بَعْضُنا بَعْضاً أَرْباباً مِنْ دُونِ اللَّهِ فَإِنْ تَوَلَّوْا فَقُولُوا اشْهَدُوا بِأَنَّا مُسْلِمُونَ»[55]

Say [O, Messenger!]:" O, people of The Book! Come to the Word of [Monotheism] which is common between us and you: That we worship none but Allah and that we shall not associate anything with Him and do not some of us take others as the god other than Allah." And if they Turn their backs, then you [Muslims] Say:" Bear witness that we are Muslims And surrender ourselves to Allah's Will."

Therefore, Allah says to His Prophet, call on Christianity (divine religions) and tell them based on the common principles of the relationship between Islam and Christianity, and these principles are:

1. We worship God;
2. Do not partner with him;
3. Lets abolish the regime of the lord and the slave and do not seek to excuse us.

So that it can abolish the regime of the lord and the slave, and no one else is praised and no one else is alive. He said: we are all God's servants. We have a paste in the name of God and a divine law, nobody does not impose his opinion on others, and what God said and we accept.

The Holy Quran in Surah Al-Anbiya states:

«إِنَّ هذِهِ أُمَّتُكُمْ أُمَّةً واحِدَةً وَ أَنَا رَبُّكُمْ فَاعْبُدُونِ»[56]

---

[55] Sura Al-e-Imran , verse 64.
[56] Anbiya Sura, Verse 92.

And [O, Messenger!]verily, the Religion Of you[Messengers]is One[based on The Divine Unity and submission to Allah's Will]and I am your Creator and Nurturer, so worship Me and Be obedient to Me;

That is, not only Muslims are the same people, but Muslims, Christians, Jews, and all followers of the divine prophets of one nation because they believe in a reference and resurrection and believe in the principle of mission.

3-5. Relations with non-monotheistic governments;

Non-monotheistic governments are called to governments that the rulers and peoples of that land do not have the unity of God. Allah Almighty in the verses of the Holy Quran, after depicting the Islamic state's relationship with the other Islamic state and the non-Muslim state, considers the principle of communication and mutual respect, as long as the policy of sedition, conspiracy and war is not. Hence, the Quran's verses explain the quality of the relationship between Muslims and others who are not at all following any Divine school:

« لا يَنْهاكُمُ اللَّهُ عَنِ الَّذينَ لَمْ يُقاتِلُوكُمْ فِي الدِّينِ وَ لَمْ يُخْرِجُوكُمْ مِنْ دِيارِكُمْ أَنْ تَبَرُّوهُمْ وَ تُقْسِطُوا إِلَيْهِمْ إِنَّ اللَّهَ يُحِبُّ الْمُقْسِطينَ»[57]

Allah dose not forbid you having Relationship with those who have not Fought you on the account of Religion And have not driven you out of your Homeland and He does not forbid you From doing good and regarding justice To them: Verily, Allah likes those who Consider justice towards other people;

The idolaters and disbelievers were two groups: some were conspiratorial and tried to kill Muslims, exile or imprison them or confiscate and rob them of their property. The other group did not work with the Muslims. If the infidels from the second group are favored by the Muslims, it is not only bad, but it is God's favorite work. God does not read that you do not have peaceful people with the disbelievers or do not apply them to justice, but he says: Do not be persuaded, if a

---

[57] Sura Mumtahanah, Verse 8.

group does not wrong you, although they are not Muslims, you also have a peaceful life with justice and justice with Establish them.

In another verse, Allah says to the Prophet (peace be upon him): the maintenance of infidel security is politically, socially and economically necessary to the extent that they are based on the logic of reward. The Holy Quran says:

» وَ إِنْ أَحَدٌ مِنَ الْمُشْرِكِينَ اسْتَجَارَكَ فَأَجِرْهُ حَتَّى يَسْمَعَ كَلامَ اللَّهِ ثُمَّ أَبْلِغْهُ مَأْمَنَهُ ذلِكَ بِأَنَّهُمْ قَوْمٌ لا يَعْلَمُونَ«[58]؛

And if any one of the idolaters Seeks refuge in you,[O, Messenger]Grant him, so that he may hear The Word of Allah {The Holy Qur'an} and then escort him To where he can be secured, that is Because they are a people who lack Knowledge[and their disbelief is due to Their ignorance]

That is, if one of the idolaters wants to establish a cultural and political relationship with you and come to your country to hear and examine the divine verses, you must: firstly: leave the border open to him; secondly, protect him when he is within the border; That he will not harm him; third, let him listen to divine speech, then if he does not accept and wants to return to his country, you are obliged to remove him from your border.

4-5. Relations with the arrogant government and the domination system
Contrary to the three preceding questions, the Lord in the Holy Quran has not left the principle of respect for political, economic and cultural relations in the Holy Quran on relations with the arrogant, arrogant, dominant, and arrogant governments. From Islamic perspective, peaceful living is not possible on the basis of mutual respect with the infidels against Islam and the oppressed, but with them only must be opposed.
In Islamic teachings, peaceful living is not possible based on mutual respect with the infidel who is struggling against Islam and Muslims, but it must only be confronted with this group (arrogant). The Qur'an is different between the infidels

---

[58] Sura Taubah , verse 6.

and the arrogant, and says: "You can have a just life with the disbelievers who are not fighting you, but you cannot live like this because they do not leave you."[59]

They (arrogant) will make your life legal. They are not willing to live without any commitment and they will not respect any treaty. If you ask for such a group to be bound by the International Covenant, they will not sign it.[60]

«وَ إِنْ نَكَثُوا أَيْمانَهُمْ مِنْ بَعْدِ عَهْدِهِمْ وَ طَعَنُوا في دينِكُمْ فَقاتِلُوا أَئِمَّةَ الْكُفْرِ إِنَّهُمْ لا أَيْمانَ لَهُمْ لَعَلَّهُمْ يَنْتَهُونَ»[61]؛

But if they break their oaths after Their covenant and treat your religion With taunt, then fight the chiefs of The disbelievers who have no respect for Their oaths, so that they may desist [Breaking their oaths and agreements];

This is while the behavior of this group is such that if you want to transfer your thoughts and culture, they will prevent them and try to impose their thought and disapprove of your thinking. And if you establish a political relationship, they want to impose their policies and reject your political votes. In business and industrial relations, you will want to use your industrial experiences and advancements, but do not make any progress or achievements. Consequently, such a group cannot live. They are, in any case, credible. Therefore, the Holy Quran says: Enemy with this group:

«فقاتلوا ائمه الكفر»

What is meant by "murderous", here, is not just murder, it is enmity, retaliation, and taking right from the infidels. Because they do not respect the covenant, covenant, and the like, and they do not adhere to it. With such a group you cannot live. International relations mean the connection between people who are not arrogant in any of them.

The Holy Quran gives us the same message about the Jews:

«وَ مِنْهُمْ أُمِّيُّونَ لا يَعْلَمُونَ الْكِتابَ إِلاَّ أَمانِيَّ وَ إِنْ هُمْ إِلاَّ يَظُنُّونَ»[62]؛

---

[59] Tabatabaei, Mohammad Hussein, "the translation of Al-Mizan," Tehran, Islamic Qom Publication , 1996, p. 97.

[60] Ibid , p. 97.

[61] Sura Taubah , verse 12.

[62] Surah Baqarah ,Verse 78.

And there are among them unlettered And common folks, not knowing The Book,{ The Taurat} so they hold only to their Own desires, [from what they have Learned by hearsay] and they do only Conjecture;

Then in another verse he says:

«وَ مِنْهُمْ مَنْ إِنْ تَأْمَنْهُ بِدِينارٍ لا يُؤَدِّهِ إِلَيْكَ إِلاَّ ما دُمْتَ عَلَيْهِ قائِماً ذلِكَ بِأَنَّهُمْ قالُوا لَيْسَ عَلَيْنا فِي الْأُمِّيِّينَ سَبِيلٌ وَ يَقُولُونَ عَلَى اللَّهِ الْكَذِبَ وَ هُمْ يَعْلَمُونَ؛» [63]

And there is a sect of the Jewish rabbis, Who[while reciting their own writing]Twist their tongues[in a way]that you May suppose it as a part of the Book,{The Taurat} Yet it is not a part of the Taurat; and They say:" It is from Allah" though it is Not from Allah; and knowingly they tell Lie about Allah, and they know it only So well[that they lie.]

Trust is part of international principles; but they betray, however, they consider themselves to be from the book and even say: "The wealth and blood of them (Muslims) is lawful to us." Such a group is not co-existent; therefore, God has issued a commemorative order against the mustahabs.

Finally, it is necessary to point out that Allah Almighty has not only failed to recognize the mutual respect for this group (arrogant governments), but also forbade the relationship between the heart and the secret of it. The Quran says about not having a heart transplant with the infidels:

« يا أَيُّهَا الَّذِينَ آمَنُوا لا تَتَّخِذُوا بِطانَةً مِنْ دُونِكُمْ لا يَأْلُونَكُمْ خَبالاً وَدُّوا ما عَنِتُّمْ قَدْ بَدَتِ الْبَغْضاءُ مِنْ أَفْواهِهِمْ وَ ما تُخْفِي صُدُورُهُمْ أَكْبَرُ قَدْ بَيَّنَّا لَكُمُ الْآياتِ إِنْ كُنْتُمْ تَعْقِلُونَ؛» [64]

O, you who believe! Do not take as your intimate friends, those who are outside your religion, since they will not fail to do their best to betray you. They desire affliction for you; hatred has already appeared from their Mouths [through their words], but what their breasts conceal is far worse. Indeed we have made clear to you The Words of Revelation [to be your Guide about them]; and if you use your Reason [you will understand.]

---

[63] Sura Al-e-Imran, verse 75.
[64] Sura Al-e-Imran, verse 118.

You should not allow the secrets of your aliens. Do not throw them into your heart, To love within them. Islam is in a state of emergency if international relations are permissible even with infidels. So, you can sell and buy commodities in an emergency, you can trade military supplies and you can trade political issues.

6.   Principle of Invitation (Peacemaking)

Explaining the two concepts of the principle of invocation (peaceful) or jihad (the originality of the war) is important in contributing to the nature of the principles of foreign relations from the point of view of Islam and is more than the other principles discussed and debated. The wide-ranging debate over the principle of invasion and jihad led to the mention of both principles under one heading, because, as some Muslim scholars have said, if only to mention the title of "invitation," the existing views on the principle of war or peace in Islamic foreign relations are ignored. And if we make the principle legitimate for jihad and war, the plan for the title of the principle of invitation will remain unfinished.

We discuss the details of this argument with a fundamental question of the nature of foreign relations from the point of view of Islam: Is Islam in conflict with non-Islamic societies, or peace? In other words, is peace a rule and war, necessity or vice versa?

If the principle of jihad, as one of the principles of foreign policy of Islam, is emphasized, according to some Muslim scholars and the general Orient lists, is the principle of war-oriented foreign relations in Islam, and peace is a matter of special situations and exceptions to the rule. But if the principle is invoked, the case will be different.[65] In order to explain the principle of invitation and jihad, several issues are stated below.

Diplomacy based on the authenticity of the invitation

The expansion of Islamic culture is one of the major goals of the political system of Islam, in the domestic and international arena. This is done in the form of

---

[65] Seyyed Abdul Qaim Sajjadi, "Principles of Foreign Policy in the Qur'an", *Journal of Political Science, (Iran)*, 2003, Vol.4, No.15, p 88.

diplomacy of invitation and propaganda; if the Qur'an addresses this issue and says:

«الَّذِينَ يُبَلِّغُونَ رِسالاتِ اللَّهِ وَ يَخْشَوْنَهُ وَ لا يَخْشَوْنَ أَحَداً إِلاَّ اللَّهَ وَ كَفى بِاللَّهِ حَسِيباً؛»[66]

This is a rule for those who deliver The Messages of Allah and who fear Him and none but Allah; and Allah's Taking account are only what matters;

The ultimate goal of the Prophet of Islam, "peace is upon him," is to invoke uniqueness and submissiveness against God. They did not use it to invite violence and war. But also promoted guidance and guidance, and included in the discussion the important points that are used today in the context of public diplomacy:

1. Target elite and influential people. So they sent letters to tribal chiefs and empires, and wrote non-political dimensions to the intellectual leaders of the letter and invited them to Islam. 2. Use of Tolerance and Tolerance: The Prophet (s) did not accept the invitation and acceptance of the law and the law in promulgating religion or inviting them promptly. They gradually progressed and, accepting the invite from the other side, accepted his word without any inquiry, which would have assured the opposing side.67 3. Flexibility in Invitation 4. Avoiding War,

The Prophet (peace be upon him) initially invited his relatives to Islam and then invited them and invited others to Islam. Allah says in the Quran:

«. قُلْ يا أَيُّهَا النَّاسُ إِنِّي رَسُولُ اللَّهِ إِلَيْكُمْ جَمِيعاً الَّذِي لَهُ مُلْكُ السَّماواتِ وَ الْأَرْضِ لا إِلهَ إِلاَّ هُوَ يُحيِي وَ يُمِيتُ فَآمِنُوا بِاللَّهِ وَ رَسُولِهِ النَّبِيِّ الْأُمِّيِّ الَّذِي يُؤْمِنُ بِاللَّهِ وَ كَلِماتِهِ وَ اتَّبِعُوهُ لَعَلَّكُمْ تَهْتَدُونَ؛»[68]

Say [O, Messenger!]:" O, people! I am sent to you all, as the Messenger of Allah, the One to Whom belongs The Dominion of the heavens and the earth; there is no God but Allah, The Almighty Who gives life and Causes death. So believe in Allah and His unlettered Messenger who believes In Allah and Allah's Words; follow The Messenger so that you may be guided."

---

[66] Surah al-Ahzab, verse 39.
[67] Andisheh Magazine, Mashhad, No. 1, spring 1991, pp. 88-86.
[68] Sura A'rafi ,verse 158.

This wrong claim that the Prophet Muhammad (peace be upon him) at the beginning of the advent of Islam just wanted to invite the Quraysh to Islam, but with the advancement and attractiveness of Islam, he made his call public. Pure falsehood and a cynical word that attributes Islam, because in the Qur'anic verses, the words "or 'al-'Arb" and "or al-Qurash" have never been brought, but it has always been his general statement, and from "يا ايّها الذين أمنوا" / O you who believe. "And" يا ايّها النّاس /O people" Used.[69]

Priority to the invitation to war

The Prophet (peace be upon him), in his political life, has used mechanisms to invite, each of which indicates the primacy of inviting other instruments; the need to invite before jihad and the unreliability of jihad before invoking the affairs Islamic jurisprudents and commentators.[70]

In the following, the emphasis placed in Islam on the priority of inviting peace is to be examined:

1. Negotiations with Ambassadors and Representatives: The formation of the government by the Prophet (peace be upon him) in Medina to date, the negotiation has enjoyed a special significance in the Islamic world, including the invitation of tribal leaders. The Prophet Muhammad (peace be upon him), called for negotiations for all his ambassadors, was a religious duty and ordered them to take diplomacy in front of other methods.[71]

    2. dispatching missionaries and sending messages to the heads of state and tribes, including the message to the empires of Iran, Rome, Egypt and the king of Nijah, and dispatching propaganda to Yemen and Najd and Rajay;[72]

    3. Use of well-known and experienced diplomats such as Imam Ali (PBUH) and Mu'taz ibn Habil to Yemen or Ja'far ibn Abi Abu Talib;[73]

---

[69] Mortaza, Motahari, Book of Jihad, Tehran, Sadra Publication, 2006, p. 232.

[70] bdul Qayum, Sajjadi, *"Diplomacy and Political Behavior in Islam"*, Book Boostan, Qom, 2010, p. 54.

[71] Abdul Qayum, Sajjadi, "Foreign Policy in the Viewpoint of Imam Ali (as)," *Political Science Quarterly, (Iran)*, 2000, Vol. 3, No.11, P. 99

[72] Amid-Zanjani, Abbas Ali, *"Political of Jurisprudence,"* Tehran, Amir Kabir Publications, 1989, P. 296.

[73] Ibid,

4. Contracts and political agreements such as the Medina Charter, the Hedibiyyah Peace Agreement and the Permanent Peace Treaty with the Christians of Najran are examples of the peace mechanism of the political form of the Prophet's policy.[74]

5. Another feature of the invitation, in Islamic teachings, is that the audience at the invitation is the whole generation of human beings, not a particular stratum. [75]This is also about the universality of Islam. Therefore, in most of the Qur'an's words, especially after Islam absorbed the island of Al-Arab, it was("يا ايّها النّاس" all people) and below all its political, religious, social and cultural goals.

As stated, in the diplomacy of the Prophet Muhammad (peace be upon him), Islam has been the main priority against Islam. In principle, the political behavior of the Prophet Muhammad was in the field of invoking politics, and this method of political behavior continued at the beginning of the mission in Mecca, and then migrated to Medina and the formation of an Islamic government. Invitation to the precepts of Islam is one of the essential elements of religion and is rooted in a clear source of revelation and is one of the most important and most important goals of the mission of divine prophets, especially the Prophet.[76]

The mistake of spreading Islam with the sword:

From the point of view of Islam, reluctance and coercion are not a means of guidance, it is a great mistake that some have committed and said that Islam has spread its religion with a sword. Because faith and faith are not something that is replaced by force, sword, and compulsion in the hearts, but the hearts are only tolerant of the argument, the argument, and the logic of the humble and permeable.[77] Since Islam is not anxious in accepting religion, Islam does not force

---

[74] Nazari, Bahram and Mazaheri Majid, "Ethics and Behavior of the Prophet's Diplomacy", *Journal of Ethics (Iran)*, 2010, No. 26, p. 51.

[75] Abdul Qaim, Sajjadi, *"Diplomacy and Political Behavior in Islam"*, Qom, Boostan Book, 2010, P. 170.

[76] Nazari, Bahram and Mazaheri Majid, "Ethics and Behavior of the Prophet's Diplomacy", *Journal of Ethics (Iran)*, 2010, No. 26, p. 54.

[77] Islamic Publications Office, *"Scientific Issues in the Interpretation of Al-Mizan "Allameh "Seyyed Mohammad Hossein Tabatabaei"*, Islamic Publishing of Qom, Tehran, 1996, p. 48.

the infidels to accept the religion of Islam, but deals with them with tolerance and intercourse, and advises them with soft language, releasing them and listening to their words. And friendly answers. Because this is the only way to attract them and has a great impact on them, The Holy Quran also says:

» لا اكراه فِى الدّين قد تبين الرّشد مِنَ الغى؛[78]

There is no compulsion in accepting Religion,[since]Truth has verily Become distinct from Falsehood[in The Qur'an and through The Messenger and Miracles];

If the Muslims took a sword at some point in history and chose the war, it was not for the development of the realm of government and for compulsory inflicting religion on the infidels, but for defending the aggressive enemies and defending Muslims and Islam. Basically, Islam does not accept the invitation that accompanies violence; invitation and propaganda in Islam cannot be reluctant and compulsory.[79] So some people mistakenly point out that Islam is the religion of the sword and its expansion is also with a sword, they intend to make Islam a warring and power seeker. If the sword was used in Islam, it was only to defend the privacy of Islam, the monotheism and the soul of the Muslims, not the conquest of other countries.[80]

The difference between the religion of Islam and Christianity is that the Christianity has not paid attention to social, political, and economic affairs, and has only addressed a set of moral orders that do not require the defense of jihad. But Islam has put forward a comprehensive plan for human life, and it is definitely a matter of defending, jihad and having an army of great importance. Because if one day was raped by another country, they would not lose their values and dignity under the oppression and the rule of others .But the objection that Islam is a religion of war does not enter, because The principle of self-defense and values is a matter of fact and rationality.[81] Each state and government defends its geographical and cultural boundaries, so the jihad in Islam has a defensive aspect, and the absolute violence attributed to Islam is not true. Because God in the

---

[78] Surah Baqara, verse 256.
[79] Morteza, Motahari, "*Siri Dar Sera-e Nabavi*," Tehran, Sadra Publication, 2005, p. 214.
[80] Ibid, p. 218.
[81] Mortaza, Motahari, "*Book of Jihad*," Tehran, Sadra Publication, 2006, p. 234

Qur'an orders you to invite the people rightfully with wisdom and preaching, And with jihad, the lives and the property of Muslims, but also human beings from the yoke of oppressors of the mercenaries.

» ادْعُ إِلَى سَبِيلِ رَبِّكَ بِالْحِكْمَةِ وَ الْمَوْعِظَةِ الْحَسَنَةِ وَ جادِلْهُمْ بِالَّتِي هِيَ أَحْسَنُ إِنَّ رَبَّكَ هُوَ أَعْلَمُ بِمَنْ ضَلَّ عَنْ سَبِيلِهِ وَ هُوَ أَعْلَمُ بِالْمُهْتَدِينَ؛ «[82]

[O, Messenger!]Invite mankind to The Way of your Creator and Nurturer with Divine Reasoning and fair Preaching and argue with them in the best manner. Truly, you're Creator and Nurturer is the Supreme Position to know who has gone astray From His Path and who the guided Ones is.

The innate defense

There are different opinions about the legitimacy of the war, but all the scholars have agreed conscientiously that defense is innate, and humans and animals respond to unconscious attacks by others.[83] From the point of view of Islam, war is not necessary for human nature; therefore, the Qur'an has considered the war unfavorable.

» كُتِبَ عَلَيْكُمُ الْقِتالُ وَ هُوَ كُرْهٌ لَكُمْ وَ عَسى أَنْ تَكْرَهُوا شَيْئاً وَ هُوَ خَيْرٌ لَكُمْ وَ عَسى أَنْ تُحِبُّوا شَيْئاً وَ هُوَ شَرٌّ لَكُمْ وَ اللَّهُ يَعْلَمُ وَ أَنْتُمْ لا تَعْلَمُونَ؛ «[84]

Fighting is Ordained upon you though It is resented by you; but,[it happens That]you resent a thing whereas it is Good for you, and perhaps you like Something whereas it is evil for you, And verily, Allah knows[what is best]While you do not know.[Since Allah's Knowledge is infinite, but man's is Limited]

As previously said, Islam is basically the opposite of war. Therefore, peace and invasion are prior to war. Foreign relations in Islam are based on peace and war is exceptional. In other words, the military doctrine in Islam is inherently defensive,

---

[82] Surah Nahl , verse 125.

[83] Haghighat, Seyyed Sadegh,"*Principles and Objectives of Foreign Policy of the Islamic State*," Qom, Islamic Center of Science and Culture press, 2006, P. 325.

[84] Surah Baqara, verse 216.

not dominant and interferential.[85] God advises on a peaceful relationship with others:

يا أَيُّهَا الَّذِينَ آمَنُوا ادْخُلُوا فِي السِّلْمِ كَافَّةً؛[86]

O, you who believe! Enter you all into Submission to Allah [in peace and without dispute] and do not follow the footsteps of Satan; for verily, he is to you an evident enemy;

In the Holy Shariah of Islam, war and jihad have been accepted as a necessity and as the last resort. It is not to invite and accept Islamic religion and beliefs to others, but to repatriate harm and danger.[87] In the practice of the Prophet Muhammad (PBUH), as regards dealing with other tribes, we are seeing many peaceful treaties with Jews and other tribes.[88] Amir al-Mu'minin Ali (as) also says: "Never refuse peace offerings on the part of the enemy that God's pleasure is in it, that the comfort of your warriors and your peace of mind and the security of the country will be met by peace."[89] But if there is a need to defend the monotheism and morals of the Muslims and oppression as much as possible in the face of Islam's freedom, it will use the most advanced possibilities available, which is, of course, normal.

There are some misgivings that Islam has obligated jihad like fasting and prayer, and this is a sign of legitimizing a war. In other words, why Islam considers the war to advance its goals in the form of an "Ebtedaei jihad" in order to promote the teachings of Islam? To answer this claim, we begin by defining the elemental jihad, and we will respond to the objection according to the interpretation of

---

[85] Ali Asghar, Kazemi, *"the Role of Power in Society and International Relations,"* Tehran, Qomes Publications, 1991, p. 132.

[86] Surah Baqara, verse 208.

[87] Sheikh Mahmoud, Shaltot, *"War and Peace in Islam, translated by Sharif Rahmani,"* Cairo, Dar al-Sharouq Publication , 2001, p. 52.

[88] Mohammad Ibrahim, Ayati, *"The History of the Prophet of Islam,"* Qom, Dar al-Fakr, 2007, p. 209.

[89] Dashti, Mohammad, *"Translation of Nahj al-Balaghah,"* Qom, Mosharqin Publishing, 2000, p.569.

Allamah Tabatabai. Shahid Sani for the jihad-e Ebtebaei has given the definition that:

»جهادُ المشرکین ابتدائاً. لِدُعاتُهِم الى الاسلامِ و جهادُ مَن یَدُهُم على المُسلمینَ على الکفار؛«[90]

Initially, the war with the idolaters which invites them to Islam, as well as the jihad with the infidels who attack the Muslims, according to the definition given, the "Ebtedaei jihad" is a war with the motive of publishing, propagating and inviting monotheism, and purging society from evil, some believe that "Ebtedaei jihad"is the result of preventing the propagation of Muslims who themselves have entered into unwanted warfare. As a result of the "Ebtedaei jihad", it is only relevant to the enemy's military aggression and to the prohibition of Muslim propaganda. If the enemy does not fight against the propagation of the Muslims, or does not create a problem in the way of the propagation of Islam, the "Ebtedaei jihad" is essentially abandoned.[91]

Originality of peace According to Negation (Without) of the Aggression

Peace means the compromise and compromise of one nation with other peoples, [92] and the meaning of "Originality of peace" in the teachings of Islam is that Islam is the basis of communication with others peace, friendship, cooperation and peaceful relations. And war in a limited number of cases.[93] In other words, despite the outrageous depiction of Islam by Western countries, Islam is the religion of mercy and peace. In Quranic verses, Karim not only failed to emphasize the war as a factor in the expansion and influence of countries and governments, but also prohibited it.[94] In Islam, domination, tyranny, and compulsion of people to accept divine orders have been rejected in Islam. The verses of the Holy Qur'an also

---

[90] Zayn al-Din al-Bin Ali, Shahid Sani, "*Al-Rousta al-Bahiyah Fe Sharhe Allomato Aldameshghye*", Qom, , 2009, p. 329.

[91] Islamic Publications Office, "*Scientific Issues in the Interpretation of Al-Mizan "Allameh "Seyyed Mohammad Hossein Tabatabaei"*, Islamic Publishing of Qom, Tehran, 1996, p. 329.

[92] Ibn-e- manzor, Muhammad Makrom, "*Lassan al-Arab,*" Qom , Adib al-Huzeh Publishing, 1988, p. 384.

[93] Haghighat, Seyyed Sadegh, "*Transnational Responsibilities in Islamic State Foreign Policy,*" Tehran, Presidential Strategic Research Center Publishing, 1997, P. 342.

[94] Such as the verses of peace (Surah Anfal, verse 61)

emphasize the supremacy of peace over hostility and conflict.[95] The best way to prove the truth is to make a reminder and invite. The Qur'an also has instructions on the propagation of religion in which any mastery has been ruled out. So he says:

»ٌ فَذَكِّرْ إِنَّما أَنْتَ مُذَكِّرٌ ـ لَسْتَ عَلَيْهِمْ بِمُصَيْطِرٍ؛«[96]

So (O, Messenger) Remind them since you are the one to admonish, - But you are not a compeller over them, [So you cannot force them to Faith].

If non-Muslim nations respect the rights of Muslims and respect Muslims, Islam will have friendly relations based on cooperation and reconciliation. In this regard, the Holy Qur'an orders Muslims to welcome peace, peace and peaceful coexistence:

» وَ إِنْ جَنَحُوا لِلسَّلْمِ فَاجْنَحْ لَها...؛«[97]

But if the enemy shows tendency towards peace, you [O, Messenger] also tend to it and put your trust in Allah; verily, Allah is the Knowing Hearer;»

From the general point of the verse, it is deduced that Islam is not a warlord, but a war is a defensive one, and Islam, when it comes to the peaceful coexistence of unbelievers, has nothing to do with it.[98]

7.   The principle of diplomatic immunity

Diplomatic immunity is one of the major issues in diplomatic and international law that the process of fulfilling the transnational responsibilities of each country and the implementation of its foreign policy decisions, beyond the boundaries of the geography that are outside the sovereignty and power of that state, and, They are considered to be an enemy to the government and their diplomatic agents are in need of security, financial, and occupational security. This security can be called diplomatic immunity. Diplomatic immunity generally means that its holder is safe

---

[95] Hashemi Rafsanjani, Ali Akbar and researchers of the Center for Islamic Culture and Education, "*Quranic Culture,*" Qom, Boostan Ketab Publishing, 2007, p. 433.

[96] Qa'isha Sura, verses 21-22.

[97] Anfal Sura, verse 61.

[98] Qareati, Mohsen, "*Tafsir Noor,*" Vol. 4, Tehran, Cultural Center Publications, Lessons from the Koran, 1996, p. 355.

from pursuing the law and the agents of the country, or, in other words, the law and the law enforcement agents can not pursue the person who holds it.[99]

Diplomatic immunity today is one of the recognized principles of international relations, and its various dimensions are regulated and of universal concern. What is needed in this discussion is the background and theoretical basis of this right and how Islam will be treated.

Given the available sources, it can be argued that Islamic teachings have been pioneered in discussions on diplomatic rights, in particular the political immunity of deputies. If today the theorists of science and law and international relations state that the history of diplomatic rights and the regulation of diplomatic immunity issues, including personal, political, residential and family immunity, came back to the "Vienna Convention of 1961" decades ago, in Islamic law The very beginning of Islam has paid special attention to this matter in the words of 14 centuries ago.[100]

Ambassadors and diplomats have long been the language and speaker of the world's nations. When the ruling powers of the two countries have been able to reach agreement and have more peaceful behavior, their ambassadors played an active role. Today, it has also been tasked with protecting the national interests of the country, raising the level of relations and establishing friendly relations, the role of the government's representative, conducting negotiations for the achievement of understanding and cooperation, collecting possible information, and commenting and participating in government policies. They have included themselves for ambassadors and diplomats. The need for these duties in a foreign country is subject to political immunity.

Diplomatic relations and diplomatic rights are a special place in the legal system of Islam, because the prerequisite for inviting and guiding is the requirement for wisdom, active diplomacy and wisdom. In order to guide mankind and build a relationship with Ashraf, God sent the creatures (human beings) the ambassadors and taught them the best way to negotiate and diplomacy:

---

[99] Sadr, Javad, *"Diplomatic and Consular Rights,"* Tehran, Tehran University Press, 2007, P. 77.

[100] Sajjadi, Abdul-Qaim, *"Diplomacy and Political Behavior in Islam",* Qom, Book Bostan Publishing, 2010, pp. 84-85.

» اذْعُ إِلَى سَبِيلِ رَبِّكَ بِالْحِكْمَةِ وَ الْمَوْعِظَةِ الْحَسَنَةِ وَ جَادِلْهُمْ بِالَّتِي هِيَ أَحْسَنُ إِنَّ رَبَّكَ هُوَ أَعْلَمُ بِمَنْ ضَلَّ عَنْ سَبِيلِهِ وَ هُوَ أَعْلَمُ بِالْمُهْتَدِينَ؛[101]

[O, Messenger!]Invite mankind to The Way of your Creator and Nurturer with Divine Reasoning and fair Preaching and argue with them in the best manner. Truly, you're Creator and Nurturer is the Supreme Position to know who has gone astray From His Path and who the guided Ones is.

To regulate the social and international relations of mankind and direct human beings to human life and social justice, it is not possible to do such a great mission, except with active and wise diplomacy.

Undoubtedly, the prophets have played a great role as divine ambassadors in the creation of civilization, the development of social and international relations and the promotion of the culture of justice.

» لَقَدْ أَرْسَلْنَا رُسُلَنَا بِالْبَيِّنَاتِ وَأَنزَلْنَا مَعَهُمُ الْكِتَابَ وَالْمِيزَانَ لِيَقُومَ النَّاسُ بِالْقِسْطِ[102]؛

Indeed we sent Our Messengers with Signs and Miracles and revealed to them Books of Religion and gave them The Criterion for establishing justice among the people.

Diplomacy in the government of Prophet Muhammad (peace be upon him), the last divine ambassador has a special manifestation. History has recorded examples of the conduct of his diplomacy. By following the Qur'anic teachings during his reign, he sent a number of ambassadors to the heads of other countries and embassed other ambassadors from other countries. Attending or accepting the ambassador also met certain formalities. Undoubtedly, his work on international relations and diplomatic rights includes valuable and inspirational points.

In Islam, the principle of the granting of diplomatic immunity has been accepted as a rational custom and rationale. In addition, the supreme goal of the Prophet Muhammad (PBUH), which is the fulfillment of the universal mission, required more and more the necessity of political immunity and security for his ambassadors and propagandists of the Islamic school among other tribes and

---

[101] Surah Nahl , verse 125.
[102] Surah Hadid, Verse 25.

nations of the world. Therefore, the Islamic government of the Prophet (peace is upon him) had a special immunity not only for the representatives of the governments, but also for the representatives of the false claimants. In the famous book "Sira Ibn Hisham" It is said about the Mosailame Kazzab,

Despite their false claims and their ambassadors, they were immune from immunity from the ambassadors of the Prophet Muhammad.[103]

Today, diplomatic immunity and ambassadors in war and peace are of particular importance, and diplomatic relations have existed since the advent of Islam, and the Prophet (peace be upon him) has also used propaganda for his divine mission and the affairs of the Muslim community. With the spread of Islam, diplomatic relations were also widespread and organized. Representatives and ambassadors were negotiating and signing contracts with the powers and authority entrusted to them by the Prophet of Islam. At the beginning of Islam, the important duties of the ambassadors were the invitation to Islam and the negotiations for peace, the exchange of prisoners and the conclusion of a partnership and friendship treaty.

8. Principle of The truth of the treaty

The troth of the covenant means accepting the treaties and contracts and doing them. [104] The principle of vindication of the covenant is one of the main commands of Islam, which many verses have recommended.[105] The fulfilment of the promise is one of the principles of Islamic State foreign policy. The Islamic State is obligated to respect all pledged political and military treaties and treaties with other societies with respect and respect for its commitment.

The Islamic State is obligated to respect all pledged political and military treaties and treaties with other societies with respect and respect for its commitment. In some verses of the Quran, absolute reference is made to the observance of the treaties, while others claim responsibility for the treaty. Also, some of the verses emphasize the vindication of pledges and pledges of treaties,

---

[103] Ibn Hisham, *"Al-Sireet al-Nibawiyah,"* Cairo, Al-M aktab Al kolliat Alzaabi Publishing, 1978, Volume 3, p. 204.

[104] Fakhr al-Din bin Muhammad al-Tariyah, *"Majma Al Bahrain,"* Volume 3, Beirut, Al-Wafa Institute of Publications, 1986, p. 103.

[105] Many verses, including the following, emphasize the fulfillment of obligations and treaties: Asra (17) verse 34, Baghera (2), verse 177, Moamenon (23) verse 8, Maarej (70) verse 32, maedeh (15) verse 1, and al e Emron (3) Verse 76.

the consequences of the breach of the treaty. The principle of the obligation to commit and commit to treaties is the case of commentators, and everyone has acknowledged the need to respect the promise of betrayal and deception in the rights of Muslims and non-Muslims.[106]

Many Islamic scholars and scholars believe that it is not necessary to devote itself to certain contracts and includes all contracts that do not contradict law, morality and reason. They are in the process of preparing the main rule that, in cases of doubt, they will order the contract and increase the scope of the required transactions.[107]

One of the important principles in relations between countries is the principle of commitment to the covenants and treaties between the two countries. According to it, the Islamic State has a duty to accept and adhere to all its political and military treaties and agreements with Islamic societies. In some verses of the Qur'an, reference is made to the observance of obligations and treaties, and in others, the obligation to enter into a pledge and responsibility is mentioned. A number of verses, while emphasizing commitment to the promise, pose harmful consequences to the violation of the treaty.[108]

Summing up

This chapter attempts to explain the principles of foreign policy of Islam while explaining the necessity of the relationship between the governments in terms of Islamic teachings. The main principles of analyzing the principles of foreign policy in Islam were the teachings of the Holy Qur'an, the hadith and the sirah of the Prophet of Islam. The main purpose of explaining the principles of foreign policy of Islam is to establish a monotheistic system, invite Islam, administer justice, establish security and peace, and defend the oppressed, and reject any authoritarian control.

---

[106] Nadie Mahmoud Mostafa, Allaqat al-Dowlia Phi-al-Islam Vaghte alharb, Beirut, Al-Ma'ad al-Alami Lalfakar al-Islami Publications, 1996, p. 103.

[107] Tabatabaei, Mohammad Hussein, *the translation of Al-Mizan,* Tehran, vol. 5, Islamic Qom Publication, 1996 , pp. 167

Islamic State foreign policy does not fit into any of my two dominant domains in international relations (realism and liberalism), since the nature of foreign relations from the point of view of Islam is not entirely war-oriented, not peace-cantered, but the nature of these relations due to the two-dimensional nature of man , Carries both things with it, though ultimately peace is considered to be a good thing and in accordance with the nature of man's perfection, so war is an exceptional situation that is prescribed only after the failure of peaceful efforts.

The foreign policy of Islam is debatable as a manifestation of soft power in terms of both politically and politically, because there is a red line from the perspective of Islam, each of which provides conditions for the empowerment of a political system. In terms of solidarity, anti-Semitism, oppression and tyranny, and in the context of the debate, there is the challenge of cooperation and flexibility. One of the factors behind the success of foreign policy of the Islamic state is the perseverance and persistence of Muslims in the belief and defense of it. This belief and stamina have caused the enemies to fail, no matter how hard endeavours and beliefs are shaken, the enemy will gain more influence.[109] The main objective in the foreign policy of the Islamic State is to reach the United Nation, and to create a single universal nation. That is, the philosophy of the activities of the diplomacy of Islam, based on the globalization and rule of law of the single world.[110]

---

[109] Vaseghy Rad, Mohammad Hussein, *"a New Approach to Islamic History"*, Qom, Afagh Ghadir Publications, 2004, P. 464.

[110] Nazari, Bahram and Mazaheri Majid, "Ethics and Behavior of the Prophet's Diplomacy", *Journal of Ethics (Iran)*, 2010, No. 26, p. 58.

»جهادُ المشركين ابتداءاً. لِدُعاتُهم الى الاسلامِ و جهادُ مَن يَدُهُم على المُسلمينَ على الكفار؛[90]

CHAPTER III

Foreign Policy Issues of the Islamic Republic of Iran

Foreign Policy Issues of the Islamic Republic of Iran

Considering what was mentioned in the first and second chapters, the main issues of foreign policy of the Islamic Republic of Iran have been considered in this chapter. As stated in the first chapter, despite the ability of some of the ideas in the presentation and analysis of some of the realities of foreign policy of the Islamic Republic of Iran, it has been substantiated that the shortcomings in the international relations theory have forced analysts and researchers to seek It would lead to a more complete theory in order to analyze all the facts of Iranian foreign policy on the basis of it. Therefore, it was concluded that the best theory is based on Islamic sources and teachings. Therefore, in the second chapter, the principles of foreign policy of Islam were expressed. Principles such as the principle of the negation of the of Nafye Sabil (principle of dignity), the principle of expediency, the issues of peace and war in Islam, the principle of devotion, the principle of coping, the principle of diplomatic immunity, the principle of unity, interaction and cooperation, the emphasis on commonalities, all of which are the lights and the mirror of the position The basis of foreign policy was Islam and was studied.

The principles of foreign policy of Islam determine the orientation of the Islamic State's foreign policy and the Islamic state must move on this basis. And Iran, as an Islamic state, must place its foreign policy on the basis of these principles. And the constitution of the Islamic Republic, which is based on Islam, in which the Constitution states the principles of foreign policy based on Islamic teachings.

In this chapter, the principles outlined in the Iranian Constitution that outline the orientation of Iran's foreign policy are examined first and then issues, principles and orientations of Iran's foreign policy are examined. Of course, the events and issues in Iran's foreign policy are huge and it is not possible to address them all, but try to outline the most important of them in this chapter.

The study will try to answer the following questions in this section, and if it is possible to answer these questions well, the understanding of the foreign policy of the Islamic Republic of Iran will be made easier.

Questions:

1. what are the principles governing Iran's foreign policy?

2. What is the purpose of the Islamic Republic of Iran for helping some countries and liberation movements?

3. Are these contributions not involved in the internal affairs of other countries?

4. What is the position of the expedient in the foreign policy of the Islamic Republic of Iran?

5. Why are Iranian politicians in isolation and sanctioned, but not in countries like the United States, despite the threat to national interests of Iran?

6. Is the Islamic Republic of Iran willing to pass on its material interests in the direction of foreign policy for the sake of the law and religious teachings?

7. How long will the Islamic Republic of Iran continue its opposition to Israel?

8. What is the purpose of Iranian politicians to invest and spend on material and spiritual burdens for countries like Palestine and Syria?

9. Why was the Islamic Republic of Iran contrary to the initial slogan of the revolution, which was "neither east nor west", but now with a country like Russia?

10. What is the role of Shiite geopolitics in Iran's relations with neighbouring countries, including West Asian region?

Before entering the main topics in this chapter, mention the following points.
1. The imperative of the comprehensive understanding of Islam, as expressed in Chapter II, is that this religion is always dynamic in every aspect of the political, social, and cultural context. Foreign policy is one of the most important areas that indicate the orientation of an Islamic state (Islamic Republic of Iran) towards the behaviors, actions and practices of other states. The Islamic State's foreign policy theory is both an explanatory and prescriptive for the Islamic state like the foreign policy of the Islamic Republic of Iran. The explanatory theory seeks to explain, explain and analyze the motives, decisions, actions and behavior of foreign policy, is an explanatory theory, since the ideal and desirable condition of foreign policy of an ideal state and Islamic right and its goals draw and recommends a

prescription. The foreign policy decision-makers of the Salam Hussein government should decide and act on their norms and values.[1]

2. The Islamic Republic of Iran has made every effort to establish all its legal bases and decisions based on Islamic Shari'a. Therefore, foreign policy is one of the most important issues of any system and country, and the whole system of action in the Islamic Republic of Iran has tried to move on the basis of the principles of foreign policy in Islam.

3. Contrary to the approach of realism and liberalism, which emphasize the centrality of the state and the individual in the process of relations and international relations, Islamic orientation is based on religion. In the Islamic approach (Islamic State), the most important principle governing the international system is neither absolute nor permanent peace, but in the international system, peace and war can be ruled out, although originality is with peace. In this sense, if nature is preceded by instinct, peace can be permanent. But if the instinct overtakes and precedes nature, then war and struggle will replace peace, peace and cooperation. With regard to what the Islamic Republic of Iran views as an Islamic state in relation to other countries based on the priority of peace, cooperation and interaction with all governments.

4. The author intends to prove that, despite the goal of the Islamic State of Iran (Islamic Republic of Iran), the attempt to reach the utopia is that the integrity of the laws of Islam is to be implemented and the basis for decision making, and the efforts of the cast And government decision-makers in Iran to enforce Islamic Sharia laws, but never claim that 100 percent of what it has done in foreign policy means the strict implementation of Islamic orders.

5. Some may have some drawbacks caused by contradictions, shortcomings and dichotomies in the foreign policy decisions of the Islamic Republic of Iran. Therefore, before discussing the issues of foreign policy of the republic, it is necessary to consider the names of Iran as the main rational and religious subject of expediency. When it comes to expediency, it does not mean the personal expediency of a particular group or specific people from the community, but rather

---

[1] Seyyed Jalal Dehghani Firoozabadi, "Islamic Theory of Foreign Policy: A Framework for Foreign Policy Analysis of the Islamic Republic of Iran," *Foreign Relations Quarterly (Iran),* Vol .3, No .9, 2011, p. 13.

the interest of Islam and the preservation of its achievements. Ayatollah Khamenei says:

"But it is expedient; it is not my personal interest to you that if we did this, it may cost us a lot. No, it will be expensive, unless we are, if it is in the interest of the country and in the interests of the revolution, But it is not my own interest to me, what matters, and the expediency means the expediency of the revolution, and this interest is immutable, that is, from our personal behavior."[2]

Hence the head of the Islamic government, in spite of the existence of certain principles embodied in the Qur'an and Islamic sources, may act in the course of decision-making against the principles in his political decision-making, and therefore may somehow move towards a strategy Cooperate and peace, fight elsewhere, or even take on silence.

The pursuit of expediency does not mean retreat from the ideals of the revolution, but as a source of the principles and ideals of the Islamic Revolution and national goals and interests according to the current state of affairs. In the foreign policy of the Islamic Republic of Iran, there are no demands and interests of individual, party or factional. The interest of the Islamic society is preceded by individual interests and national interests in the Islamic system are linked to the interests of the Islamic nation and there is no contradiction in the work,[3] but we must gradually evaluate the goals of the country according to the priorities and needs.

Acting in the Islamic State of Iran (Islamic Republic of Iran), considering the interest, while understanding the principles and principles of Islamic dignity, based on some of the most important issues and in the interests of the Islamic system, put some preferences on the agenda of its foreign policy. Although the likelihood of the expediency of a secondary ruling[4] appearing in Islamic jurisprudence may not

---

[2] Statement by Ayatollah Khamenei, "Supreme Leader of the Islamic Revolution of Iran" in a meeting with officials of the Ministry of Foreign Affairs - 09/07/1997 - (http://farsi.khamenei.ir/speech-topic)

[3] Alireza Davoodi, "The Ideals of the Revolutionary Point of Height of the Triangle of Dignity", Wisdom and Expectation, *The Younger Journal*, 06/06/2015

[4] "secondary ruling", a new religious law that replaces the first ruling by creating certain conditions, such as urgency, disagreement, and hajj, which aims to achieve the best decision on the basis of conditions and facilities, Such as the unnecessary hajj of particular circumstances.

be correct, it can be exploited in one direction, and that is to achieve a higher goal. Because the Islamic ruler, in the secondary ruling, establishes a new religious law due to the creation of special conditions, Therefore a preliminary ruling may be changed, such as being obligatory or forbidden, for a particular reason. For example, the duty of the Islamic State (Islamic Republic of Iran) to help all Muslims be full resistance to arrogance and support for Islamic movements and freedom-loving ones. But in the meantime, it pays more attention to other priorities. For example, if, at some point in time, the Islamic Republic of Iran is eclipsed in a particular economic or security context, it is undoubtedly not necessary to give assistance to Muslims of other countries. Because the wisdom and wisdom requirement is created, the Islamic State first has to strengthen its economic and political foundation. Afterwards, it will seek the help of others, because if the Islamic government is weak, or at different levels in danger, it will not be possible to help others, and maintaining the Islamic state is more compulsory.

6. The relationship between foreign policy of the Islamic Republic of Iran and international opinion can only be used for analyzing and assisting foreign policy orientation and prescription.

7. This chapter, which is intended to address the foreign policy issues of the Islamic Republic of Iran, does not intend to consider all foreign policy issues of the Islamic Republic of Iran after the revolution. Because this is not feasible and does not lead us to the main goal, First of all, the foreign policy issues of the Islamic Republic of Iran are so high that more than a few of these issues may occur every day. It's very difficult to check each one. Secondly, examining examples for a reader and one who wants to obtain information from a foreign policy of a country provides a clear and good view. Because the positions of other countries are constantly changing against the foreign policy of a country that has fixed principles and a case study may only be answerable at a single point in time. Therefore, it is necessary and necessary to examine the general foreign policy issues based on some principles and principles, in which the positioning on these issues is unchangeable in all circumstances and times.

8. The foreign policy of Iran, despite the fact that the principles and principles of the foreign policy of the Islamic Republic of Iran are constantly established, but

the strategies and orientations have varied in different periods of time, according to the time and place conditions.

9. The exact judgment of Iran's foreign policy requires the recognition of the principles and principles of foreign policy of Islam.[5] Because the culture, the constitution, beliefs and beliefs of the Iranian man are based on the teachings of Islam, and this is institutionalized among people. Basically, the direction of foreign policy behaviour of countries is the result of analyzing the dominant theories in international relations. But none of the analyzes of the conventional theorists, who as the dominant discourse in the two areas of the theorizing of international relations and foreign policy, are not intended to explain why and how the foreign policy of the Islamic Republic of Iran is behaving. The impossibility of analyzing the foreign policy of the Islamic Republic of Iran results from a significant difference in the principles and principles of foreign policy of the Islamic Republic of Iran, which has made Iran's foreign policy different. Iranian foreign policy has Islamic identity and foundations.[6]

---

[5] Arasta, Mohammad Javad, *"A look at the analytical foundations of the Islamic Republic of Iran, reflections on political jurisprudence and jurisprudential principles of the constitution of the Islamic Republic of Iran,"* Qom, Bostan-e ketab Publishing, 2012, p.144.
[6] Ibid, p. 157.

A. Principles of Iranian Foreign Policy in the Constitution

The Islamic Republic constitution' limits, goals, and rules regarding foreign politics are important before thinking critically of its transnational security oriented politics and its reproduction and transformation over the years. The constitution of the Islamic Republic is very important to understand the impulse behind the Iranian transnational ambitions, because of the Iranian constitution's emphasis on the revolutionary aspect of the state's ideology. For example, on the one hand, it advocates from refraining interference in the domestic affairs of other states, on the other hand, it declares itself as a guardian of the "oppressed". Basically, Iran declares that it has the duty to protect oppressed people regardless nation, which means intervening other nations.

Iran has idealistic promises and a universal role in the world including the universal validity of its own ideology, which was specified in the constitution. Therefore, the constitution is the main text to analyze the basic concepts and the starting point of the Iranian foreign policy and transnational activities. The first constitution of the Islamic Republic was declared in 1979 and it was amended in 1989 before the death of Khomeini. The constitution of Iran clearly states that the regime of the Iranian Republic has been established on the belief "the one God's exclusive sovereignty and right to legislate" and "divine revelation and its fundamental role in setting forth laws" (Article 2). "All law in the country must obey the Islamic criteria" (Article 4), and "ultimate political power lies in the hands of the *faqih*" (Article 5 and 110). Originally, the *faqih* was an ultimate guide that would take care of the *ummah* during the absence of the Hidden *Imam*. The Iranian constitution is based on the supremacy of the clergy. The constitution has strong legitimacy, and it is unique and the strongest text ever to be established by God's sovereignty.

The foreign policy of the Islamic Republic of Iran is based upon the rejection of all forms of domination, both the exertion of it and submission to it, the preservation of the independence of the country in all respects and its territorial integrity, the defence of the rights of all Muslims, non-alignment with respect to the hegemonist superpowers, and the maintenance of mutually peaceful relations with all non-belligerent states.

In the constitution of the Islamic Republic of Iran, the principles of the foreign policy are based on the principles of the Qur'an verses, the traditions and practices of the Prophet and the infallibles (as). Principles such as denial of domination and domination and preservation of the country's absolute independence and how to interact with Islamic and non-Islamic governments, as well as defending the right-wing struggle of the oppressed against the oppressed, and the denial of the alien domination over natural, economic, cultural and military resources and other The country is forbidden. [7] These cases are mentioned in the constitution of the Islamic Republic of Iran and outline the orientation and orientation of the foreign policy of the Islamic Republic of Iran. Of course, in the second chapter, the principles of religious and Islamic principles were fully mentioned. Below are the principles referred to in the constitution, Some of the constitutional principles outline the general lines of foreign policy of the Islamic Republic of Iran, including:

Article 9

In the Islamic Republic of Iran, the freedom, independence, unity, and territorial integrity of the country are inseparable from one another, and their preservation is the duty of the government and all individual citizens. No individual, group, or authority, has the right to infringe in the slightest way upon the political, cultural, economic, and military independence or the territorial integrity of Iran under the pretext of exercising freedom. Similarly, no authority has the right to abrogate legitimate freedoms, not even by enacting laws and regulations for that purpose, under the pretext of preserving the independence and territorial integrity of the country.[8]

Article 11

In accordance with the sacred verse of the Qur'an ("This your community is a single community, and I am your Lord, so worship Me" [21:92]), all Muslims form a single nation, and the government of the Islamic Republic of Iran has the duty of formulating its general policies with a view to cultivating the friendship and unity

---

[7] Nazpour, Mehdi, *"Introduction to the Constitution of the Islamic Republic of Iran,"* Tehran, Ma'araf Publishing, 2015, pp. 187-204.
[8] Ibid. (Article 9), p. 181.

of all Muslim peoples, and it must constantly strive to bring about the political, economic, and cultural unity of the Islamic world.

According to these principles, the general lines of foreign policy of the Islamic Republic of Iran can be used as follows: 1 negation of domination, 2 preservation of total independence 3 prohibiting contracts that lead to foreign domination over the country, 4 The ideal of self-knowledge of human prosperity in the whole of human society, 5 The recognition of independence and freedom and the rule of law and justice as the rights of all people of the world, 6 Absolute full repression of any interference in the internal affairs of other nations, 7 Protecting the rights of the oppressed against the oppressed in The whole world, 8 Accepting political asylum, 9 Inseparable freedom, independence and unity and territorial integrity of the country, 10 Defending the rights of all Muslims in the world, 11 Non-alignment with the dominant powers, 12 Mutual and peaceful relations with non-aggressive states, 13 Respect for international treaties and treaties 14 Resolving international disputes through peaceful and peaceful means Its arbitrariness on the basis of justice and justice, 15 Co-operation and participation and active role in international affairs, 16 Coping with the paradigm in the necessary cases, 17 Preferring relations with Islamic countries on non-Islamic countries, 18 Respecting dignity, wisdom and expediency in foreign policy. "[9]

Article 152

The revolutionary aims were to ensure the continuation of the revolution "at home and abroad". Being a single unified entity was the duty of all Muslims and Iran would consult and formulate all the Islamic governments as a task of the Islamic Republic of Iran. Iran had the potential and energy to undertake the role of a supreme leader for the Muslim *ummah*. Iran would have the supremacy on all newly established Islamic states for the sake of formulating general Islamic policies. The Islamic Republic saw itself as state that must fulfill the holy goals for the sake of Islam and has the best Islamic features among the Muslim world. Iran basically was trying to create a world based on advisory and supremacy of the Islamic Republic. It also was trying to create a Muslim federation and to hold all

---

[9] Ibid. (Article 11), p. 196.

the power in hand. Although Iranian legitimacy is very strong, it attempted transnational politics in a very pragmatic manner in the world after Khomeini.

The foreign policy of the Islamic Republic of Iran is based upon the rejection of all forms of domination, both the exertion of it and submission to it, the preservation of the independence of the country in all respects and its territorial integrity, the defense of the rights of all Muslims, non-alignment with respect to the hegemonies superpowers, and the maintenance of mutually peaceful relations with all non-belligerent States.[10]

Article 153

Any form of agreement resulting in foreign control over the natural resources, economy, army, or culture of the country, as well as other aspects of the national life, is forbidden.[11]

Article 154

The Islamic Republic of Iran has as its ideal human felicity throughout human society, and considers the attainment of independence, freedom, and rule of justice and truth to be the right of all people of the world. Accordingly, while scrupulously refraining from all forms of interference in the internal affairs of other nations, it supports the just struggles of the mustad'afun against the mustakbirun (The oppressed against the oppressor) in every corner of the globe.[12]

Article 155

The government of the Islamic Republic of Iran may grant political asylum to those who seek it unless they are regarded as traitors and saboteurs according to the laws of Iran.[13]

---

[10] Ibid. (Article 152), p. 289.
[11] Ibid. (Article 153), p. 294.
[12] Ibid. (Article 154), p. 298.
[13] Ibid. (Article 155), p. 299.

According to the principles stated in the constitution, two types of positive and positive policies can be pointed out in the direction of the foreign relations of the Islamic Republic of Iran.

A) Positive policy: Establishing unity between Muslims is part of the Islamic Republic of Iran's positive foreign policy. Since the beginning of the Islamic Revolution, unity has been one of the key slogans of this revolution, and has been made as much as possible to non-Muslim countries, to invite, engage and cooperate and to have peaceful relations. Imam Khomeini, peace be upon him, says: "We want to convey to all nations that Islam is a unity religion, a religion that none of the peoples are superior to the other, except for the virtue and following the teachings of Islam."[14]

B. Political policy: The foreign policy of the Islamic Republic of Iran does not accept any domination and domination (negation of the mustache) in its political manifestation with others, and never pledges itself against the tyrannical countries and does not go under their burden of oppression. Imam Khomeini, peace be upon him, says: "They are not afraid of Islam, which they confirm, but they are afraid of Islam, Ali Ibn Abi Talib (as), who is opposed to oppression. They are from Islam, who sit in a corner and worship and do something to They are not afraid of others, they are fearful of Islam for the sake of justice and justice in the battle of Jamal, Siffin, and Nehron. [15]"They are afraid of Islam, which does not allow silence against the wrongdoers.[16]

B. The most important issues of Iranian foreign policy after the 1979 Islamic Revolution

In this section, we are going to discuss the foreign policy issues of the Islamic Republic of Iran. Undoubtedly, in any of the issues that will be expressed, there may be opportunities, threats and challenges that we will face. The issues surrounding Iran's foreign policy are very high and cannot be addressed in this

---

[14] Rohullah, Khomeini (Imam), *"Sahifeh Noor"*, vol. 13, Tehran, Ministry of Culture and Islamic Guidance publication, 1992, P. 226.
[15] Ibid. vol.18, p. 4
[16] Ibid. vol.1, p. 337

research, and only the most important issues will be expressed. Before the discussion, two points to note.

One: Some issues of foreign policy are important for the Islamic Republic of Iran at a time, but it is not important at this time and will not be addressed in this study due to the emergence of new issues regarding Iran's foreign policy. Like the Iran-Iraq war[17], the occupation of the US embassy in Tehran and the kidnapping of their diplomats,[18] the slogan neither "Neither East nor the West";

Two: Due to changes in the content and titles of some foreign policy issues, they will also be discussed in the form and title. For example, the issue of issuing a revolution today can be viewed in the form of a Shiite geopolitical (resistance axis).

The policy of issuing the Islamic Revolution of Iran is a strategy that believes in the issuance of the teachings of the Islamic Revolution of Iran to carry out similar instances in other Islamic countries and even non-Islamic. This policy has been announced explicitly and at various times by Imam Khomeini and some officials and theorists.[19]

---

[17] The imposed Iraq war with Iran (holy defense) began with Saddam Hassan's invasion of Iran on September 31, 1979, on September 22, 1980. And the longest war in the twentieth century after the Vietnam War, which lasted nearly eight years. Some of the main causes of the war are borderline and ideological differences and rivalry over the region's gendarmes. Eventually, after eight years, this war ended in August 1988 with a ceasefire by the two sides and after leaving one million people dead and $ 1190 billion in damage to the two countries by endorsing Iran's resolution 598, Iraq was recognized as an aggressor country.

[18] The capture of the US Embassy siege (US Embassy siege), or the question of the hostage taking of American diplomats in Iran, "Conquer the Spy Nest", is said to have lasted 444 days of political-military hostility between the revolutionary government of Iran and the United States. On November 13, 1358 Sh (November 4, 1979), began with the arrival of a number of student activists, the followers of the Imam's line, to the American Embassy in Tehran, and became hostage to one of the major international crises with the hostage taking of the 66 American diplomats. The hostage taking on December 30, 1980 (January 20, 1981) ended with the acceptance of Algeria by the governments of Iran and the United States.

[19] Sajjadi, Seyyed Abdul-Qaim, "Imam Khomeini and the Contemporary Islamic Movements," *Political Science Quarterly (Iran),* Vol. 2, No. 5, 2007, p. 56.

This slogan has led to the position of Islamic countries, especially the Persian Gulf countries, and has led to an escalation of tension and disputes with Iran. With the onset of the Iran-Iraq war and the necessity of rebuilding Iran, the literature of the issuance of the revolution was forgotten due to the problems of the war. Although the title of the slogan of the issuance of the revolution is not heard today, the Islamic Republic of Iran is always thinking of enhancing its military, scientific, political, economic and cultural power, and it is trying to become a model for other Islamic countries and freedom-loving ones by promoting power. And through this, as well as the help of its software power in other countries without using the key word for the issuance of revolution in political and diplomatic literature, In the 20-year-old program of the Islamic Republic of Iran, which outlines the horizons of the 20-year perspective, since 200, it has been referred to the issuance of the revolution entitled "Inspirational in the Muslim World."

With regard to what has been said, some of the foreign policy issues of the Islamic Republic of Iran, which have been important at some point in time and are not relevant now, are not being explored in this study. But we are trying to examine the important issues of the current foreign policy of the Islamic Republic of Iran. Of course, some issues may also be important from the very beginning of the revolution, and it is now important that they be examined.

1. The issue of sanctions;

2. The Axis of Resistance (Issues of Palestine, Lebanon and Syria);

3. Iran's nuclear activities;

4. Relationships with new global powers such as India;

5. Human rights;

6. Relations with America;

7. Domination of technologies and global culture;

8. The Israeli Question;

9. Pass the security crises around;

10. Communication with the international system and international politics is another issue. How to interact with the world and great powers;

11. Maintaining Iran's power in the West Asia region;

12. Relations between Iran and the Arab states (Alliance and Coalition or Competition and Conflict);

13. Relationship with Saudi Arabia;

1. Foreign Policy and International Organizations

There is a two-way relationship between the international organizations and foreign policy and bilateral interaction. In fact, foreign policy is a channel through which countries interact with the rest of the international system in general and with international organizations in particular.[20] International organizations can have important implications for foreign policy of the country and, in contrast to the foreign policy orientation of a country, can also exert a widespread influence on international organizations. In other words, the interaction and the relationship between international organizations and foreign policy is subject to the strength and weakness of foreign policy of the countries, so that if the foreign policy of a country is weak, international organizations affect the country and if it is a powerful country, The decisions of international organizations are affected.

One of the most important international organizations that was formed before the United Nations was the League of Nations, and Iran was the first Muslim country in the Middle East, since the beginning of 1922 the National Assembly approved Iran's membership in the League of Nations[21] And given the fact that the first Muslim country was appointed at the General Assembly of the League of Nations to be representative of the Islamic world.[22]

---

[20] Mustafa Maleki, Mojtaba Babaei, "Iran's Relations with the UN after Victory of the Islamic Revolution," *Studies of International Relations Journal (Iran),* Vol. 5, No. 18, 2012 , p. 161.
[21] Ibid.

[22] Mojani, Seyyed Ali, "Iran from the League of Nations to the United Nations," *Foreign Policy Quarterly (Iran),* Vol. 9, No. 3, 1995, p. 75.

International organizations in the current international system are one of the most important and influential actors in the global management process.[23] With regard to the formation of international organizations and the developments that have taken place, the international system as a whole is formed of national governments, their mutual interactions, international organizations and the interaction of private actors, while national governments and major international organizations Most actors in the international arena, and in the direction of the development of the phenomenon of organization, the idea of international organizations, both in words and in practice, is gradually becoming more complex and important. Although governments have not gone so far as to surrender their authority to international organizations, they sometimes have to perform duties that are imposed on international countries by international organizations. Of course, the newly emerging states have weakened their willingness to accept the United Nations. In spite of the extreme differences and perspectives, it seems that great powers are eager to leave these organizations. Nowadays, all governments are useful international organizations for their ideas and communication, and a means to address some of their needs, they know.[24] The conditions in international relations and its complexities in foreign relations and the orientation of countries in foreign policy necessitate the need for international organizations to be more involved. Today, the international organization has grown so expanded that countries, in some cases, annually pay money to facilitate their relations and to avoid isolation and to defend their rights, even in some cases.

The record of Iran's relationship with international organizations such as the United Nations, after the victory of the Islamic Revolution, shows that Iran, after 40 years of the Islamic Revolution, has not been able to play an effective, effective and proportionate role and place Iran in this organization at the outset, although this may be affected by the main actors of the United Nations and other international organizations, the lack of involvement of Iran in regional and international developments. Or it may be due to the shattering of great powers by increasing Iran's influence and strength. But the lack of a coherent, lofty and targeted strategy

---

[23] Zarder, Fereydoun, *"Iran and the League of Nations"*, Tehran, Shirazi Publishing, 1998, p. 3.

[24] Ali Babaei, "Iran's relationship with international organizations (International)," *Ma'aref Magazine (Iran),* Vol. 18, No.1, 2009 , p. 54.

to promote Iran's position in the United Nations and other organizations, as well as the lack of use of the potential of Iran's soft power for lobbying and consensus in international institutions, plays an important role in Iran's very bad situation. It has an important international organization.[25]

The Islamic Republic of Iran still has no effective ability to determine the UN agenda. The way in which the existing capabilities of the United Nations are used is that, if the states want and insist on a demand, they can use this opportunity to achieve their goals. Unfortunately, the Islamic Republic of Iran is only announcing positions from the United Nations tribunals and other international organizations, and in practice it does not have an active presence to direct the minds of countries in line with its own interests. The Islamic Republic of Iran has not even been able to play a pivotal and constructive role for important issues of the Islamic world, such as the Palestinian issue, using the UN's capacity.[26]

One of the important discussions in the early Islamic Revolution of Iran was the necessity or unwillingness of participation in many international organizations and associations; there were two attitudes in this regard. Some believed that although organizations could not be expected, they could use their capacity to deliver the message of the Islamic Revolution. But another group believed that the main audience of the revolution was people, not governments, so that they should engage in popular investments and support public streams.[27] In practice, the first attitude prevailed and Iran participated in international gatherings.

In this section, we intend to analyze the relationship of the Islamic Republic of Iran with international organizations after the 1979 revolution. In order to understand and provide the correct analysis, it is very important from the point of view of Iran's relations with international organizations to understand the goals and principles of the Islamic Revolution. Because the principles of foreign policy of the Islamic Republic of Iran are based on principles that are in contradiction with

---

[25] Mustafa Maleki, Mojtaba Babaei, "Iran's Relations with the UN after Victory of the Islamic Revolution," *Studies of International Relations Journal (Iran),* Vol. 5, No. 18, 2012 , p. 155.

[26] Ibid.

[27] Yahya Fawzi Tasirkani, *"Organization of the Islamic Conference,"* Tehran, Islamic Revolution Documentation Center Publication, 1998, p. 138.

many governing systems and regulations existing in international organizations, Issues such as self-seeking, the negation of the control of foreigners, the defense of the oppressed and the oppressed of the world, anti-Semitism, which is part of the principles of the foreign policy of the Islamic Republic, is in some cases contradictory to some of the rules and laws existing in international organizations. This controversy has led to different approaches to international organizations in different governments in Iran. It seems that all post-revolutionary governments have always been in the process of implementing the principles governing international relations and foreign policy, but their approaches to achieving different goals are different. The main orientation of the Islamic system in foreign policy is based on the principles of foreign policy, as outlined in the constitution of our country, and the observance of the three principles of dignity, wisdom and expediency, which, in this regard, has a relatively stable trend and in different periods, that is, the time of life Imam Khomeini, as well as during the leadership of Ayatollah Khamenei, as well as in the constitutions, reformist, principality, and moderate, was almost constant. However, with regard to determining the conditions and requirements, tactics and methods of governments and their orientations in the field of foreign policy, we are witnessing some minor and sometimes important changes. As the type of literature and discourses of the reformist government and fundamentalist foreign policy differed.

Therefore, there are six courses for Islamic Republic of Iran relations with international organizations.

A tough time in deciding to reform

With the victory of the Islamic Revolution and the coming of the interim government, Iran's foreign policy was undergoing change. The foreign policy of the country, on the one hand, was influenced by the revolutionary conditions and the new demands of the people, and on the other hand, because of the revisionist nature of the revolution, it seriously threatened the interests of the countries. This duality can also be seen in the ideal nature of the revolution and the realism of the forces forming the interim government.[28]

At that time, due to instability in the interior, there was no specific trend and direction in the field of foreign policy, but the interim government was trying to move within the framework of existing international laws and regulations and avoid interfering in the internal affairs of other countries. During the reign of the interim government, relations with the international organizations were limited to a limited extent, and Iran joined the Non-Aligned Movement during this period. Relations with the Organization of Islamic Conference continued in the past. But in front of the interim government, there was a revolutionary and radical majority that looked at international and regional organizations from the outset.[29]

Tension period (1979-1989)

This period, which began from the very early days after the interim administration of Bazargan's engineer and the acceptance of the Iranian governing body in accepting Iran's membership in international organizations, was more influenced by revolutionary conditions and conditions, almost until the end of the Iran-Iraq War (1989) continued. The most important events that occurred in this period include the occupation and hostage taking of the American Embassy in Tehran, the issues related to the issuance of the revolution, the politics of the nine eastern and western countries, the Iran-Iraq war, and withdrawal from the Treaty of Santo.[30]

Rationalist conservatism (1989-1997)

By adopting Resolution 598 of the Security Council in July 1988, the Islamic Republic of Iran took the first steps towards working with the international organization. This has led many analysts to analyze the change in Iran's approach

---

[28] Alireza Azghandi, *"Foreign Policy of the Islamic Republic of Iran,"* Tehran, Ghomes Publication, 2002, p. 101.

[29] Karimi, Gholamreza," Islamic Republic of Iran and International Organizations, A survey of development of Islamic Republic of Iran's relationships with international organizations," *Political Sciences Quarterly (Iran),* Vol. 9, No. 36 , 2006, p. 129.

[30] Mojarrad, Mohsen, *"Effect of the Islamic Revolution on International Politics",* Tehran, Islamic Revolution Documentation Center, 2007, p. 142.

to dealing with international issues. During this period, the slogan of the issuance of the revolution diminished, and the Islamic Republic of Iran, who had been emancipated from a civil war, most of its power in the right direction destroyed. The relations between Iran and the Islamic countries that had become obscured by the slogan of the issuance of the revolution, Iran was the first to attend the highest level of the Islamic Conference, and in November 1997, the summit of Islamic countries with the presence of more than 50 Islamic high-ranking officials in Tehran Was held.

Relatively active engagement (1997-2005):

During this period, which began with the presidency of Seyyed Mohammad Khatami, the officials in this period believed that in order to uphold the rights of the Islamic Republic of Iran and realize its values, despite the differences in the principles and nature of Iran's foreign policy with some countries and organizations, Available for revolutionary purposes. The process of deconstruction in foreign policy that began at the time of Hashemi Rafsanjani's presidency accelerated more seriously; the ruling discourse in this period was based on the use of concepts such as tension, political development, and dialogue of civilizations that sought to be a peace figure Call for Iran to the world public opinion. During this period, communication with European countries and international organizations grew dramatically. Even the plan to resume the normalization of Iran-US relations was raised. Of course, America's hostile policies, the determination of the Supreme Leader of Iran (Ayatollah Ali Khamenei) to maintain Islamic values and revolutionary aspirations do not go a long way.[31]

In spite of Iran's good cooperation with countries and international organizations, the country continues to be sanctioned and is called by the President of the United States (George W. Bush) the axis of evil that violates human rights and supports terrorism. The main reason for these hostilities seemed to be the nature of the Islamic Revolutionary Guard System of Iran.

---

[31] Salehi Amiri, Seyed Reza and Mohammadi, Saeed, "*Cultural Diplomacy*", Tehran, Phoenix Publishing, 2010, pp. 56-89

Radical role play along with relative return of tension (2005-2013)

Despite the comprehensive engagement of Iran with the international community during the presidency of Seyyed Mohammad Khatami, but the dual clash of Western countries with Iran's core issue, Iran's repeated condemnation of human rights abuses, the advocacy of Iran's readiness for terrorism and the centerpiece of Iran's wickedness Along with North Korea and Iraq, one of the reasons that the people in 2005, with the election of Mahmoud Ahmadinejad, reacted to Iran's cooperation and interaction with international organizations and some countries. This indicates a change in the discourse of the Islamic Republic of Iran with the mainly Western countries and international organizations.[32]

Ahmadinejad's government has been working on the revival of the values of revolution and Islam, and this approach has had a significant impact on Iran's political and economic developments on the domestic and international levels. Ahmadinejad's government, in a dual clash with international issues, wanted an active presence in international organizations, on the one hand, and emphasized their lack of legitimacy. In the nuclear case, the government entered a position of authority and continued nuclear activities with authority. The government also tried to challenge Israel by supporting Palestine and always criticized international organizations that discriminated against countries, such as the veto power of the UN Security Council and forceful powers such as the United States in international affairs.

Of course, a very important difference that this period was with the period of tension in Iran's relations with international organizations during the first revolution was that the people and senior officials of Iran did not feel in this period and tried to take into account the principle of dignity, Wisdom and expediency and defend their rights within the frameworks of the international system. High-level authorities at that time tried to communicate with countries and international organizations, provided that their dignity was not compromised. During his eight years in office, Mahmoud Ahmadinejad traveled to the United Nations each year and lectured there. But despite all these activities, Iranian President's speeches on

---

[32] Rasoul Afzali; Vahid Kiani, "The Qualitative Assessment and Evaluation of Iran's Foreign Relations in the Fourth Development Plan", *Quarterly Journal of the Macro and Strategic Policies (Iran)*, Vol. 1, No. 1, 2013, pp. 106-118.

the Holocaust and the UN's controversial statements made Iran more isolated. In the course of this period, Iran was subject to the most stringent economic and military sanctions and sanctions, despite the accumulation of scientific advances and self-sufficiency in some economic areas, which caused irreparable damage to the country. Entered And Iran was politically very secure and economically very risky.[33]

It seems that all that Ahmadinejad spoke was the main word of the revolution and the people. Even many governments and nations of the world defended their speeches, but the fears or national interests of those countries did not require Iran to stand behind the discriminatory practices of the international system. Hence, one of the major drawbacks in Ahmadinejad's aggressive policy in foreign policy was that he did not pay attention to the realities of the international system, which would have imposed a lot of costs on Iran.[34]

 Instead of focusing more on security, instead of a cooperative and cooperative approach, there was a tightening up of costs. Even during this period, Saudi-dominated Arab-dominated Arab countries introduced Iran as a centerpiece of threats and insecurity in the region, as well as trying to prevent any openness in Iran's possible relationship with the West over a nuclear case.

 To make this caused the Iranian people to choose Ahmadinejad's political rival in 2013 and to show their protest to the foreign policy ruling discourse with the election of a moderate government.

Second de-stress period (2013 -2018)
Hassan Rouhani's government's view of foreign policy was that the result of the foreign policy of the country should be to secure the national interests and national security of Iran. If foreign policy is not able to provide national interests, the country cannot take the path of development and opportunities are eliminated.

All post-revolutionary governments in Iran have sought Islamic values and adhered to the constitutional principles of the country. And the current Iranian government (Rouhani) is also no exception, but their strategies are very different in reaching the goals and principles of revolution, so that some in Iran and abroad thought

---

[33] Ibid. pp.122-125
[34] https://irlip.um.ac.ir/index.php/jipr/article/view/49042

incorrectly that there were different principles of foreign policy in different governments. Is. In the discourse of the moderate spirit of the clerical government, it is believed that the ruling order of the relations and the international system has a lot of discriminations and desirability, but contrary to the administration, Mr. Ahmadinejad believes that the transformation of the order and the international system from The process of gradual and peaceful reform, interaction and multilateral cooperation should take place. And with radical ideas and aggressive policies, we cannot do anything.

To illustrate this, two examples are given:

A: Nuclear Issues: One of the most important issues in the foreign policy of the Islamic Republic of Iran has been and continues to be a nuclear issue. The issue has become a crisis for the foreign policy of the Islamic Republic, and many sanctions have been on the pretext of these nuclear issues.[35] Of course, we will explain in detail the core issue in the other part. Here it is briefly pointed out that the diplomacy apparatus in Rouhani's government over a two-year period after the election victory, with the endless effort of the foreign minister, the support of Dr. Rouhani and the support of the Supreme Leader of the Islamic Revolution, the crisis of 12 The year ahead of the Republic will resolve Iran's policies and policies. Although the nuclear deal has serious opponents in Iran, it was able to capture nuclear-related sanctions, as well as its nuclear program, as an excuse from Western countries about Iran's nuclear activities. Most importantly, the lifting of the United Nations Security Council sanctions resolutions. Although today the United States and some countries, such as Israel and Saudi Arabia, are trying to call this agreement bad agreement, the other countries that have been negotiating have consistently supported this agreement and are sounding against the bad deal of the US with Iran, and this A diplomatic success for Iran.

B: The issue of oil sales: Another major Iranian problem during the boycott was the issue of reducing Iranian oil sales. Following the signing of the nuclear deal, the Iranian Oil Ministry, with strong backing after the nuclear talks, was able to withdraw its share of OPEC from the OPEC with economic diplomacy, which

---

[35] http://www.news.bbc.co.uk,June1,2003.

forced Saudi Arabia to cut its oil production, Oil prices did not rise, but increased oil prices.[36]

Some Important Features in Foreign Policy of President Hassan Rouhani After the revolution, the foreign policy of the Islamic Republic of Iran has been more successful and more measured than other areas. But a few features about the foreign policy of the government of Rouhani are noteworthy:

1. The use of 35 years of experience, actors and system in foreign policy decision making, without excitement and adventure in the direction of dignity, interest and interests of Iran;

2. Understanding of international realities and existing capacities;

3. Interaction with the West to replace diplomatic efforts and diplomacy rather than threatening issues, which resulted in their withdrawal from the threat posed by the Islamic Republic of Iran.

4. To play an active role in important issues in the region, such as Syria, to oppose Israel by maintaining the fundamental positions of the Iranian Revolution;

5. Provide practical solutions to Iran's problems in the international arena, such as Iran's nuclear issue, sanctions and problems in OPEC;

Unfortunately, there is an irrefutable fact in the structure of the system and the international organizations and the rules governing it, which, contrary to the most primitive principle in the ruling circle of countries, which is the absolute equality of countries, has brought countries powerful and weak. Which indicates inequality and injustice in international relations and the use of international institutions;[37] this has led many countries, such as non-aligned countries, to interpret multinational and bullying countries for countries like the United States.[38]

---

[36] http://www.alef.ir/news/3961008016.

[37] Seyyed Hassan Amin, "International System and Islamic Republic of Iran," Tehran, *Journal of Cultural Research (Iran),* Vol. 5, No. 12-13, 1999, p. 143.
[38] Ibid , p. 148.

The Islamic Republic of Iran requires itself to respect and respect all obligations, contracts based on religious teachings, and respect all international protocols that have accepted them. Although Iran is opposed to some of the governing systems in international organizations, such as the veto power of the permanent members of the Security Council, it is always seeking to eliminate discrimination and inequality with advisers, but has never tried to move beyond these systems. But also tried to get the most out of the available opportunities to reach its goals, but did not choose isolation in any way. Although they believe that the decision-making process in some international organizations, such as the Security Council, is contrary to the dignity and integrity of Islam, it has temporarily accepted the wisdom and wisdom of it, and undoubtedly, if it becomes a powerful day, it will certainly not be under the burden of it, Because neither the constitution nor the Islamic teachings have given such a permission.

The differences between Iran and the international system on issues such as human rights, the defense of liberation movements, the struggle against arrogance and Israel are the result of the contradiction between the principles and nature of the Islamic Republic of Iran with the systems governing international relations. Fundamental principles and values in Iran are based on the Shari'a of Islam, the central principle of monotheism that these values do not exist in the West and are based on secularism, rationalism and humanism.[39]

---

[39] Ibid , p. 145.

2. Challenges and constraints of Iran's foreign policy with the international system

The Islamic Republic of Iran believes that the problems caused by the domination of the great powers and the oppression of the weak countries are due to the nature of the international system, which is mentally, structurally and politically conditioned to create the present situation in the world. Imam Khomeini believed that he should stop the injustice and injustice in accordance with the capabilities and abilities, and in the Islamic teachings of the Shari'a, that everyone should be able to prevent oppression, he should act on his religious duty. They say:

If we had power, if we had the power, we should go all the cruelty and sorts out of the world. Our religious duty is ours, but we cannot, what is that is, that the Prophet (s) will fill the world with justice; you will not abandon your prayers, nor will you have any other duties.[40]

The structure of the international system, by challenging the revisionist policy of the Islamic Republic of Iran, tried to use the means of sanctions, the war (Iraq and Iran), the coup, the military siege, and the limitation of the revolution and its issuance.[41]

The stimulus value system in the Islamic Revolution has led to different behaviours in the Islamic Republic's behavioural pattern, and these behavioural patterns fluctuate with a range of interactions to confrontation. The analysis of the Islamic Revolution of Iran at the macro level shows that the Iranian revolution was essentially in conflict with the international system. This revolution raised the values and norms that were in conflict with the interests of the supportive powers of preserving the present situation, and also the activation of religious thought in the political arena of Iran was rooted in the ineffectiveness and dependence of the

---

[40] Rouhollah, Khomeini (Imam), *"Sahifeh Noor,"* Tehran, Ministry of Culture and Islamic Guidance, vol. 15, 1992 , p. 81.

[41] Enayatollah Yazdani; Dariush Qasemi; Safiollah Shahghaleh, "Islamic Revolution of Iran, International System and Critical Theory," *political knowledge Quarterly (Iran)*, Vol. 7, No. 14, 2013, p. 209.

governments of the time. [42] As Kissinger, the Shi'a, Islamic fundamentalism reminds them of the Iranian-Soviet revolution as a threat to the Gulf States. [43]

One of the main goals of the Islamic Republic of Iran is to achieve unconstitutionality in the West Asian[44] region. The West Asia (Middle East) region includes the Arab countries, and its neighbours, such as Turkey, Iran and Israel (Occupied Palestine). In addition to the discussion of oil and gas, the region has six different races, living side by side, and is home to three great religions of Islam, Judaism and Christianity. At present, its culture is based on the principles of Islam[45]. The Islamic Republic of Iran has made great strides to achieve this goal and has developed the 20-Year Perspective Document for Iran (2005-04-204 AD). One of the most important cases in this document is the drawing up of a foreign policy based on Islamic principles and certain ideological foundations, which expresses a new form of non-commitment in the foreign policy of the Islamic Republic of Iran.[46] The emphasis on Islamic principles and the ideological nature of the revolution created problems for Iran against other countries and organizations.[47]

Undoubtedly, Iran has many challenges and challenges to achieve this goal. This is stated below:

1. Challenges for the international system for Iran such as terrorism, nuclear and human rights;

---

[42] Saryaol Al-ghalam, Mahmoud , *"Iran and Globalization of Challenges and Solutions,"* Tehran: Strategic Research Center publication, 2007, p. 69.

[43] Sotoudeh, Mohammad, "Foreign Policy of the Islamic Republic of Iran and the Structure of the International System", *Political Science Quarterly (Iran),* Vol. 4, No. 16, 2007, p. 155.

[44] The term "West Asia" has recently been used as a substitute for the "Middle East" in Iran's Foreign Policy Dialogue.

[45] Ghanbari Ali Asghar, "The Importance of the Middle East Region and Overview of the Great Middle East Project," *Geosciences Military Journal (Iran) ,* Vol. 4, No. 15, 2003, p.3.

[46] Asadi Bijan, *"Foreign Policy of the Islamic Republic of Iran",* Qom, Publicity Office of the Islamic Translation Office, 1992, pp. 80-81.

[47]. Haji Yousefi, Amir Mohammad, *"Iran and the Zionist regime from cooperation to conflict,"* Tehran, Imam Sadiq University Press , 2002, p. 68.

2. Restrictions imposed by major powers to restrict Iran's power in West Asia by some countries, such as the United States and the European Union;

3. The existence of hard regional rivals such as Turkey, Saudi Arabia, Israel and Egypt;

The people who revolutionized Iran in 1979 sought values and aspirations that caused many regional and transatlantic countries to find fundamental differences with Iran. The Islamic Revolution of Iran, which pursued pan-Islamism, did not legitimize Arab governments, protested secular governments like Turkey. The existence of a state like Israel has not been identified and the principle of state and sovereignty is not legitimate.[48] Tying America's interests with Israel left American hostility against Iran, and America with all its power allowed any Iranian domination and progress in the region and the world. Of course, along with the above, in the first decade of the revolution slogans such as the issuance of the revolution or conquering the US embassy, and in the second to the fourth decades of the revolution, such as human rights, nuclear, and terrorism, were a good justification for bringing the international community against Iran, and until Greatly succeeded. The obvious example of this was Iran's nuclear embargo on the United Nations Security Council, the United States, and European countries, as well as many of Iran's small and large countries, with all-round crippling sanctions. Although some believe that sanctions were an opportunity for Iran, the reality is that the need for political and trade engagement and the use of modern scientific equipment and technologies is a fundamental need of every country, and the lack of access to that development process is slowing.

Challenges for the international system for Iran such as Terrorism and Human Rights:

The Islamic Republic of Iran, after the 1979 revolution, chose a revisionist approach to its foreign policy based on Islamic principles and values. Hence, it relied on some key concepts in foreign policy, such as negation of infidel

---

[48] Alireza Samiee Esfahani; Ali Amirbaik, "International System, Superregional Powers, Regional Power, Iran-West Challenges (United States and Europe)," *Politic Quarterly (Iran)*, Vol. 41, No. 4, 2012, p. 100.

domination, anti-Semitism, support for Islamic movements and freedom-loving ones, and observance of the principle of dignity, wisdom and expediency in foreign policy decision-making. Due to these issues, the Islamic Republic of Iran faced many challenges with the governing systems of international organizations. If we look at the realities of the foreign policy of the Islamic Republic of Iran in the area of operation and decision-making, it might be possible that the source of most of Iran's challenges in opposition to Israel and the support of the resistance axis is that it is problematic for the interests of Iran. What Iran is following and insisting on in foreign policy, the structure of the international system does not allow Iran to operate, a system that, through the governing bodies (such as the United Nations), often in the domain of decision-making, is at the disposal of the great powers.

Seriousness has put a lot of obstacles and challenges in front of Iran. So that it is difficult for Iran to reach regional power and influence international affairs.[49]

An international system that influences the great powers, exercises power to distribute regional power in West Asia and it also uses international institutions in this regard. Great powers, and at the top of their minds, America does not like to relax in West Asia at all times, and their interests always depend on the creation of a challenge, insecurity and a tension-tight competition between the countries of the region. They moderate or weaken Iran's power to strengthen other powers in the region, such as Saudi Arabia and Israel.

Since the United States has a lot of strategic interests in strengthening Israel's sovereignty, it seeks to endure the main rival, Iran, with the crisis. Challenges such as sanctions, insecurity, and the containment of Iran's influence and power, Nuclear debate is one of the most important challenges facing Iran with the international system, which will be discussed in detail in this research separately. And other issues and challenges, such as terrorism, the defence of the resistance and human rights, will be further discussed in the next discussion.

---

[49] Hosseini Esfidewahani, Mehdi, "Foreign Policy of Iran and the International System," *Quarterly Journal of Political Economy (Iran),* Vol. 2, No. 225-226, 2006, pp. 89-78.

3. Iran-US relations

The history of Iran-US relations can be seen in the mid-19th century.[50] At that time, US government relations with Iran were in tandem. And it has always been a compromise state for opinion and opinion of the people, and it has a good reputation among the people and politicians of the two rival militants, namely, Russia and Britain. But the strategic interests and strategic position of Iran was not something America could ignore. Historically, the presence of the United States in Iran can be said that the years after the end of the Second World War were the beginning of its direct and influential presence in Iran. The peak of this presence in the early 1950s was in the case of the direct involvement and involvement of the United States in the *coup d'état* of 28 Mordad 1332 sh (18/8/1953), when Mossadeq's government was disbanded and Mohammad Reza Pahlavi, the US-backer, returned to power. The influence of the United States in the Iranian government was so high that it left no room for intervention by the British and the Soviet Union.

Iran-US relations became very close and warm after the *coup d'état* of 28 Mordad 1332 sh (18/8/1953). In the opinion of many people, intellectuals and religious people, during the Second Pillar II, the United States was more oppressive than Britain and the Soviet Union. Its peak was in executing the regulation of capitulation. This means giving the right to judicial review of the crimes of foreign nationals and citizens to a foreign legal representative (US). But despite the direct influence and influence of the United States on Iran, due to the Iranian attachment to the United States, he never objected to Iran's involvement in Iran's affairs.

Clergymen, intellectuals, marketers and various people have considered rules like capitalization contrary to Islamic teachings and considered it a kind of obvious oppression of Muslim domination, and this is denied in Islam. At the head of the opposition were the US and Pahlavi regime of Imam Khomeini. He began to openly oppose the United States since 1963, and he considered the root of all the misery, delusions and backwardness in Iran as American domination and dependence on Mohammad Reza Pahlavi. Although Imam Khomeini was exiled

---

[50] Hossein Hamidinia, *"United States of America, First edition,"* Tehran, Political and International Bureau of Political Studies and International Publications, 2003, p. 56.

from Iran through protest, people refused to comply with Mohammad Reza Pahlavi's policies and were constantly abandoning relations with the United States.

But the attachment of the Shah of Iran to the United States prevented the interruption of relations. People opposed the Shah with different occasions. With the escape of the Shah of Iran in December 1978 and the entrance of Imam Khomeini to the country on February 11, 1979, (22 Bahman 1357 Sh) the kingdom was ruled out in Iran, and the regime of the Islamic republic came to power after the Iranian revolution. Imam Khomeini and the people, who saw the tyranny of Americans in their own right during the time of Pahlavi II (Mohammad Reza Shah), sought to break the relationship with the United States.

Imam Khomeini, who in the pre-revolutionary affairs, like the Treaty of SENTO, who saw the American plan for Iran, had seen the capitulation and humiliation of the Iranian nation before the revolution, and, on the other hand, saw the conspiracy of the United States in Muslim countries, called the United States the Great Satan.[51]

Following are some of Imam Khomeini's and Ayatollah Khamenei's speeches and stances about Iran-US relations:

A. Some Imam Khomeini's Speech on Relations with America:

Imam Khomeini called for re-engagement with the United States, subject to a change in the regime's approach to dealing with the Iranian nation. And they say:

> 1. We will not establish relations with the United States unless we can change (behave) and stop the tyranny and do not come from the rest of the world in Lebanon, and will not extend its hand to the Persian Gulf.[52]

> 2. If the purpose of the relations is those relations that have existed between Iran and the United States, it was during the time of the former Shah between Iran and the United States, it was not a relationship. It was a gentleman with whom he wanted whatever he wanted, whatever he could. If

---

[51] Rouhollah, Khomeini (Imam), "Sahifeh Noor," vol.20, Tehran, Ministry of Culture and Islamic Guidance, 1992, p. 151.
[52] Ibid. vol. 19, p. 95.

you say - if we want to advance Islam, we should no longer be worthy of it. If you are not a girlfriend, he will interrupt his relationship with us, we ask God to make the relationship cut off. It's better to have no relationship with those who want to mess us up until one day they come to know that the East is in the universe. The day that they realize that the East is also where the civilization has gone before them[53].

3. I have been reminded that our relationship with the likes of America is the relationship between the oppressed nation and the world.[54]

4. We will not establish relations with the United States, unless we are Adam and abandon the oppression.[55]

B: Some of Ayatollah Khamenei's words about relationship with America:

The leader of the Islamic Revolution of Iran, Ayatollah Khamenei, according to the circumstances we are in, not only does not accept a relationship with a country like the United States, but considers any kind of negotiation and dialogue about political issues, etc., as harmful and useless.

1. "One of our basic policies is to cut off relations with the United States. We never said that we would end the relationship forever; no, there is no reason for us to permanently disconnect any country with any state. The problem is that the conditions of this state (America) are in such a way that his relationship with him is harmful to us. Man creates an interest in relation with any country in defining a benefit; where we do not benefit, we do not pursue the relationship; now if it is a loss, we don't go.[56]

---

[53] Ibid. vol. 11, p. 34.
[54] Ibid. vol. 12, p. 40.
[55] Ibid. vol. 19, p. 94.
[56] Statement by Ayatollah Khamenei, "Supreme Leader of the Islamic Revolution of Iran "on visiting students of Yazd University Universities -(http://farsi.khamenei.ir/speech-topic)01/03/2018

2. Relationship with the United States and the negotiation of this country, except in certain cases for the Islamic Republic, is not only worthless but also harmful, and which is wise to pursue ill-will?[57]

3. Negotiation with the United States is forbidden because of the numerous losses it has and the benefits it does not have; this is different from negotiating with a government that has neither such facilities nor so much incentive; these are different, they do not understand it.[58]

4. The political relationship with America is harmful to us. First, it does not reduce America's risk. The United States invaded Iraq, while having a political relationship, they had ambassadors; it was an ambassador there, and there was an ambassador there. The relationship that no maladministration and suppressive threat of no power is to be eliminated. Secondly, the existence of a relationship for the Americans - not today - has always been this - has been a means of penetrating mercenary corps in that country.[59]

5. It is not that some say that we are going to negotiate with the United States to resolve these hostilities, no. America's hostility to negotiation does not go away. The United States is pursuing its own interests in Iran.[60]

6. The policy of not negotiating and communicating with America remains in place until its policies change.

Iran's logic in hostility to the United States is based on the Islamic values and national interests of Iran. The Islamic Republic of Iran has never said until the end of the intention to engage with the United States. Iran believes that if the United

---

[57] Statement by Ayatollah Khamenei, "Supreme Leader of the Islamic Revolution of Iran" in a meeting with Foreign Ministry officials with the leader of the revolution - (http://farsi.khamenei.ir/speech-topic) 13/8/2014.

[58] Statement by Ayatollah Khamenei, "Supreme Leader of the Islamic Revolution of Iran" on the meeting of the Islamic Revolutionary Guards Corps' navy commanders and personnel -(http://farsi.khamenei.ir/speech-topic)7 / 10/2015.

[59] Statement by Ayatollah Khamenei, "Supreme Leader of the Islamic Revolution of Iran" on visiting students of Yazd University Universities - (http://farsi.khamenei.ir/speech-topic)01/03/2018.

[60] Statement by Ayatollah Khamenei, "Supreme Leader of the Islamic Revolution of Iran" in the great community of pilgrims and adherents of Imam Reza (http://farsi.khamenei.ir/speech-topic)26/3/2000.

States abandons domination and arrogance and respects the national interests of Iran, it will undoubtedly associate with the United States.

After the revolution, the Islamic Republic of Iran, in terms of relations with countries, only excluded two countries and did not have a relationship, but with the rest of the countries there was no problem in continuing to cooperate. One was Israel, which, in addition to folklore, was occupying and aggressive and as long as it has such a structure, it is not legitimate for Iran. The other was South Africa, which also had a racist regime. But when Mandela's supporters and the racist regime were reformed, Iran was among the first countries to establish ties with South Africa. Therefore, the lack of communication with the United States was not first and foremost illegal because, according to Imam Khomeini (Iran's Islamic Republic of Iran), although the United States had taken an evil course in foreign policy, it was not legally legitimate in law.[61]

Despite intense criticism of Imam Khomeini during the early days of the revolution about interrupting relations with the United States, he did not think that they would have been cut off with the United States, but the biggest mistake by the Americans was to indirectly seek to overthrow the Iranian government instead of constructively engaging with Iran. They also launched an economic boycott, which ultimately ended up being completely interrupted by the students' conquest of the spy nest. And, of course, Imam Khomeini even welcomed the US economic sanctions against Iran for self-determination and self-reliance.[62]

Isolation and separation cannot be permanent, and religious teachings always emphasize communication and cooperation. In the political thought of Imam Khomeini, there are some established principles that are unchangeable and emphasized by Islamic teachings such as lack of oppression and domination. Adoption of the oppression and domination of others creates irreparable spiritual and material harm to the country, such as dependence, lack of independence in decision making and positioning, lack of dignity, including such damage and damage.

---

[61] http://www.imam-khomeini.ir/fa/c76_21134/

[62] Ibid.

If you look at the principles of the constitution, the positions of Imam Khomeini and Ayatollah Khamenei on the relations between the states, there are a few points to make:

1. Relationship with the United States is not eternal, but until the United States changes its view on Iran, the relationship will not be created.

2. The reason for the interruption of relations with the United States is due to the domination and morale of the country's arrogance.

3. America should change its sight to Iran. Foreign policy after the Islamic Revolution on the site of the foreign policy of the Islamic Republic of Iran, after the revolution, was preceded by a 100% paradigm shift. Iran is in no way accepting a relationship based on dependence and is willing to pay a heavy price for its independence. Understanding this issue for the resumption of relations between Iran and the United States is very important for the United States.

4. Given the aggressive US policy since the first revolution, so much this country has oppressed Iran, Such as sanctions, political and security pressures and attempts to overthrow the Iranian government.

5. The US aims to negotiate the imposition of demands, and this is not acceptable to Iran.

6. US engagement in international and international agreements to eliminate the rights of the Iranian nation.

7. The loss of the relationship and even the negotiation with the United States is greater than its interests. If one day the Islamic Republic of Iran concludes that the relationship to the negotiation of a particular position will bring its interests. Undoubtedly, the negotiators will welcome.

8. The Islamic Republic of Iran welcomes mutual respect relations, Neither Islamic teachings nor the constitution of Iran, will not allow a relationship that will undermine the dignity of the Muslim nation of Iran.

They have this vacuum in Iran; they need a base; they do not have a base; they want it. They need free and diligent travel by the spy officers and their intelligence agents and their illegitimate communications with the hermits, but they do not. Communication provides this to them. Now sit down and talk and argue gentlemen, that the lack of relations with America is harmful to us. No sir! The lack of a relationship with America is useful to us. On the day when it is useful for a relationship with the United States, I am a servant who first tells us to create a relationship.[63]

Of course, in the aftermath of the victory of the Islamic Revolution, US interests in the South West Asia region (the Middle East) were also fundamentally under threat. Firstly, with the Iranian Revolution, a colluding government (Mohammad Reza Pahlavi), who had strategic ties with the United States, fell. Secondly, issues such as the Middle East peace, the axis of resistance, Israel, ISIL, Syria, show deep divisions between Iran and the United States. On the other hand, the existence of common interests has revealed the need for dialogue and cooperation between the two countries. These factors indicate the complexity and ambiguity in the horizons of relations between the two countries. The disagreements between Iran and the United States are really more complicated than being negotiable or solvable. For example, Iran does not accept the principle of Israel's legitimacy, and considers it a usurper country that must be eliminated, in the face of the United States, it is always defending Israel and the vital interests of the two countries in West Asia, except through cooperation. Another example is the defence of the resistance axis, including Hezbollah, Lebanon, Syria, Palestinian, Iraqi, Yemeni and Afghan groups, as part of the Islamic Republic of Iran's unique principles and strategies, but the United States has always sought to eliminate the axis of resistance. And they consider them a terrorist. These deep divisions, which are the result of the strategic depth of the two countries and cannot be changed, have made it difficult to establish close ties between the United States and Iran. It would seem that if Iran's disagreement on human rights, nuclear, and so on, can be resolved.

---

[63] Statement by Ayatollah Khamenei, "Supreme Leader of the Islamic Revolution of Iran" on visiting students of Yazd University Universities - (http://farsi.khamenei.ir/speech-topic) 01/03/2018.

But, as stated, the disagreements between Iran and the United States are more than these. The need for communication and cooperation requires the abandonment of one side of its principles and its vital interests, which is unreasonable and irrational. Unless something goes wrong in the future, or if the two countries are more interested in matters of common interest.

Issues and Challenges of the Foreign Relations of the Islamic Republic of Iran after the Iranian Revolution is so much the first post-revolutionary subject to the seizure of the American Embassy in Tehran by revolutionary forces, then perhaps more than a dozen important issues in Iran-US foreign policy has happened. But according to the research goal, they are not allowed to pay for this research. But more key issues that illustrate the causes of hostilities between the two countries will be examined.

How much did I say during the nuclear negotiations that Americans are cheating, lying, do not keep up with their words; now you see! Today, the one who says that they do not want me, I'm not alone; the respectable officials of the country, our negotiators, who are so bothered, say. [64]

My insistence on the need to negotiate with the United States is for this reason, and the experience has proven that Americans are seeking to impose their demands instead of understanding, a clear example of which is the same recent case.

The main causes of the differences between Iran and the United States
1. Basic disputes arising from intellectual and ideological foundations
The origins of fundamental and profound differences between the Islamic State of Iran and secularism (US) With the roots of the two Islamic-secular governments' thinking of the Iranian and American examples, the fundamental depth of the differences between the two countries is manifested religiously and creatively. Undoubtedly, the dependency of each of these countries has a great influence on the decision making of foreign policy actors in their unique ideology. As stated in the Islamic teachings and the constitution of the Islamic Republic of Iran, al-

---

[64] Statement by Ayatollah Khamenei, "Supreme Leader of the Islamic Revolution of Iran" Meet students and students - (http://farsi.khamenei.ir/speech-topic) 2016/11/02

Khidhari is a principle at the top of all affairs. But the ontological basis of the political thought of the United States is based on humanism. These two opposing thoughts will result in two fruits and a result. First: In Islamic thought (Islamic Republic of Iran), the government is rooted in revelation and Imamate is considered to be a worthy endeavour. But in Western thought (America), government is a custom and rooted in the understanding of people and thinkers. Second, Islamic thought is the legitimacy of laws and rulers on the part of God, but in Western thought (secular thinking); legitimacy is achieved through law and the rule of the ruling ruler and people.[65]

Governance, sovereignty, and power must be instrumental in the development of society and social justice and the revival of divine values. In fact, it is not the goal but an instrument for human development in the dimension of moral and divine values. Earning power in Western discourse is a goal. In this discourse, which is practical and theoretical in the international arena, they are allowed to achieve (power) by any means and in any way possible.[66]

In fact, acquiring power is like a tool that should be a facilitator and a way to achieve another goal.[67] Imam Khomeini proclaims: Power is from the Islamic point of view a condition of tangibility. Accordingly, the goal is to achieve power in the international arena, in order to achieve human goals, divine teachings, defence against intruders, deterrence and peace and security, fight against oppression and domination. Therefore, according to Imam Khomeini, gaining political power must be aimed at achieving the sovereignty of God over the world.[68]

In the Islamic Republic of Iran, all laws must be within the framework of the Islamic teachings (Qur'an and Sunnah) and aim at the perfection of mankind. But in western thought (America), human primarily is characterized by its freedom from the rules of divine law.[69]

---

[65] Nowroozi, Mohammad Javad, *"Introduction to the Political System of Islam,"* Qom, Imam Khomeini Raad Research Institute, 2011, p. 51.

[66] Mansoor, Mir Ahmadi and Hadi Ajeli " Introduction to the Meaning and Meaning of Power in International Relations: Islamic Approach," *Quarterly political and international approaches (Iran),* Vol. 5, No. 19, 2009, p. 136.

[67] Ibid,PP. 136-137

[68] Ibid,PP. 138-139

[69] Nowroozi, Mohammad Javad, *"Introduction to the Political System of Islam,"* Qom, Imam Khomeini Raad Research Institute, 2011, p. 57.

Another disagreement between Islam (Islamic Republic of Iran) and West (US) is related to the two words of the Ummah and the government. The government is one of the main concepts in the realism approach, and this concept holds true for countries like the United States.

The concept of "Ummah" is merely an ideological concept. "Ummah" refers to a collection of human beings that bring together their single purpose and purpose. The border between the "nations" is an ideological frontier. All those who focus on tawhid, prophet hood, and resurrection form the united Islamic nation. From the point of view of Islam, "the Ummah" is the most important criterion for the division of human societies.

The constitution of the Islamic Republic of Iran is based on religious principles and principles, and in this regard, in its various principles, the unity of the Islamic Ummah and the support of Muslims in every corner of the world have been considered by the world as an important and essential task:

"انّ هذه امتكم امّة واحدة و انا ربّكُم فاعبدون"[70]

Article 11

In accordance with the sacred verse of the Qur'an ("This your community is a single community, and I am your Lord, so worship Me" [21:92]), all Muslims form a single nation, and the government of the Islamic Republic of Iran has the duty of formulating its general policies with a view to cultivating the friendship and unity of all Muslim peoples, and it must constantly strive to bring about the political, economic, and cultural unity of the Islamic world.[71]

The third principle of the constitution, which consists of 16 clauses, is one of the most important principles of the constitution that expresses the various policies of the state. In the last paragraph of this article, the government of the Islamic Republic of Iran is obligated to use all its facilities to "regulate the foreign policy of the country based on Islamic criteria, brotherly commitment to all Muslims, and the indisputable support of the oppressed people of the world."

---

[70] Nazpour, Mehdi, *"Introduction to the Constitution of the Islamic Republic of Iran,"* Tehran, Ma'araf Publishing, 2015 (Article 11), p. 144.
[71] Ibid.

What has been mentioned in paragraph 16 of the third principle referred to in Chapter 10, which is devoted to the foreign policy of the Islamic Republic of Iran, has been explicitly emphasized.

Article 152

The foreign policy of the Islamic Republic of Iran is based upon the rejection of all forms of domination, both the exertion of it and submission to it, the preservation of the independence of the country in all respects and its territorial integrity, the defense of the rights of all Muslims, non-alignment with respect to the hegemonies superpowers, and the maintenance of mutually peaceful relations with all non-belligerent States.

With regard to the above principles, it can be concluded that in the constitution, such as "all Muslims are one", "the defence of the rights of all Muslims" and the "protection of the right-wing struggle of the oppressed against the oppressed in any part of the world", one of the "criteria of Islam" Is. And therefore, it is one of the principles of the foreign policy of the Islamic Republic of Iran.

2. Disputes arising from national interests

Along with the deep-seated divisions between Iran and the United States, each of which is the subject of secular and secular thought. There are very significant differences in national interests between the two countries. These disputes are debatable in three areas: political, economic, and security.

Political and economic tensions between Iran and the United States have been two-sided since the revolution. This means that some of Iran's actions against the United States and some of America's actions against Iran after the Islamic Revolution have jeopardized the national interests of each other.

Iran's actions to jeopardize US interests:

1. Reviving the concept of pure Islam based on self-respect and oppression;

2. Belief in the rule of Islam in all aspects and propagating this thought among Islamic countries with the motive of destroying the hegemony of Western thought;

3. Occupation of the US Embassy in Tehran;

4. The excessive influence of Iran in the countries of the region (if countries like Afghanistan, Iraq, Yemen were threatened for Iran a few years ago, they have become an opportunity today.)

5. Non-admission of American goods to Iran after signature;

7. Antagonism and hostility with US strategic partner in West Asia (Middle East) Israel;

Efforts to increase oil and gas prices;

8. Explaining and disclosing the dual role of the United States in supporting its united royal regimes and strict and discriminatory treatment of the opposition;

9. Advancing the goals of Iran in Syria and Iraq despite US opposition (Arica intended to overthrow Bashar al-Assad and create insecurity and disintegration of Iraq).

10. Support the resistance axis (Hezbollah, Lebanon, Syria, Yemen, Iraq, and Palestinian movements);

11. Non-cooperation with the United States after the invasion of Iraq and Afghanistan (lack of cooperation in stabilizing the two countries);

12. Iran's attempt to provoke Muslim nations against American domination policies;

13. Opposition to the Middle East peace process;

14. The proximity of Iran's relations with China and Russia;

15. Supporting the conscious movement of the Muslim countries of the region in the form of Islamic Awakening;

16. Loss of 80 Million Iranian Markets;

17. The humiliating behavior of Iranians with the United States on national and religious occasions in antagonism to the country's arrogant behavior (such as the slogans of the death of America and the burning of its flag on Jerusalem, the anniversary of the victory of the revolution, the day of Arafah in Arafat of Mecca);

18. Iran's Nuclear and Scientific Progress;

US actions in jeopardizing Iran's interests:

1. Supporting the enemies of Iran in the region;

2. The proximity of Israel and Saudi Arabia and some Arab countries to Iran's regional policies with American provocation and support;

3. Assisting and supporting the militant groups and subversion of the Islamic Revolution and the Islamic Revolution;

4. Security of foreign policy activities of the Islamic Republic of Iran;

5. Iran's Political and Economic Sanctions under Excuses for Supporting Terrorism, Nuclear and Human Rights;

6. Stimulate the Arab countries of the region against Iran;

7. Supporting Saddam Hussein in Iraq's imposed Iraq war against Iran;

8. Insecurity of the borders of Iran and campaign against two important Iran's neighbours - Afghanistan and Iraq - in controlling Iran;

9. Establishment of numerous military bases in the region;

10. Military Attack (Operation Peaks);

11. Military *coup d'état*;

12. An attempt to defuse Iran by supporting the hypocrites and Saddam in the first years of the revolution and ISIL in recent years;

13. Unconditional support from Israel;

14. US consensus on Iran on Iran's nuclear activities and the withdrawal of Iran's case to the UN Security Council (this American action in the political and economic field was one of Iran's most important activities in isolating Iran);

15. The attempt to curb Iran's power (the United States has made a lot of efforts to influence Iran)

16. America's failure to commit new sanctions to missile pretexts;

There are many reasons to consider the tension in the relationship between Iran and the United States. If we want to discuss this issue from a religious point of view, the most important reason for breaking the relationship between Iran and the United States can be the authoritarian, authoritarian, and authoritarian behaviour of the United States. The Islamic Republic of Iran has links to nearly two hundred countries in the world, except Israel and the United States. The reason for the interruption of Iran's relations with Israel is due to the lack of legitimacy of the sovereignty of Israel, which will be dealt with in its place. But in the case of the

United States, the main cause of its viciousness has been to prevent the establishment of relations between the two countries. The constitution and dignity of the people of Iran have always been oppressive. Religiously, the main document of this issue is a verse from the Qur'an, explained in detail in the second part:

«﴿ وَلَن يَجْعَلَ اللَّهُ لِلْكَافِرِينَ عَلَى الْمُؤْمِنِينَ سَبِيلاً﴾[72]».

And Allah will not give the disbelievers any way (of success) against the believers.

According to this verse, in order to preserve the Islamic Republic of Iran, the dignity of Muslims, the way of any infiltration and domination of the infidels should be blocked on Islamic societies in various political, military, economic and cultural areas. Today, according to the Islamic Republic of Iran, America is the manifestation of oppression, arrogance and interference in internal and external affairs, and should stand against it, although it may be politically and economically pressured on Iran. Of course, confronting American domination is one side of the matter, and the other side is Iran's support for the countries that have been oppressed.

4. Supporting the Axis of Resistance and the Foreign Policy of the Islamic Republic of Iran;

The body of the sceptic is one of the most important foreign policy issues of the Islamic Republic of Iran after the revolution, supporting the Axis of Resistance. If the foreign policy issues of the Islamic Republic of Iran are thoroughly analyzed, it can be understood that the issue of Iran's support for the resistance to other issues of Iranian foreign policy directly affects Iran. Iran's relationship with the Arab countries, neighbouring countries, Russia, the European Union, the United States and many other countries is all influential in Iran's support of the resistance axis. Western countries always pressure the Islamic Republic of Iran because of Iran's support for the resistance axis. Some Arab countries like Saudi Arabia, the UAE, and Bahrain, with the support of the United States, are always trying to weaken the axis of resistance. In general, it can be said that the fears of some Arab countries

---

[72] Surah Nisa , verse 141.

that Iran's influence over Iran and its supreme powers in the region and in the Western countries have always been pressing Iran for supporting Israel. But in contrast to Russia, it has always supported the Axis of Resistance, because of the prevention of further US influence in the region.

Define Axis of Resistance

If we want to present a comprehensive definition of the Axis of Resistance that explains that concept, one can say that the resistance axis comes from two major state actors (Iran, Yemen, Syria and Lebanon) and non-state actors (Hamas, Islamic Jihad and Hezbollah Lebanon) Composed. Which has formed a geopolitical alliance in line with the excesses of the United States and some Arab countries and attempts to eliminate the sovereignty and interests of Israel, due to the interests of the convergence, another definition of the resistance axis can be given which is more discursive. Which is a part of that negation and the other part is positive and "affirmative." In the centre of the resurgence of resistance discourse, there is "domination". The most important element of the discourse of resistance is the negation of domination and domination. Second, the negation of arrogance and autocracy, But the most important positive and positive aspects of the discourse of resistance, cantered on this discourse, are justice and justice, Islamism, pacifism, self-determination and authority, independence, liberty, spirituality, wisdom and rationality, Expediency and idealism and realism.[73]

Explain the position of the Axis of Resistance in the teachings of Islam:

The defence of Islam and the rejection of domination and oppression, the preservation of independence and dignity, the defence of the oppressed and the oppressed are among the fundamental principles of the Islamic State's foreign policy, which the Islamic Republic of Iran has also emphasized. In the second chapter, these principles are explained in detail; henceforth in this section we only mention the titles. The formation of the resistance axis due to the violation of these principles has the duty to defend the Islamic Ummah. In other words, self-

---

[73] Faramarz Mirzazadeh Ahmad Biglou, Ali Harbizadeh, The Perspective of Identical Challenges that Originated from Recent Middle Eastern Changes, World Politics Quarterly(Iran), Vol. 2, No. 4, 2013, pp. 203-208.

affirmation is against the support of groups and countries of the resistance axis in the part of the divine assignments, which is obligatory in practice.

Although the Islamic Republic of Iran has suffered considerable moral and material losses for supporting the resistance axis, it has been able to introduce itself as an influential country in the region and the world, and today it is introduced as an active actor in the region. Today, if Iran does not solve the problem in the region, then the crisis will not be resolved. Given the strategic and strategic engagement of Iran with the countries and the resistance movement, Iran's border today is not limited to its geography. The Islamic Republic of Iran Syria, Lebanon, Yemen knows Iraq as its geographical borders with other countries. Therefore, Iran, with its interactions with Syria and Lebanon, sees itself on its side along the Israeli border. This has put Israeli interests at risk more than ever before.

The most important reason for Iran's support for Syria as one of the Axis of Resistance and tensions with Saudi Arabia as one of the opponents of the resistance is their opposition to the policies and policies of the two countries in opposition to Israel, the domination of foreigners, Islamic sovereignty and oppression. That is the root of all these religious doctrines. To further clarify the topic, this chapter will focus on issues of resistance to this topic. A discussion of the axis of resistance, a lot of things can be designed, but it is more important to consider in terms of a few topics that we will explain. Those issues are: the Syrian crisis, the relationship between Iran and Saudi Arabia and the Shiite crescent. Before discussing these three issues, we will explain the Axis of Resistance issue.

Axis of Resistance

With the victory of the Islamic Revolution, the support of the freedom-loving and Muslim movements that was at the head of the Palestinian issue and protecting the freedom and independence of its people, became one of the most important pillars of identification to the Islamic Revolution and thus shaped the foreign policy of the Islamic Republic of Iran. Over the course of time, affecting the Middle East security system, this led to the formation of a security-oriented sub-system of resistance to the leadership of the Islamic Republic of Iran, which, under the influence of the vast majority of identity sources, conveyed to the Islamic Republic of Iran, as opposed to global colonialism and its regional imprisonment, Israel, Considered the legitimacy of the Israeli regime. [74]

Iran's geopolitical capacities have been heavily influenced by the regional security of the Middle East .After the Islamic Revolution, the formation of a coalition from the Sunni countries of the Persian Gulf to Saudi Arabia, inevitably forced Iran to oppose resistance within the framework of the resistance axis. The axis that came with the Shiite government in Iraq was doubled. Iran's security performance in the developments of Islamic awakening, the support of Shiite groups in Yemen and Bahrain, as well as active participation in Iraq and Syria, can be considered as an effort to maintain and increase the strength of the security-assembled resistor and, in fact, to secure Iran's national security.[75]

Undoubtedly, Hezbollah's victory in the 33-day war in 2006 and the victory of the Gazans in the 2008 and 2014 battle against Israel, Iraq's and Syria's victory in 2017 against the ISIL invaders and the resistance of the Yemenis against the invasion of Saudi Arabia, with the support of the resistance axis, Of the people, groups and governments of Iran, Iraq, Syria, Lebanon, Palestine and Yemen. In the coming years or decades, Saudi Shiites and Bahrainis, or the Alevis of Turkey, may also join the resistance axis. Putting Shaykh Isa Qassim and Sheikh Mohammad Baqer Nemar, Shiite scholars of Bahrain and Saudi Arabia alongside photos of Sayyid Badr al-Din Houthi (Yemen) Ayatollah Sistani (Iraq) Imam Khomeini and Ayatollah Khamenei (Iran) Seyyed Hassan Nasrallah (Lebanon), and sometimes Vladimir Putin (Russia) could be a sign of danger to the national interests of Saudi Arabia and Bahrain. Of course, these two countries, with the execution of Sheikh Nemr and the imprisonment of Sheikh Isa Qassim, have apparently been able to suppress the main factors.

---

[74] Karimi, Abolfazl, "The role of the Islamic Republic of Iran in identifying part of the security-based resistance system," *Quarterly Journal of Research on the Nations (Iran)*, Vol. 2, No. 20, 2017, p. 7.

[75] Ali Adami, Elham Keshavarz-Moghaddam, "The Security Complex of Axis of Resistance in Foreign Policies of Islamic Republic of Iran," *The journal of "Political Studies of Islamic World"(Iran),* Vol . 4, No. 2, 2015, pp. 9-10.

The axis of resistance is a political term that was first put forward by the Libyan newspaper against the "axis of evil" that was introduced by George W. Bush in 2002, stating that the countries that the president of the United States called "the Axis of Evil" The win is essentially the "axis of resistance" against the United States and its attempt to dominate other countries. [76]

Indeed, the resistance axis has become an effective force and effective act with the modelling of the Islamic Revolution under the leadership of the Islamic Republic of Iran. Without a doubt, the security suite in the Axis of Resistance, as one of the security subsidiaries in the Middle East region, has been able to change the security order of this region and undermine Israel's security and the interests of its allies, especially the United States.[77] Israel is the country that is the main protector of the interests of the West, especially the United States in the region. It can be said that the Axis of Resistance, in the security structure of the Middle East, is the only effective power against the domination system, and in particular Israel. In particular, in recent years, the security and survival of Israel have been threatened by the Axis of Resistance under totally unequal conditions in an asymmetric manner, relying on faith and on its people, in the light of the ideals derived from the Islamic Revolution of Iran.[78]

Ayatollah Khamenei, the Supreme Leader of the Islamic Republic of Iran, said about the oppression and support of the resistance: "In the resistance issue, the Americans decided to establish the root of resistance in West Asia, they were sure they would do it; we stood, we said. Today, for the whole world, it has been proven today that he wanted and could not, and we wanted it and we could understand it all in the world. "In contrast, oppression must cease, now it was foreign oppression, (but) domestic oppression is also the same.[79] And it may be a priority in some ways. "In another speech, he says: The Islamic Republic of Iran defends the ideals of the right, human rights, the national and Islamic identity of its

---

[76] Karimi, Abolfazl, "The role of the Islamic Republic of Iran in identifying part of the security-based resistance system," *Quarterly Journal of Research on the Nations (Iran),* Vol . 2, No. 20, 2017, p .2.

[77] Ibid , p. 12.

[78] Ibid, p. 6.

[79] Statement by Ayatollah Khamenei, "Supreme Leader of the Islamic Revolution of Iran" on Army Air Force Commanders and Staff, - (http://farsi.khamenei.ir/speech-topic)February 2, 2018

people and the pride of a nation deserving of pride, and does not retreat from oppression. [80]

> In analyzing the positions of the Islamic Republic's resistance and foreign policy toward Israel, the Islamic Shiite Islamic Revolution has a decisive role in defining the interests and goals of foreign policy of the Islamic Republic of Iran. [81]

The Supreme Leader of the Islamic Revolution Ayatollah Khamenei, based on the practice of Islamic teachings, advocates support for the Islamic Resistance axis as part of Iran's foreign policy principles. He even emphasizes the defense of the axis of resistance during the negotiations with the world powers around the nuclear issue and states: "Whether this text is approved or not, we will not stop supporting our friends in the region (the axis of resistance): from The oppressed Palestinian people, from the oppressed Yemeni people, from the Syrian people and government, from the Iraqi people and government, from the oppressed Bahraini people, from the true resistance mujahedeen in Lebanon and Palestine; they will always be our supporters. "[82]

The resistance axis has had a great deal of influence in the Middle East. But three of the more important are the following: 1. the contrast between the resistance axis and the Israeli entity, 2. Avoiding resistance to the Middle East peace process , 3. Addressing military threats such as resistance to ISIS, Most of the Arab states consider Iran a threat to themselves, so they are trying to confront Iranian influence

---

[80] Statement by Ayatollah Khamenei, "Supreme Leader of the Islamic Revolution of Iran" after visiting the military achievements of the IRGC Air Force, - (http://farsi.khamenei.ir/speech-topic)2003/7/20

[81] Karimi, Abolfazl, "The role of the Islamic Republic of Iran in identifying part of the security-based resistance system," Quarterly Journal of Research on the Nations (Iran), Vol. 2, No. 20, 2017, p. 8.

[82] Ayatollah Khamenei's statements in Eid al-Fitr prayers sermons, - (http://farsi.khamenei.ir/speech-topic) 18/8/2015 .

and power. [83]The Arab countries have set up a coalition and cooperation against Iran, in pursuit of their goal, between themselves and with the cooperation of Western countries. The Arab countries of the region believe that Iran has played a destructive role in Middle East policy in the past decade, supporting Lebanon and Hamas, support for a wide range of Shiite militias in Iraq, supporting the Assad regime and Shiite revolutionaries in Bahrain and Yemen is part of a destructive and threatening act of their own.[84]

The Arab countries believe that Iran is a vicious circle of government that is unilaterally seeking a large part of its influence, from the west to the Mediterranean, not by military forces, but by its close and follower allies. What the Sunni Arab countries have not been able to accomplish. [85] In such an environment, Iran wants to be treated like a great regional power. A power whose interests and security are defined at the level of the region, This view, along with the type of relations between Iran and the Arab states of the Sunni region, the active presence in Syria and Iraq, and the support of the Yemeni and Bahrain people during the course of Islamic Awakening, have contributed to the growth of the anger and counter-opposing policies of other countries in the region against the axis of resistance. But the most important question that comes to mind in this regard is what factors have triggered Iran's susceptibility to the developments in Islamic awakening in Syria, Iraq, Bahrain and Yemen.[86]

The coming of a Shiite government in Bahrain and Yemen, of course, will increase the strategic depth of Iran in the region. And may strengthen the Shi'ite discourse

---

[83] Boozan, Barry, *"People, Government, Panic. Translation of the Research Institute for Strategic Studies,"* Tehran, 1999, p. 103.

[84] Ali Adami, Elham Keshavarz-Moghaddam, "The Security Complex of Axis of Resistance in Foreign Policies of Islamic Republic of Iran," *The journal of "Political Studies of Islamic World"(Iran)*, Vol. 4, No. 2, 2015 , p. 9.

[85] Fishman, Brian, the Conflict in Syria An Assessment of US Strategic Interests, RAND Corp, New America Foundation, March 2013, pp. 5-6.

[86] Boozan, Barry, *"People, Government, Panic. Translation of the Research Institute for Strategic Studies,"* Tehran, 1999, p. 9.

in the region and increase the strength of the security-oriented component and increase the security of Iran significantly.

Shiite geopolitical -Shiite crescent

The Shiite Crescent is an ideological and constructive issue posed by the West and the countries of the region in the direction of Shiite and Iranian fears and is more unrealistic, but Shiite geopolitics is a real and geopolitical sequence of Shiite Middle East countries that is coherent and sustainable.[87] Aware of this fact, there are debates about Shiite-Shiite Shiite geopolitics.

There are two positive and reciprocal theories around the issue of the Shi'ite Crescent. Some countries with a majority of Sunni religious communities, such as Saudi Arabia, the United Arab Emirates, Jordan, and others believe that after the US invasion of Iraq and the overthrow of Saddam Hussein, Iran was able to form a Shiite crescent along with Iraq. Part of the Shiite crescent is Syria and Lebanon.[88] Most Arab authorities consider Iran's influence in Lebanon, Bahrain, Syria, Iraq, and Yemen to be a threat to their interests and sovereignty, so that countries like Saudi Arabia and Bahrain are also afraid of Iran's influence. What the Arab states say about the Shiite crescent. In practice, it is the same resistance axis that maintains Iran against the dangers of Israel, ISIS and foreign pressures.

The purpose of the Shiite in the Shiite Crescent is not only the Shi'a of the Imam, but it is a religious flow that extends across the geographic and vast parts of India, Pakistan, the whole of Iran, the majority of Iraq and Bahrain, East of Saudi Arabia, important parts of Turkey, Lebanon, Syria and Africa Are present. Shiite sects in this geographic area are in addition to twelve Shiite Shiites including Ismaili, Zaidi, Turkish Alawites, Syrian Alevis, and Turkey's Bektashiyah. The geographic extension of this encompasses an integrated cultural environment. From this point of view, Iran's historical influence over the Middle East Shiites is considered a factor in the political impediment of the Middle East's political security, and insists

---

[87] Bazin Zarghami, Seyyed Mohammad Javad Shooshtari, Salman Ansari Zadeh, "Shiite Geopolitics or Shiite Crescent (Foundations, Objectives, and Options)," *Human Geography Research (Iran),* Vol. 46, No. 1, 2014, p. 212.

[88] Haji Yousefi, Amir Mohammad, "The Shia Crescent: Opportunities and Threats for the Islamic Republic of Iran, Arab Countries and the United States," *Political knowledge Quarterly (Iran),* Vol. 5, No. 9, 2009, p. 159.

on using this term strongly. On the one hand, this concept reflects the rise of Shi'a in international politics and the Middle East, and on the other hand, it is a kind of direction to the negative sensitivities of the media.[89]

The word "Shiite Crescent" was first introduced by King Abdullah II of Jordan. The purpose of this discussion is to eliminate Israel through the development of Iran and support for the Hamas and Hezbollah field operations. The term is, according to the Iranian authorities, a plan that is not realistic and aims to bring the Arab, American and European countries closer to pressure on Iran, on the one hand, and to confront the wave of demands of the people's freedom in the Arab countries on the other[90]. During which the threat of Shiites in the region was raised. After Abdullah II, Hosni Mubarak in Egypt and some Saudi officials, including those who posed the threat of a Shiite crescent in the region,[91] they believe that the Islamic Republic of Iran can, by exercising influence, in the form of soft power among the Shiites of Iraq, Leading the geopolitical developments in the Middle East and shifting the balance of power in favour of the Shiites and against the interests of the United States, Israel, and Sunnis. The depth of Iran's influence in the words of Hosni Mubarak, the former Egyptian president, can be seen in an interview with Al-Arabiya Network: "Shiite residents of Arab countries are more loyal to Iran than their own country."[92]

The emergence and expansion of Shiite geopolitics is the concept of changing the rules of strategic game and security in the Middle East. It is obvious that the formation of any new balance of Shiite geopolitics affects the type of behaviour

---

[89] http://www.jahannews.com/analysis/423586/

[90] Bazin Zarghami, Seyyed Mohammad Javad Shooshtari, Salman Ansari Zadeh, "Shiite Geopolitics or Shiite Crescent (Foundations, Objectives, and Options)," *Human Geography Research (Iran),* Vol. 46, No. 1, 2014, p. 210.

[91] Ebrahimi, Shahrooz, "Saudi Arabia and the Power System in the Persian Gulf," *Strategic Studies Quarterly (Iran),* Vol. 7, No. 3, 2004, p. 54.

[92] Haji Yousefi, Amir Mohammad, "The Shia Crescent: Opportunities and Threats for the Islamic Republic of Iran, Arab Countries and the United States," *Political knowledge Quarterly (Iran)*, Vol. 5, No. 9, 2009, p. 159.

and relations between the countries of the region and the pattern of friendship and hostility of governments.[93]

Shiite geopolitics means the continuation of Shiite political geography in different countries of the great Middle East. The significance of Iran is so much that the Graham Fuller calls Iran the heart of the world.[94]

The use of the concept of the Shiite Crescent as a putative theory coincided with the rise of Shiites in the Iraqi election following the 2003 US invasion of the country. Accordingly, the Shi'a power of arrival in Iraq was a crescent complement of Shi'a influence domains that included Lebanon, Syria, Iraq, Iran, Pakistan, and Afghanistan, meaning that not only in Iran, Shiites in the form of the Islamic Republic And in Lebanon, as a powerful and progressive movement, but also in Iraq and Syria, which have the government, they have a decisive role in the region.[95]

Those who raise the issue of the Shiite crescent believe that this is very important for analyzing the future developments of West Asia. Although, in terms of quantity, both the government and the Sunni population in this area are more than Shiites, but in geopolitical terms, Shiites in the region have a high power. In fact, the geographic location of Shiite or Shi'a geopolitical deployment in the Middle East is considered to be the strategic economic and political belt in the region, because Shiites are at the heart of the largest oil-rich Middle East, which holds more than 70 percent of the world's oil reserves, and " With most Shiites in Iran, Iraq and Azerbaijan have access to 30% of the oil reserves, which would add up to 50% if the east Shiite portion of Saudi Arabia is added to these figures. Thus, Arab Shiites along with Iran can control most Gulf sources.[96]

---

[93]Towal, Francois, "*Shiite geopolitics,*" Translated by Katayoun Basar, Tehran, Wistar Publication, Second Edition, 2005, p. 137.

[94] Bazin Zarghami, Seyyed Mohammad Javad Shooshtari, Salman Ansari Zadeh, "Shiite Geopolitics or Shiite Crescent (Foundations, Objectives, and Options)," *Human Geography Research (Iran),* Vol. 46, No. 1, 2014, p. 203.

[95] Pourahmadi, Hossein, "International Political Economy and American Invasion to Iraq", *Defense Strategy Quarterly (Iran),* Vol. 3, No. 2, 2004, p. 64.

[96] Javdani Moghaddam, Mehdi and Gohari, Abuzar, *"American Strategy for the Shia World",* American Strategy for the Islamic World ," Center for Strategic Research of the Expediency Council. 2008 , p. 147.

Many Arab countries in the last decade have been attempting to condemn the Shiite-Sunni-dominated Shi'ite fear of Iran as a geopolitical difference. They refer to Shiite geopolitics as the Shiite expansionist political thought beyond the boundaries of Iran, or to the extent that Iran's interests so require. These interests form the basis of Iran's vital space for dominance over the land and the geographic territory appropriate to the Iranian government or based on the creation of trans boundary geographical shields. These shields are gradually communicating with Iran so that Iran achieves the ultimate and desirable goal of a developments approach. This goal is based on the strategies and planning of decision-making centres in Iran, and has been based on these programs and strategies since the 1979 revolution victory, which is considered to be Iran's lead in the geopolitical plan. "[97]

The Islamic Republic of Iran appears to be moving towards a policy of strengthening the Shiite Crescent with its open policy in support of the resistance and resistance axis and the fight against Israel and US policies in the region. Of course, it does not announce this policy publicly. The Islamic Republic of Iran, not only among the Arab countries, but also beyond, means Nigeria, India, Pakistan and Afghanistan, are also seeking to influence these countries.[98]

Some believe that the Islamic Republic of Iran began its plan to launch a dialogue on the issuance of the revolution to reach the Shiite geopolitics.

 Subsequently, the Umm al-Qaeda theory of the Islamic world was conceptualized, which, due to lack of political experience, economic problems, the creation of excessive tension with the Arab countries and the Iran-Iraq War did not reach their goals, but ultimately they have achieved their goals by carefully designing a Shia geopolitical strategy. Although the formation of the Shiite Crescent has provided Iran with the possibility of balancing power in the region, the high ranking officials of the Islamic Republic of Iran have consistently condemned this idea as enemies of Iran and believe that this is in line with Iran's fear and Shiite fears. The Islamic Republic of Iran also recognizes the fact that the political, social and ethnic

---

[97] https://arabiangcis.org/pars (Shiite geopolitics, reality and future).

[98] Mohammad Javad Larijani, *"Issues in the National Strategy,"* Tehran; Center for Strategic Research and Future Studies, 2013, p. 46.

conditions of the countries of Iraq, Lebanon, Syria and Yemen do not allow the full cooperation and cooperation of the abovementioned governments with all policies of the Islamic Republic of Iran.[99] Here are the comments of some Iranian officials.

The Islamic Republic of Iran, in accordance with the constitution and Imam Khomeini's theory, looked at the issues of the Islamic world, the Ummahism. Islam demands the unity of the Islamic Ummah and the unification of all Muslims in the world, and the concentration and unity of the leadership and leadership of the Islamic society is a symbol of the unity of the Ummah. Islam wants a single government not only for the Islamic community, but also for the international community. [100] That some issues raise the issue of the Shiite crescent, this reflects the divisive politics, and it is certain that, given Imam Khomeini's stance on Iran's pursuit of the Shiite crescent, it is certain that it will be rejected.

The positions of some high ranking officials of the Islamic Republic of Iran regarding the Shiite Crescent:

1. Iran's Supreme Leader Ayatollah Khamenei: The plan of the "Shiite Crescent" by the agents of the United States, as well as the appeasement of the United States to terrorist currents in Iraq and Syria, such as ISIS, or their assistance, include the evidence of arrogant religious disengagement policy, adding: "Everyone, What Shiites should be aware that they will not play the enemy. [101]

2. Iran's President Hassan Rouhani announced at the World Summit Meeting of Ahlul Bayt in 2015. We have no Shiite crescent, but we have the Islamic mantra. All Muslims are united and united against disbelief and hypocrisy. He points out that Shiite and Sunni Imam Khomeini are together and the leader of the revolution has always relied on the principle of unity. Hassan Rouhani, at the 29th International Conference on Islamic Unity, reaffirmed in January 2015 that what

---

[99] Haji Yousefi, Amir Mohammad, "The Shia Crescent: Opportunities and Threats for the Islamic Republic of Iran, Arab Countries and the United States," *Political knowledge Quarterly (Iran)*, Vol. 5, No. 9, 2009, p. 171

[100] Mesbah Yazdi, Mohammad Taghi ,*"Law and Politics in the Quran"*, Qom, Imam Khomeini Institute of Education and Research, Autumn 2004, p. 280.

[101] Statement by Ayatollah Khamenei, "Supreme Leader of the Islamic Revolution of Iran on 4/6/2015 on the anniversary of Imam Khomeini's death; - (http://farsi.khamenei.ir/speech-topic)

some people called the Shiite Crescent are ill-fated and false discourses, and we have neither Shiite crests nor Sunni crests, but we have Islamic Bard. [102]

3. Qassim Soleimani, Commander of the Quds Force of Iran, in February 2013, does not consider the Shiite Crescent as a political one, describing it as an Economic Crescent, and considers oil as the most important economic issue. According to him, the 3 countries in the world (Iran, Saudi Arabia and Iraq) have the world's largest oil, the first of which is Saudi Arabia, Iran and Iraq, second and third, and almost 70% of the world's oil is located in these three countries, all of which are 70% in the Shia region It's native. [103]

Shiite Geopolitical:

• Accepting Iran's influence among nations;

• Increasing Iran's role in Arab countries;

• Increasing Iranian influence in liberation movements;

• The emergence of new regional and international alliances and the coalition of Iran with Russia internationally and with Turkey in the region, there are more likely to be a Shiite geopolitical rise.

• Increasing the Shi'a influence and influence in the region in the face of US policy in the region;

• Revitalizing the role of Iran at the regional level as a regional power;

• Supporting the oppressed peoples of the region;

• The threat of the legitimacy of some Arab powers;

• Accept the role of Iran in solving the problems of the region;

• Inhibition against Israel and the United States;

---

[102] http://fa.abna24.com/service/sixthconference/archive/2015/08/15/691501.

[103] http://www.asriran.com/fa/news/359420.

Threats from Shiite Geopolitical Shrine:

• Increasing Shiite and Sunnis' religious differences in the region;

• Distort what is called "Arab Spring Revolutions" by Sunni religious rulers in the region;

• Increased tension in relations between Iran and some countries in the region;

• Promoting the culture of "Iran phobia" and "Shi'ah" in the region;

• Increased arms competition in the Arab countries of the region;

• The weakening of national unity between Shiites and Sunnis within the geographic boundaries of Iran;

• Conversion of Shiite-Sunni religious differences into political differences;

• Tensions in Iran's political relations with some Arab and Arab countries in the region;

• The proximity of Arab countries led by Saudi Arabia and the United States against Iran;

• Give excuses to Iran's enemies for fear of Iran and Shia;

• Under the age of the slogan of unity and nation-cantered Iran;

• The intensification of the arms race in the region, which will benefit Arab countries.

• Cheap energy sales from the Arab countries to undermine Iran;

• Tension inside Iran due to the presence of Sunnis;

• Iran's lack of tools and facilities for implementing Shi'a geopolitical theory;

• The lack of economic, military, intellectual and political facilities that can solve internal crises and impose its attitude and strategy on the region and the world. Having such capabilities seems indispensable for the success of the geopolitical plan of the countries.

Considering evidence such as the formation of new Arab and Islamic alliances led by the Kingdom of Saudi Arabia, the probability of a change in the US foreign policy under Donald Trump's presidency over the region's crises and expansion of Iran's influence and the separation of the policy from politics His previous counterpart, in particular, Tramp's remarks, suggests that he will not allow Iran to extend its influence, a close look at Iran from within, and an examination of the economic situation and military power of the country to expand its influence in target countries and the size of the support of the Iranian people. This sovereignty approach can be concluded that Shi'i geopolitics is in now it's weakening and collapse. Iran is composed of a diverse population that includes not only Fars, but also various nationalities, religions and religions.

Iran's relations with Arab countries (Saudi Arabia);

The Islamic Republic of Iran and Saudi Arabia are two actors, rivals and actors of the region, which, taking into account the changing factors, affecting the relations between the two countries during different periods, have taken a variety of policies from relative cooperation to competition and opposition. In this regard, the tensions and incongruity between the two countries, with the onset of new developments in the region, have reached a wider level of disagreement that has led to more competition and more influence in the strategic areas of the region.[104]

To understand and understand the relationship between Iran and Arab countries, the study of the relationship between Iran and Saudi Arabia greatly contributes to the issue. Some Arab countries have a strategic relationship with Iran, such as Syria and Yemen. Some countries, such as Iraq, Oman and Lebanon, have close ties with Iran and Saudi Arabia. Of course they are closer to Iran. And a large number of Arab countries have close proximity to Saudi Arabia, such as Bahrain and the UAE. Hence, in this section, we will only focus on the strategic relationship between the two major countries of the region, Iran and Saudi Arabia.

---

[104] Vahid Darabi, Hamed Kazemi, "Crisis of Conflict and Balance of Power in Foreign Policy of Iran and Saudi Arabia," *Journal of Research in the Nations (Iran),* Vol. 2, No. 15, March 2016, p. 1.

The détente of the relationship between Iran and Saudi Arabia;
Perhaps the end of the presidency of Hashemi Rafsanjani and the presidency of Seyyed Mohad Khatami may be the most important period of time for having a close and unrestrained relationship between Iran and Saudi Arabia. For the first time, Mr. Hashemi Rafsanjani, who was the president after the 1991 revolution, attended the summit of the Islamic Conference. The conference, which was held in Senegal, hosted Mr. Hashemi Rafsanjani with Crown Prince Abdullah, Saudi Arabia, and criticized Saudi Arabia. Abdullah did not accept many of them, but this match later became an effective match. [105] Between 1993 and the end of the presidential term, Mr. Hashemi Rafsanjani, relations between the two countries improved day by day, and it could be highlighted at the beginning of the presidency of Seyyed Mohammad Khatami, when the Crown Prince of that time, visited Saudi Arabia for the first time in the conference summit Islam participated. Good relations between the two countries continued until the end of the presidency of Khatami. However, with the coming of Ahmadinejad, relations with Saudi Arabia became tense. Because Ahmadinejad, with the slogan of reviving the ideals of the Islamic Revolution and supporting the people against the Arab kings, made this unpleasant for Saudi Arabia.

Tensions between Iran and Saudi Arabia
Except for the two periods that were announced (the second term of Hashemi Rafsanjani's presidency and the presidency of Seyyed Mohammad Khatami), which had a high level of relations between the two countries, during other periods; relations between Iran and Saudi Arabia were tense. At different times, both countries can be mentioned as a stress factor. However, in some cases, external factors also played a role in exacerbating tension. The following is summarized in the following:

1. The Goals of the Islamic Revolution;

With the victory of the Islamic Revolution, the first spark of tensions between the two countries was struck. Saudi Arabia and some other Arab countries with an unpopular government considered the renditions of the issuance of the

---

[105] https://rafsanjani.ir

revolution as a threat to their sovereignty and always sought to prevent Iran from realizing revolutionary aspirations.

2. Different approaches of Iran and Saudi Arabia in the field of structure, identity and their status in the structure of the international system; the identity of the Islamic Republic of Iran consists of being Iranian, Shiite, and revolutionary. But Saudi identity is based on being Arab, conservative and Sunni Muslim. The Islamic Republic of Iran is in the form of republicanism and Islamism, and religious democracy is among its honours. But the Saudi government is kingdom in its own right, and democracy and democracy have no place. In the international structure, Iran considers itself to be a non-committed, genuine, and opposed metaphorical verbiage policy. But Saudi Arabia's policies are in line with the West.[106]

3. Iran-Iraq War; One of the main supporters of Iraq during the eight years of the war between Iran and Iraq was Saudi Arabia. With a lot of financial resources, the country made a lot of efforts to bring down the Iranian revolution.

4. The ritual of hatred of polytheists;

One of the plans of the Iranian pilgrimage after the revolution was the slogan against the United States, Israel and the arrogant. And Saudi Arabia considered it a crime. In 1987, Saudi security agents killed about 400 Hajjis who were slogans of Iranians and non-Iranians. This marked the peak of tension between Iran and Saudi Arabia. The incident caused the greatest blow to the relations between the two countries. At that time, Imam Khomeini proclaimed that, even if we were to blame for the crimes of Saddam, the crime of Al Saud in this incident is indescribable.[107] Following Saudi Arabia's action, some in Iran attacked the Saudi embassy in Tehran.

----

[106] Vahid Darabi, Hamed Kazemi, "Crisis of Conflict and Balance of Power in Foreign Policy of Iran and Saudi Arabia," *Journal of Research in the Nations (Iran),* Second Edition, No. 15, March 2016, p. 1.
[107] Rouhollah, Khomeini (Imam), *"Sahifeh Noor,"* vol. 13, Tehran, Ministry of Culture and Islamic Guidance, 2013, p. 226.

5. Rise of the Taliban: Another area of tension in relations between Iran and Saudi Arabia is Saudi support for the Taliban. The Taliban, which was established in 1986, was very hostile to Iran. But Saudi Arabia recognized the Taliban and supported the group.

6. The theme of the three islands: Saudi interference with the three islands of Persia, the small Tunb and the Great Tunb and Abu Musa, as well as the beginning of the establishment of Saudi Arabia, continued to be associated with the issue of Bahrain. In the Pahlavi era, with the reconciliation of the Iranian government and the British colonial game, Bahrain was separated from the geography of Iran under the pretext of the complete transfer of the three islands to Iran. However, allegations made by the Arab countries of the region, especially after the victory of the Islamic Revolution of Iran, continue to grow and increase every year. Even in the years following the signing of the 1971-1992 agreement, there was no objection to the current status of the islands, and only a year ago, there were new allegations made by the Saudis, the UAE and Egypt about these islands. They claimed that Iran's action on November 30, 1971, had taken on the development of the Greater Tunb and Lesser Tunb, and Abu Musa Islands of England, and they had not been aware of the 1971 Iranian-British talks on Iran's renewed sovereignty over the islands. Thus, the claims of the UAE, which were accompanied by the support of the Arab rulers, have come to fruition and are repeated every year.

7.   33-Day War of Israel against Lebanon: Perhaps the peak of Saudi Arabia's sense of danger at this time point was mentioned. Because Saudi Arabia preferred a Muslim country called Lebanon to defeat Israel and many Muslims were killed, but Lebanon (Hezbollah) did not win. The reason was that Saudi Arabia knew well that the victory of Lebanon's Hezbollah was the victory of Iranian politics (the axis of resistance) in the region.

8.   Shiite Crescent: This discussion, which was discussed in detail in the previous section, is a sign of Saudi Arabia's fear of Shia and Iran. Although the Islamic Republic of Iran does not believe in the existence of a Shiite crescent.

9. Shiite geopolitics: Another dominant discourse that has been tensions between Iran and Saudi Arabia is Shiite geopolitics. Saudi Arabia sees such a discourse as creating an axis of resistance against its goals and interests.

10. Shiite and Sunni differences. Ideologically, Iran and Saudi Arabia can be regarded as leaders of two tendencies and readings of Islam. Although many interests in the region and competition over regionalization are considered to be the main cause of the difference between Iran and Saudi Arabia, But differences of opinion between the two countries can also be effective in provoking tensions.

11. The case of Iran's core; another tension factor in relations between Iran and Saudi Arabia is Iran's core issue. Saudi Arabia has always tried to provoke Iran's nuclear activities as a threat by provoking Western and Israeli states. On the other hand, Saudi Arabia, using oil tools, tried to reduce the price of gas while increasing production. The move was in line with economic pressure on Iran to change Iran's behavior in support of Axis of Resistance.

12. Attack on two Iranian teenagers at the airport: This has sparked the feelings of the Iranian people and a wave of hatred in Saudi Arabia began. The peak of the protests in Iran marked the boycott of the Hajj. The people asked the authorities to shut down the Hajj.

13. Arabia's Neglect or Negligence at Mina Disaster 2015.

The number of Iranian deaths in the incident is 464.[108] Iran blames Saudi Arabia for killing its Hajji. Ayatollah Khamenei criticized the Saudi authorities for curtailing the causes of the tragedy in an announcement on the eve of the Hajj feast on 5/9/2016, blaming Saudi rulers for the catastrophe.[109]

14. Islamic Awakening: Iran's support for the wake of the Arab countries has provoked Saudi Arabia's protest. Iran was seeking to protect it from Islamic awakening against Saudi Arabia.

15. The execution of Sheikh Nemr and the attack on the Saudi embassy; the aggression against two Iranian teenagers at the airport, the catastrophe of Mana and the execution of Sheikh Nimr was the culmination of Iran's protest and hostility

---

[108] The list of Iranian casualties is MENA. "Hajj Pilgrimage Organization 28 September, 2015, p. 28.

[109] Statement by Ayatollah Khamenei, "Supreme Leader of the Islamic Revolution of Iran" Message to the Muslims of the world on the occasion of the Hajj's coming, (http://farsi.khamenei.ir/speech-topic) 5/9/2016

with Saudi Arabia. Following these incidents, some people in Iran on 2/1/2016 attacked the Saudi consulate in Mashhad and the Saudi embassy in Tehran. Although it was condemned by high-ranking Iranian officials, this action, in practice, caused great tension between the two countries. Iran did not send Haji to Saudi Arabia, and Saudi Arabia was also prosecuted by some Iranian citizens at their embassy. And brought many countries to condemn Iran, after these events, the title of the relationship between Iran and Saudi Arabia is meaningless. Because the relations between the two countries have come out of the ordinary and the two countries are declaring themselves against each other in various congresses and trying to destroy them.

16. The issue of ISIL and the axis of resistance (Syria, Yemen, Hezbollah, Lebanon, Iraq, and Palestinian groups); Perhaps one of the main areas of Iranian-Saudi arrogance in the Iraqi constituencies, Lebanon's Hezbollah, Syria, Yemen and The axis of resistance. Undoubtedly, the two countries of Iran and Saudi Arabia are the main players in the battle of Syria, Yemen, Iraq and Hezbollah in Lebanon. In fact, the two countries are in a proxy war. With the support of the resistance, the Islamic Republic of Iran has always sought to eliminate ISIL, Israel, Hussein Al-Assad in Syria, Lebanese Hezbollah, and Badr al-Din Houthi in Yemen. In contrast to Saudi Arabia, some Western countries support Iran's regional policies.

16. Lack of Democracy in Saudi Arabia; one of the major differences and tensions between Iran and Saudi Arabia may be the debate about the internal problems of Saudi Arabia, which is due to the lack of democracy in this country. The Islamic Republic of Iran is attempting to challenge the ruling system in Saudi Arabia with every opportunity, "like the Islamic Awakening", and to always point out the lack of religious democracy in the country. The activities of Iran in this area can be attributed to the Shiite share of the Saudi government.

Syria Crisis

The Syrian-Iranian coalition, which began in 1979, is one of the most stable regional alliances in the Middle East. This alliance was rooted in the cooperation of the two governments against the threats of Israel and Iraq, and then the scope of cooperation between Syria and Iran from cooperation with Israel and Iraq was extended to cooperation with other regional powers. [110]

One of the most important loop of Islamic resistance and strategic depth, and one of the fundamental strategic elements of the Islamic Republic of Iran's containment, is the crisis of destabilization in Syria, which, in fact, does not aim to balance the balance between the axes and undermine Iran's role and position.[111]

Syria's ideological ties with the Islamic Republic of Iran, especially during the Bashar al-Assad period, have strengthened the influence of strengthening the Islamic Revolutionary Islamic ideology of the region, especially in the Lebanese and Palestinian territories. Bashar al-Assad said that Syria is the leader of the Arab resistance against the devastation of the United States. In fact, he developed with this approach the continuation of the strategic alliance of Damascus in Tehran under his rule. And the two countries were ready for further cooperation, in which shared views on a range of regional and international issues, including hostility to Israel and the occupation of Iraq from America, were prepared.

One of Syria's most important attributes is the centrality of its relationship with the three continents of Africa, Europe and Asia, which is the most influential Arab state opposite the regime, with its eastern margin of the Mediterranean Sea with its 186 km of coastline, which is more important for Iran than Syria, Has given[112] .

The struggle in Syria is not due to democracy, human rights and Bashar al-Assad. Because in some Arab countries, like Saudi Arabia, the situation is far worse than Syria. The strife in Syria is the battle of two thinking. On the one hand, it is Iran and its allies, and the other is Arab, Israel and the West. This has led Syria to manoeuvre the United States and its allies with Iran and its allies. The US pushed for the exclusion of Bashar al-Assad by pushing Israel to isolate Iran, but has not

---

[110] Rajabi, Soheil, "Analyzing the strategic position of Syria in regional and international relations," *Quarterly journal of fifteen Khordad (Iran)* , Vol. 3, No. 34, 2012, p. 124.

[111] Ibid , p. 124.

[112] Hossein Salimi, Mojtaba Shariati, "Interests of the Islamic Republic of Iran Continuation or discontinuation of support for the current Syrian regime?" *Defense Policy Magazine (Iran)*, Vol. 17, No. 89, 2014, pp. 72-73.

succeeded in spite of much effort.[113] Saudi Arabia is also trying to reduce the role of Iran in infiltration by changing Bashar al-Asad, while consolidating his power.[114]

The Islamic Republic of Iran believes that Islamic awakening means the restoration of Islamic values, such as justice and other transcendental values, in the light of the teachings of genuine Islam, as well as eliminating the ambiguity of the Islamic religion and introducing it with genuine Islamic sources.[115] Islamic Awakening, some of which is called the Arab Spring, is considered to be an important factor in expanding Iran's influence in Arab countries in early 2011 in Tunisia, Egypt, Libya, Yemen and Syria. In fact, these uprisings have created a real opportunity for Iran. Some believe Iran initially called it "Islamic Awakening" and inspired by the 1979 revolution by declaring support for the rise of the Arab nations (Islamic awakening), especially in Egypt and Tunisia and Libya and Yemen. In Iran's view, at that time, these uprisings were in line with the interests of Iran in the sphere of expansion of influence and development. However, when the wave of protests came to Bashar al-Assad, Iran's ally in Syria, Iran, with all its strength, assisted Syria and retained the power of Bashar al-Assad, believing in the dictatorship of Iran's behaviour regarding Islamic awakening.

In Iran, what happened in Syria was different from that of other countries. The Islamic Republic of Iran believed that people in Syria should determine their own destiny, but the Iranian authorities believed that because Syria was the centrepiece of resistance to Israel, the dissatisfaction inside the country was more than driven abroad, but Other countries that joined the Islamic awakening were protests from inside the country against the rulers. Although some Syrians were upset about the status quo and protests, but as stated, major hostilities against Syria were due to

---

[113] Khanboluki, Farideh, "US Goals in the Syrian Crisis," *the Annals of Revolution Journal (Iran)*, No. 68, 2012, p. 24.

[114] Mansouri Moghadam, Mohammad, "The Identity Element and Its Influence on Saudi Foreign Policy toward the Islamic Republic of Iran," *Majles and Strategic Quarterly(Iran)*, Vol. 19, No. 72, 2012, p. 94.

[115] Seyyed Shamsedin Sadeghi, Kamran, Latifi, "Syria's Crisis and Analyze of The Islamic Republic of Iran's Positions against Syria Crisis," *Contemporary Political Studies Quarterly (Iran)*, Vol. 6, No. 15 2015, p. 128.

differences with Bashar al-Assad, and the Islamic Republic of Iran is naturally sponsored as a friend and ally of Syria. Made Of course, the interference of some Arab countries, Israel and Turkey in the Syrian affairs also shows the hostility of these countries with Iran's strategic alliance.

Iran and Syria, through their ties to Hezbollah, not only affect the security interests of Israel and its Western allies, but also the interests of Saudi Arabia and its allies. Hence, Saudi Arabia feels that Lebanon's Hezbollah is the force or arm of Iran in the Eastern Mediterranean equations, which has not only changed the internal balance of Lebanon in favour of Iran, but has also affected Iran's positions on the Arab-Israeli conflict. And has joined the efforts of Iran, Syria and Hamas to prevent the Arab-Israeli peace process, The Middle East and Palestinian peace issue is another important area in which Iran and Syria have worked together to prevent Saudi Arabia's plans and policies.

In addition to playing a key role against Israel and Iraq (at the time of Saddam Hussein and Iraq's invasion of Iran), as well as the disruption of US hegemony in the Middle East, a structural function against the influence of Saudi Arabia in the Eastern Mediterranean region as well as regional balance of power In the Middle East too. In the case of Palestine, Iran has established close ties with Hamas with regard to the common features of Islamic political ideology, and Saudi Arabia has turned to closer cooperation with Fatah. In Lebanon, Iran supported March 8th and Saudi Arabia to support the March 14th group. In this area, financial assistance and the similarities of political ideological tendencies and, most importantly, common security concerns have shaped the ties between Iran and Saudi Arabia and their nongovernmental allies.

One question is always raised: why does the Islamic Republic of Iran carry a lot of material and moral costs to maintain the Syrian regime?

In response to this question, many observers point out the strategic importance of Syria as the only serious and reliable ally of Iran in the region and even in the international community as a whole. In addition to the facilitator's role in Iran's relations with the Arab world (before the Syrian popular uprising began in 2011), Damascus has always been a reliable means of securing access to the Islamic Republic, whether military, political or political, to its protected groups in the field.

The periphery of Israel, in particular Lebanese Hezbollah, has provided. Therefore, it may be said that Syria is the cornerstone of Iran's strategic depth and its launch pad in terms of influence in the Middle East. At the same time, however, such a "realistic" argument of Tehran's relative lack of flexibility in replacing Assad with a similarly-minded verb - a transformation that might have endangered, or at least drastically reduced - the Syrian civil war. He does not give. Over the past years, Iranian authorities have resisted in a variety of ways, against Assad's withdrawal from power as a "prerequisite" for peace talks and for the formation of a transitional government, and against the conduct of the general election that Bashar al-Assad has been involved in. The future of Syria has been emphasized

There are several reasons why Iran's support for Syria and Bashar al-Assad's sovereignty and the full entry into the defense.

1. The strategic importance of Syria as a united and secure;

2. Compensation for Syria's aid to Iran during the sanctions and the Iraqi war against Iran;

3. With the help of Syria, Iran intends to make it clear to its other allies and friends that in no circumstances will it leave its friends alone and are always loyal to defend and support the countries and movements under its protection under any circumstances.

4. Fighting and destroying ISIL outside the borders;

5. Defending the privacy of Hazrat Zainab Salam Allah Ali;

6. Syria has always been a bridge between the Islamic Republic of Iran and Lebanon's Hezbollah in order to strengthen the military and economic strength of Hezbollah in Lebanon.

7. Tie the security of Iran to Syrian security;

8. Syria is a trusted friendship for Iran's relations with the Arabs (it is not currently possible due to the Syrian crisis, and the Syrian regime itself is under pressure in the Arab League)

9. Bringing the borders of Iran to the borders of Israel to pressure the country;

10. Defending Syria in the direction of the issuance of the revolution.

11. Iran considers the protection of the oppressed Syrian state under the pressure of the West, ISIL, Saudi Arabia and Israel. It has a religious duty and religious duty.

12. Syrian geopolitical position for Iran;

13. Assistance in balancing power in the region;

14. Show Iran's Power against Saudi Arabia and Turkey;

15. Strengthening Iran's bargaining in regional and international political affairs;

All of the above can partly solve the causes of Iran's help to Syria and answer some of the questions. But the most important reason for Iran's support for the Syrian government seems to be that Syria is in the centrepiece of resistance. The geopolitical position of Syria and the struggle and resistance of the country against the tyranny and domination of some countries in the region, especially Israel, as well as the obstruction of US goals in the region, have encouraged Iran to support Bashar al-Assad, Iran believes that supporting a country that is facing a Israel, which is the usurper of the Palestinian Territory, as well as America, which is a bullying and dominant, is a task that emphasizes both the constitution and Islamic teachings. Although Iran suffered a lot because of this support, But Iranian officials consider the value of preserving Syria's sovereignty more than these costs. Forty years ago, the Syrian government has played a big role in strengthening the opposition and the Palestinian movements against the aggressive and oppressive policies of Israel and the United States.[116] This is why Iran has always been and will be with Syria. The Islamic Republic of Iran understands well that Syria's failure for Iran will be very costly. Hence, Iran is not happy to deal with anyone in Syria's sovereignty. Talking about going to Bashar al-Assad and changing Syria's positions for Iran is a retreat. Tom Daniilon, a US national security adviser in December 2011, states: "The end of the Assad regime will lead to Iran's biggest

---

[116] Hossein Salimi, Mojtaba Shariati, "Interests of the Islamic Republic of Iran Continuation or discontinuation of support for the current Syrian regime?" *Defense Policy Magazine (Iran)*, Vol. 17, No. 89, 2014, p. 83.

retreat in the region and to overcome the balance of strategic forces and change it in the region against Iran."[117]

Some argue that Iran has kept the war within the borders of Syria and are trying to defeat the enemy there. And they argue that if we fight in Syria, we should fight ISIS inside Iran. Ayatollah Khamenei expresses this point. The leader of the Islamic Republic, Ayatollah Khamenei, during a visit in November 2016, confirmed to the families of some army commanders who had been killed in Syria. "If they were not stopped by the abusers and terrorists who were the source of American and Zionist hostility, we had to fight in Tehran, Fars, Khorasan and Esfahan, and they fired the enemy."

---

[117] Seyyed Hossein Mousavi, *"US Dual Logic for the Syrian crisis,"* Tehran, Strategic Studies Research Institute Publishers, 2011, p. 25.

5. Relations between Iran and Israel

On May 15, 1948, the Israeli regime issued a Declaration of Independence at the same time as the withdrawal of British troops from Palestine.[118] In this section, we consider one of the most important foreign policy issues of the Islamic Republic of Iran since the 1979 revolution. A clear understanding of the Iranian-Israeli approach and orientation will help a great deal of understanding of issues such as Iran's support for the resistance axis (Syria, Lebanon, the Palestinian liberation movements, Iraq and Yemen), the nuclear issue, and Iran's relations with the United States and the Arab countries. Made because the issues that have been expressed in most cases are directly linked to the relationship

Before the Revolution, Mohammad Reza Pahlavi identified Israel as a de facto in 1950. Which was recaptured during Dr. Mohammad Mossadegh's time, however, with the fall of Mossadegh's government and consolidation of the foundations of the reign of Mohammad Reza Pahlavi, after the coup of 19 August 1950, relations between the two countries were restored and lasted until the end of the Shah's fall in 1979.[119] It should be noted that under the premiership of Mohammad Sa'ed, the government of Iran, within a period of about 1 year after the formation of Israel (March 14, 1950), recognized the country in a de facto manner and established its consulate in Jerusalem.[120]

But with the victory of the Islamic Revolution, the convergence factors replaced the divergent factors, and the Israeli embassy became the embassy of Palestine, and Israel lost not only its main regional ally but also the most united country to its number one enemy. Opposition to Israel became one of the main essences of the Islamic Republic of Iran and became a constant axis of Iranian foreign policy.[121]

---

[118] Morteza Law, Hidden Diplomacy, *"an Investigation into Iran-Israel Relations in the Pahlavi Age, Reviewing the Historical Background,"* Tehran, Tabarestan Publications, 2002 , p. 173.

[119] Velayati, "Ali Akbar*, Iran and Palestinian Affairs,"* Tehran, Center for Documentation and Diplomacy, Ministry of Foreign Affairs Publishing, 2001, pp. 27-30.

[120] Alireza Azghandi, *"Iran's Foreign Relations (1941-1979),"* Tehran, Ghoos Publication, 2005, p. 410.

[121] Mousavi Far, Rezaie, Iran-US Relations; the Israeli Question, Political Quarterly (Iran), Vol. 46, No. 2, 2016, p. 501.

Indeed, the policy of "neither East nor West" was the rejection of the East and West bloc. This transformed the Middle East's relationship, which at its head was challenging the principle of Israel's existence, the country that was then a regional actor, had a strong backer in the United States. This has cost enmity to Israel for Iran. Because the US government is influenced by Israel in its regional policy in the Middle East, the United States does not allow Israel to threaten anyone.[122]

The existence of Israel has provided a privilege for the supranational powers in order to secure their own interests in the region through this regime. Israel, as a threat to regional opposition governments, has always been a source of control and control over the Muslim states of the Middle East. The influence of the political and economic dominance of the superpowers and the reduction of the costs of direct military presence in the region are among other consequences of the existence of a regime such as Israel. Transatlantic powers will not deny their diplomatic and economic assistance to Israel, in order to remain an active, powerful, and loyal element of the Middle East to serve their interests. The Islamic Republic of Iran regards Israel as an instrument of arrogance and has always fought for the colonial purposes of the superpowers, and is trying to awaken other Muslim nations to awareness and combat them. [123]

At the very beginning of Iran's revolution, Imam Khomeini described Iran-Israel relations as "the political relationship with Israel and America as the main threat to Islam and Muslims."[124] In the same vein, the interim government of the Islamic Republic of Iran, on February 18, 1979, announced that Iran had broken ties with Israel, invited Yasser Arafat to Iran as a sign of opposition to the Zionist regime.[125] Ayatollah Khamenei states in the entry of the Palestine Encyclopaedia on

---

[122] Seyyed Hassan Amin, "International System and Islamic Republic of Iran," Tehran, *Journal of Cultural Research (Iran),* Vol. 5, No. 12-13, 1999, p. 72.
[123] Mehdi Nateghpour, Abbas Mehri and Fariba Azimi, *"The Causes and Consequences of the Hosniyad Khomeini's Hostage Regime with the Islamic Republic of Iran,"* Tehran, Thesis, 2013, p. 12.
[124] Seyyed Hassan Amin, "International System and Islamic Republic of Iran," Tehran, *Journal of Cultural Research (Iran),* Vol. 5, No. 12-13, 1999, p. 73.
[125] Majid Safatagh, *"Palestine Distinguished Faculty,"* Tehran, Center for Palestinian Studies, 1994, pp. 516-517.

September 8, 1994: "The Islamic Iran stands firmly and firmly in principle and consistently, and it always emphasizes that Israel must be eliminated."[126]

Along with Israel's hard-core threats against Iran, there are software threats that propagate the media against the regime and the Islamic Republic of Iran, which has created a wave of psychological warfare against Iran.

In the past 40 years, the Islamic Republic of Iran has been a constant advocate of the rights of the Palestinian people, emphasizing Islamic unity and value. Meanwhile, while some "compromise" Arabs of the Arab world are in favor of cooperating and building a peaceful and respectful relationship with Israel, Iran calls for a "peace deal" to continue the full Palestinian right, under the slogan "Death to Israel". But the majority of Arab League member states are dissatisfied with the slogans of the Islamic Republic of Iran and the direct and indirect provocations of Iran's political and religious authorities.

The main complaint of Arab governments from Iran is that the Islamic Republic of Iran, for reasons of value, with Islamic emotions and justice-based arguments, is central to the issue in which Iran really has a marginal power. For this reason, many Arab governments took on Iraq in the Iran-Iraq war, and, while silenced against Israel, they found Islamism and the issuance of revolution from Israel as dangerous for themselves. Israel attacked southern Lebanon, causing a rebellion against Palestinian resistance. [127] The Arab countries did not even support Israel at any time in the 33-day war (2006) against an Arab country (Lebanon) because of the weakening of Iran's resistance to Lebanon's resistance, preferring Israel to win.

Iran's foreign policy has had many ups and downs during the four decades following the Islamic Revolution. At a time with Saudi Arabia, South Africa's relations were in bad shape, but not only did they not break the political and economic relationship with them, but today we see good relations between Iran and Iraq and South Africa. In the case of a country like Saudi Arabia, there are serious differences over the relations between the two countries, but such differences are commonplace among the countries of the world. And Iran, despite being aware of

---

[126] Ibid, p.15.

[127] Seyyed Hassan Amin, "International System and Islamic Republic of Iran," Tehran, *Journal of Cultural Research (Iran),* Vol. 5, No. 12-13, 1999, p. 73.

some of the mistakes made by Saudi Arabia, does not in any way regard the complete failure of the relationship with a major Muslim country to be of interest to the Islamic world.

Also, it is against the principles of foreign policy of the Islamic State of Iran. Iran, even in spite of fundamental differences with the United States, negotiated a number of issues, such as Iraq and the nuclear issue, at a high level (at the level of Foreign Minister). But Israel is the only exception to Iran's relationship with Iran. The Islamic Republic of Iran basically does not regard the existence of a foreign country as legitimate, and believes that the principle and sovereignty of this country should disappear from the scene of political and economic relations of the world, so there was no appeasement in establishing relations with this Israel. When the Thesis of the Dialogue of Civilizations was presented internationally by the Iranian President (Seyyed Mohammad Khatami), the Jews of the world were not negotiated. [128]

Since the creation of Israel by the European and American Zionists in 1948, the preservation and recognition of this regime has been the central issue in the Middle East. With the advent of the Islamic Revolution of Iran, the Islamic Republic as one of the Muslim states of the region has declared its opposition to this regime and questioned its legitimacy.

The ideological conflict is considered to be the most important and root cause of the Islamic Republic of Iran's opposition to the occupation regime of Qods. The Zionist radical theories that come from the distorted Torah justify the Zionist oppression and occupation. Jewish rabbis carry out activities of more than one religious institution in society and act as pressure groups on political leaders. They consider Palestine to be the Promised Land and Divine Gifts, and therefore they do not have any rights for the Palestinians as residents and owners.

Among the other theories posed by Israel is Zionist pre-eminence. Zionists believe that the Jewish race is superior to all ethnicities and races. As well as the idea of the superiority of the Jewish religion to other religions, such thoughts of the rights of other nations are worthless and worthless. In contrast, the Islamic Republic of

---

[128] Ibid , p. 72.

Iran respects the legal rights of all ethnicities and nations and opposes this extreme Zionist idea.

The Islamic nature and values in the Iranian revolution have prevented any kind of cooperation and communication between Iran and Israel. The Islamic Republic of Iran considers itself bound to support freedom-loving movements and oppressed countries, and believes that Israel has seized and oppressed a Muslim homeland, so it is essentially problematic and does not accept the legitimacy of this regime.

Some argue that the difference between Iran and Israel is not about ideology and religion, but rather because of the rivalry over dominance over the Middle East. This theory, of course, does not seem to be right, because the Islamic Republic of Iran does not essentially accept the legitimacy of Israel as a country; hence competition does not make sense, so the difference between them is much more fundamental than this.

Although Israel at the beginning of the revolution was reluctant to have a relationship with Iran and even claimed assistance in the war between Iran and Iraq,[129] But with the victory of the Islamic Revolution, the orientation of foreign policy in Iran has changed. Iran withdrew from the West and the United States, and moved to support the Third World, not committing to colonialism and anti-Semitism, and, in this regard, took back the identification of the previous government's backwardness from the Israeli regime .And called it a cancerous cancer that must be eliminated and cut off any economic, political or cultural ties with this regime. [130]

If for Imam Khomeini the establishment of an Islamic government was their priority in Iran (internal dimension), abroad, freedom of Jerusalem and the land of Palestine were the main concern of their political thought and politics. Imam Khomeini, referring to the Zionist bond with the major Western capitalists (especially the United States), believes that the origins of the emergence of Israel are the governments of the West and the East. Israel is today supported and

---

[129] Shahbazi, Elham, Iran and Israel from Cooperation to Controversy," *Khordaman magazine (Iran)* , Vol. 1, No. 1, 2014, pp . 100-101.

[130] Ibid, pp. 101-102.

supported by all the colonialists. Britain and the United States, with military and political reinforcements, have put Israel at the disposal of Israel's deadly weapons to repeated aggression against Arabs and Muslims. [131]

Reasons for the hostility of the Islamic Republic of Iran and Israel

1. The religious nature of the Islamic Republic of Iran system

Many scholars believe that the most important reason for not recognizing the regime of Israel by the Islamic Republic of Iran is the ideological reason. For this reason, it is argued that the Israeli regime is a usurper of Palestinian territory and has no legitimacy. Hence, the Islamic Republic of Iran, as a religious government that calls itself human democracy, has cut off its relationship with the Israeli regime and called for it to be destroyed. [132]

The Islamic Republic of Iran has essentially humanitarian, anti-oppression and oppressive beliefs. Accordingly, the principles and ideals of the Islamic Revolution undermine the racist existence of the Israeli regime. In this regard, Imam Khomeini called for the formation of a state of Israel and the recognition of this regime for Muslims a catastrophe, and for Islamic governments, a suicide bombing and opposition to it was considered by the great Islamic prayer. While emphasizing the interruption of relations with the Israeli regime and the declaration of the state of war between Muslims with this regime, they declared any political, trade, and military affiliation with this Forbidden and illegitimate regime because, in their view, this illegitimate regime, the usurper and the enemy of all Muslims in the world is. [133]

2. Position of the Islamic Republic of Iran;

---

[131] Rouhollah, Khomeini (Imam), *"Sahifeh Noor,"* vol. 1, Tehran, Ministry of Culture and Islamic Guidance, 1992, p. 259.

[132] Shahbazi, Elham, *Iran and Israel from Cooperation to Controversy*, Khordaman: Spring and summer 2014, No. 1, p. 102.

[133] Mohammad Hosseini Moghaddam, *Negin Iran Journal*, No. 3, the Strategy of Israel in the Iran-Iraq War, 2002, p. 52.

The positions of the Islamic Republic of Iran towards Israel clearly and mainly on three pillars have created anger for the authorities of the Israeli regime:

A: Neglect and the lack of legitimacy of the sovereignty and state of Israel;

B. Support for anti-Israeli groups in the Middle East, and in particular the Palestinian and Lebanese groups involved with Israel;

C: Opposition to the Arab-Israeli peace process and the leadership of anti-Israeli movements on the international scene. [134]

In the eyes of the Israeli regime's officials, the policies and values pursued by Iran are a major threat to Israel. The regime also claims that the Islamic Republic of Iran will support Hamas and Islamic jihad, and this will end the flood of the Intifada. [135]

Mutual threats of the Islamic Republic of Iran and the Israeli regime

A: Threats of the Islamic Republic of Iran against the Israeli regime

As stated, one of the principles of foreign policy of the Islamic Republic of Iran is based on Israel's lack of legitimacy. Iran's politicians believe that Israel should disappear from the ground. Imam Khomeini says: Israel should disappear from the page. [136]

Imam Khomeini never considered fruitful political negotiations and talks with Israel to solve Palestinian issues and problems because in the eyes of this divine leader, political talks are an instrument for the continuation of the sovereignty of Israel and are the tricks that confirm the legitimacy of this occupying regime. Thus, by denying political negotiations on the part of Imam Khomeini, one way remains, and that is a military struggle to destroy this regime. As the following statements by the rejection of political games lead to the continued persecution of the Zionist

---

[134] Morteza Shams, *Israeli military security threats against the Islamic Republic of Iran"*, Strategic Studies Quarterly, Preliminary Edition No. 2, 1998, p. 177.

[135] Jafari Voldani, Asghar, *Iran's Foreign Relations (after the Islamic Revolution)*, Tehran, Ava Nour Publisher, 2003, p. 83.

[136] Rouhollah, Khomeini (Imam), *"Sahifeh Noor,"* vol. 16, Tehran, Ministry of Culture and Islamic Guidance, 1992 , p. 490.

regime's crimes, military confrontation is the only way and the basic method for the salvation of the Palestinian Muslims:

"How long has he neglected to fight the enemy of Islam and save Jerusalem from the firearm and the military and divine power, and has spent time with political work and compromise with the superpowers, and has given Israel an unrelenting period of crimes and witnessed massacres Was." [137]

From the perspective of Imam Khomeini, Camp David's agreement is one example of concurrence with the Israeli regime and the cause of his continued crimes. Imam Khomeini explicitly stated:

Camp David's agreement, and so on, is a plot to legitimize the Israeli aggression, which has changed the situation in favour of Israel and at the expense of the Arabs and Palestinians. [138]

Ayatollah Khamenei expresses the stance and framework of the foreign policy of the Islamic Republic of Iran explicitly about the plan for the compilation and identification of Israel, and considers any legitimating of Israel and assistance in the Middle East peace plan as a substitute for Muslims. He says about it:

What is called the Middle East peace process is, in our view, not a peace but a cowardly process and a compromise, and it is against Muslims to oppose any way with the Zionist enemy and the usurpers of the Palestinian Territory. Our opposition to what the Middle East peace talks say is unfair, arrogant, humiliating, and finally illegitimate. [139]

Imam Khomeini's political thoughts repeatedly point to Israel's usurpation. Take note of the following:

The selfishness and surrender of some Arab states to the direct influence of foreigners is a hindrance. Which tens of millions of Arabs can dispel Palestine from occupation and usurpation of Israel?[140]

The Islamic Republic of Iran, based on the constitution and political thought of Imam Khomeini, has always tried to reveal the essence of Israel, which is a

---

[137] Ibid , p, 60.

[138] Ibid.

[139] Soleimani, Mohammad Bagher, *"Actors in the Middle East Peace Process,"* Tehran, Ministry of Foreign Affairs Publishers, 2000, pp. 231-234.

[140] Rohullah, Khomeini (Imam), *"Islamic Revolution's Revolution and ideas of Imam Khomeini,"*Tehran, Institute of Publishing and Imam Khomeini, 2008, p. 404.

usurped state for Muslims and free nations of the world. And call this regime illegal.

In the first place, the main strategy of the Islamic Republic of Iran in the Middle East to undermine the Israeli regime has been to keep this regime within its borders. [141]

Because of the influence that the Lebanese Shiites and Islamic Palestinian groups took from the Islamic Revolution of Iran, the best strategy for Iran was to strengthen these groups in confrontation with the Israeli regime. Iran also launched a kind of alliance with the Syrian government to confront the Israeli regime.

One of the main goals of the strategic alliance with Syria is to strengthen the country against the regime of Israel. [142] In fact, Syria also plays a strategic role in Iran's relationship with the axis of resistance to help Palestine and Lebanon.

In sum, the most important actions of the Islamic Republic of Iran over the past four decades against the Israeli regime are:

• Supporting the resistance axis at the head of Syria and Lebanon.

• Creating a Popular and Military Base (Syria and Lebanon);

• The influence of software power of Iran;

• Extensive relationship and constructive engagement of Iran with international organizations and Western countries;

• Strengthening Iran's missile defense capabilities with the ability to target Israel;

• Possibility to use the psychological weakness of the ruling people of Israel in the event of a war;

• Strategic partnership with Russia in opposition to US policies;

• Supporting Liberation Movements in Palestine;

• Disclosure of the policy of support in arming the Israeli intelligence groups;

• An attempt to question the legitimacy and actions of Israel in international organizations;

• Strengthening the country's defensive and aggressive base;

• Helping hostile countries with Israel;

• Propaganda war by strengthening the Lebanese Hezbollah Foundation;

---

[141] Shahbazi, Elham, Iran and Israel from Cooperation to Controversy," *Khordaman magazine (Iran)* , Vol. 1, No. 1, 2014, p . 105.

[142] Haji Yousefi, Amir Mohammad, *"Iran and the Zionist regime from cooperation to conflict"*, Tehran, Imam Sadiq University Press, 2003 , p. 148.

• To play a key role in the development of war zones in the form of military advisers;

• Disrupting the Middle East peace process by supporting Palestinian groups;

• Strengthening the nuclear program;

• Increasing scientific growth at various levels (nano, nuclear, medical, aerospace, etc.);

• Supporting anti-Zionist anti-Jews and non-Jews. [143]

B. the threats of the Israeli regime against the Islamic Republic of Iran

Israeli leaders are calling for a global response to Iran, citing the Islamic Republic's announcement of the destruction of Israel. The post-revolutionary Israeli authorities have repeatedly and openly considered their greatest security risk to be the Islamic Republic of Iran. Former Israeli Prime Minister Shimon Peres says:

"Israel is not threatened by any country other than Iran, and this state is the greatest threat to the security and the existence of Israel." [144]

The Islamic Republic of Iran is considered as the most important threat to Israel, and hostility to Iran is clearly expressed. Israel's foreign policy is based on the isolation of Iran after the Islamic Revolution. For this reason, and given the high level of conflict between the Islamic Republic of Iran and the Israeli regime, the threats posed by the Israeli regime can be viewed in the political, security, economic and military spheres.

One of Israel's policies towards the Islamic Republic of Iran is to isolate it in the security sector. Israel is struggling to curtail Iran's influence through pressure on the United States and the West, and in cooperation with regional adversaries. Unfortunately, some positions and political decisions in Iran have strengthened the fence of other countries against Iran and have been given to Israel by excuse. Israel tries to portray the Islamic Republic of Iran as a threat to regional governments. It threatens the danger of Islamic fundamentalism originating from Iran in large Central Asian countries, and it has a key role to play in countering the danger of Islamists and introduces the Iranian government as the center of Islamic

---

[143] Javad Sharbaf, "Balance Threat; Islamic Republic and Zionist Regime," *Defense Diplomacy Journal (Iran),* Vol. 1, No. 4, 2012, p. 60.

[144] Jafari Voldani, Asghar," *Iran's Foreign Relations (after the Islamic Revolution), "* Tehran, Ava Nour Publisher, 2003, pp. 83-84.

fundamentalism in the region and the world. In this way, Iran is introduced as a threat to the internal stability of these countries. [145]

In the political dimension, Israel has always been at the heart of destroying the rule of Iran and always destroying the political image of Iran. In some cases, such as the blast of the Jewish Centre of Argentina and the condemnation of the Islamic Republic of Iran for human rights violations with the help of the United States has also been successful. [146]

Israel was the largest economic partner of Israel before the Iranian revolution. Most of the exports and imports of agricultural products were made between the two countries. But the 1979 Revolution caused a complete disruption of relations between the two countries. This caused Israel to press Iran with economic instruments. Israel's economic strength is being pursued simultaneously with the objective of weakening the economy of other countries in the region, especially Iran. Especially considering that any attempt to balance military forces requires a strong backing of economic ability. Also, the role of economic weaknesses is itself a major threat.

Therefore, Israel is pursuing a growing economic weakness of the Islamic Republic of Iran as a serious policy. On the other hand, some groups believe that US economic sanctions against Iran have been dramatically overshadowed by Israeli provocations. Economically, one of the main goals of the sanctions (in the form of missile and nuclear sanctions) is Iran's economic weakness and isolation. [147] One of the reasons why Israel was unhappy with the outcome was that the country believes it has opened the way to breathing Iran for several years. If the sanctions continued, unrest would bring the country closer to collapse.

Israel's economic policy in the form of economic supremacy in the region has threatened and threatened regional powers such as Iran. In the view of Shimon Peres (the ninth president of Israel), the Middle East is an economic region, not a cultural mix that Israel can play in the first place; this view threatens Iran's national security. [148] In this regard, the Israeli regime is trying to prevent Iran's economy

---

[145] Ibid , p, 84.

[146] Morteza Shams, "Israeli military security threats against the Islamic Republic of Iran", *Strategic Studies Quarterly (Iran),* Vol. 1, No. 2, 1998, p. 189.

[147] https://donya-e-eqtesad.com.

[148] www.irdc.ir, 1392/09/01.

from flourishing and its scientific and technical development by creating an obstacle to the cooperation of the Islamic Republic of Iran in the world. [149] In general, Israel's attempt to remove itself from the scope of sanctions and economic isolation, on the contrary, seeks to impose such sanctions on Iran.

In the military dimension, equipping the Israeli army with a nuclear bomb is the greatest military threat against Iran. Israeli weapons are such that their range extends beyond the territory of the neighbouring countries of the Islamic Republic of Iran. The Islamic Republic of Iran, despite its assertion of its military power in defence of its country, still considers Israel to be a threat to itself, given its predecessor's history of starting a war with other countries. Threats to Israel's nuclear threat although serious for the whole of the Middle East, its threat reflects Iran more at risk. [150]

Religious Foundations in Opposition to Israel

The defence of the Islamic Ummah is a fundamental principle in the foreign policy of the Islamic State (Islamic Republic of Iran), and in the second chapter it is explained in detail about this principle. One of the indisputable religious duties of each Muslim, as well as one of the general principles of foreign policy of Islamic states, is to defend the Islamic Ummah.

In the religious foundations, helping those who have been expelled and oppressed from their homeland is considered an obligatory divine duty. And some verses of the Qur'an indicate this. Allah says in the Quran around this.

"أُذِنَ لِلَّذِينَ يُقَاتَلُونَ بِأَنَّهُمْ ظُلِمُوا وَإِنَّ اللَّهَ عَلَى نَصْرِهِمْ لَقَدِيرٌ [151]"

Permission [to fight] has been given to those who are being fought, because they were wronged. And indeed, Allah is competent to give them victory.

الَّذِينَ أُخْرِجُوا مِنْ دِيَارِهِمْ بِغَيْرِ حَقٍّ إِلَّا أَنْ يَقُولُوا رَبُّنَا اللَّهُ وَلَوْلَا دَفْعُ اللَّهِ النَّاسَ بَعْضَهُمْ بِبَعْضٍ لَهُدِّمَتْ صَوَامِعُ وَبِيَعٌ وَصَلَوَاتٌ وَمَسَاجِدُ يُذْكَرُ فِيهَا اسْمُ اللَّهِ كَثِيرًا وَلَيَنْصُرَنَّ اللَّهُ مَنْ يَنْصُرُهُ إِنَّ اللَّهَ لَقَوِيٌّ عَزِيزٌ [152]

---

[149] Morteza Shams, "Israeli military security threats against the Islamic Republic of Iran", *Strategic Studies Quarterly (Iran)*, Vol. 1, No. 2, 1998, p. 189.

[150] Ebrahim Mottaghi, "Analysis of the Behavior of Israel against the Islamic Republic of Iran", *Journal of Defense Policy (Iran)*, Vol. 5, No. 18, 1997, p. 182.

[151] Hajj surah, verse 39.

[152] Hajj surah, verse 40.

"[They are] those who have been evicted from their homes without right - only because they say, "Our Lord is Allah." And were it not that Allah checks the people, some by means of others, there would have been demolished monasteries, churches, synagogues, and mosques in which the name of Allah is much mentioned. And Allah will surely support those who support Him. Indeed, Allah is Powerful and Exalted in Might."

Those believers who were unjustly displaced from their homes (and had no crime), but said: Our Lord is one God. And if God (do not let warts) and repentance of some people to others, then the monasteries and the late, the churches and the mosques where (prayer) and the mention of God will be great, all will be ruined and ruined. And whoever helps God, of course God will help him, that God is the ultimate authority and ability.

Therefore, ideologically and religiously, it is obligatory to help the people of Palestine and fight and hostility with Israel. In the Israeli-Palestinian issue of Islamic esteem, the Ummah of Islam has been disturbed and Muslims should not be religiously dominated by the influence of foreigners and if it happens in such circumstances, it is obligatory for other Muslims to help. Because Palestine is part of the body of Islam, Another religious factor is the need for hostility against Israel to occupy Jerusalem as the capital of Israel, and this year the president of the United States (Trump) declared Jerusalem the capital for Israel. Jerusalem is the land that each of the religions of Islam, Christianity, and Jews give it a special sacredness. This place is very important for Muslims due to the lack of a mosque that preceded Mecca's first qiblah Muslims.

In a narration from the great Prophet Muhammad (PBUH), it is quoted that: "Anyone who cries out to sue any oppressed (whether Muslim or non-Muslim) who needs help from Muslims, but who is not helping him, is not a Muslim. [153]
In Sahih Bukhari, the Prophet also narrated that "All Muslims are brothers, do not oppress each other, and resist each other in front of enemies and do not let them go. [154]

---

[153] Naser Makarem Shirazi, *"the Message of the Qur'an,"* Qom, Amir Al-Momenin Publications, 2009, p. 358.

In the mosque of Ahmad ibn Hanbal, it is also narrated from the Prophet that: "Whosoever despised unto him a believer, but does not help him, while he is able to receive his help, Almighty in the day of resurrection shall he dishonour him. [155]

What was said was the need to support Palestine and fight against Israel as a usurped state in a documented Islamist state based on religious principles. But rationally, this can be proven. The rationale is that all Muslims are considered a unitary nation, in which case any oppressor to any Islamic country or Muslim population would be oppressed to all of them, defending them is self-defense and is required by reason of reason. Therefore, some jurisprudents consider the need for defensive jihad against the infidel infidels and Zionists against Islamic countries, the killing of women men, property stealing, the destruction of temples and mosques as a necessary and rational necessity. [156] It can also be reasonably stated that the defence of oppression and hostility with the oppressors and invaders is one of the most prominent rationales that are always cited in the context of rational goodness.

Allameh Morteza Motahari says about the human and religious duty of helping the Palestinians:

"Whenever a group does not fight with us, it has committed a gross oppression to a number of human beings, and we have the power to save those other people who have been raped, if we do not save, in fact, the oppression of this tyrannies, We have helped against that oppressor. Wherever we are, no one has violated us, but

---

[154] Mohammad bin al-Hassan al-Hur al-Amli, Wasā'il al-Shī'a, vol. 11, vol. 59, 2014, p. 108.

من سمع مناديا ينادى يا للمسلمين فلم يجبه فليس بمسلم. »

Whoever hears and does not answer the Muslim help is not Muslim.

[155] Mohammad Hassanin Hikel, Al-Jihad and Al-Taqul al-Sayyas al-Shariah, Beirut, Vol. 1, 2003 p. 83.

"المسلم اخو المسلم لا يظلمه و لا يسلمه » اى «يدافع عنه و لا يسلمه عنه و لا يسلمه لمن يريد به مكروها او اعتداء"..

[156] Abdolmolk Ibn Hisham, *Sira Ibn Hisham*, Volume 1, Beirut, Dar al-Kotb Al-Ulamyyah Publications, 2006, p. 141-142.

"لقد شهدت فى دار عبدالله بن جدعان حلفا ما احب ان لى به حمر النعم ولو ادعى به فى الاسلام لا جبت "

Indeed, I witnessed a covenant at Abdu'llah bin Jayatan's house that I am not happy to exchange it with anything else, and if I am invited to do so in Islam, I will respond and accept.

some other people who may be Muslims and may not be Muslims, if they are Muslims, such as the Palestinians, whose Israelis have displaced them from their homes, They have taken their property, they have committed various types of oppression to them, but they do not do anything for us now, is it lawful for us to resort to these Muslim oppressions to save them? Yes, this is also permissible, but it is obligatory, this is not an elementary one. This, too, is helping the oppressed person to escape the oppression of the oppressed Muslim in particular. "[157]

6. Iran's Nuclear issue and Sanctions

The use of economic sanctions has a long history of international relations. The oldest sanctions are Pericles's limitation on imports of goods from Megara to the Athens market in 432 BC. [158] Today, economic sanctions are a substitute for wars and conflicts and as an important tool in foreign policy[159].

The boycott is a negative economic strategy that is used instead of hard tools such as war.[160] Galtung "action by one or more international players against one or more other actors to punish the sanctions objectives by depriving them of some of their privileges and compelling them to comply with some of the important norms for sanctioning"[161]

The United States has imposed the most sanctions against other countries, so that two thirds (67%) of sanctions against the United States before the 1990s were

---

[157] Morteza Motahhari, "*Jihad*," Tehran, Sadra Publication, 2005, pp. 29-30

[158] Thucydides ، "*History of the Peloponnesian War ،New York (translated by Warner R.)*," Penguin Books , 1972, p. 56.

[159] Toghani, Mehdi, Derakhshan, Morteza, "Analysis of the Effect of Economic Sanctions on Iran and its Coping Strategies," *Strategic Quarterly*, No. 73, 2014, p. 119.

[160] Ayatollah Khamenei's statement among students: 6/8/2016-

(http://farsi.khamenei.ir/speech-topic).

[161] Galtung, J. *On the Effects of International Economic Sanctions,* World Politics , 1967, vol. 19 , p. 15.

committed by other countries.[162] And after 1990 (the collapse of the Soviet Union), the US share in the number of sanctions increased to about 92 percent of the sanctions in the United States between 1990 and 1999. And 35 countries (42% of the world's population) were in the US sanctions, and now the US is using this foreign policy tool to influence its demands against other countries.[163]

One of the most widely used words in Iran's political relations (after the 1959 Islamic Revolution) and the West is the sanctions keyword, which was first introduced by the United States in 1979 (due to the attack on the US Embassy in Tehran). After several years in the United States, under Bill Clinton's presidency, they imposed a boycott of investment in the Iranian oil industry by the Demento law.[164]

But some of the world's oil giants invested in Iran without paying attention to the law of Delta due to the high profitability of oil investments. In George Bush's time, despite the cooperation and cooperation of the Iranian government (Seyyed Mohammad Khatami) with Western governments, Iran was again the centrepiece of evil, and sanctions against Iran were laid down on terrorism and human rights. But despite all these sanctions due to high oil revenues and the lack of significant political and economic ties between Iran and the United States, US sanctions did not have much impact on the development of Iran. But at the time of Mahmoud Ahmadinejad's presidency, the situation changed, and the United States was not alone in boycott. After the adoption of six United Nations Security Council resolutions passed between 2006 and 2010 against Iran's nuclear program, in addition to the United States, the EU also boycotted Iran. The success of the US in building a consensus on Iran was a success for US foreign policy, they brought with them strong countries like China and Russia and some of its neighbours, like Qatar and the United Arab Emirates, which was unprecedented and isolated. Iran

---

[162] Doxey, Margaret P. *"Economic Sanctions and International Enforcement*, London: Basingstoke, Macmillan, 1980.p. 42.

[163] Alexander, Kern ,"*Economic Sanctions Law and Public Policy*," published in Palgrave Macmillan, 2009.pp. 8-16.

[164] R Feathers, L, "Economic Sanctions and Their Effect on the Energy Industry", *Texas International Law Journal* (Iran) , Vol. 1, No. 1, 18, 2001 , p .55.

led Insurance, aviation, petrochemicals, Iranian oil sales, transferring money to Iran, shipping, the Central Bank of Iran, some Iranian personalities and many other crippling sanctions against Iran, and the economic and political situation in Iran was in a very bad condition.

The boycott is now being applied as a punitive measure against the people, the government and the government of Iran. Many sanctions have been imposed by the United States and some of its allies against Iran on various grounds, such as human rights abuses by Iran, support for terrorist groups, missile sanctions and sanctions against Iran due to Iran's nuclear activities. But among the statements made, the nuclear sanctions against Iran, which were carried out since 2006 with the referral of Iran's case to the UN Security Council, resulted in Iran's political and economic pressures in the form of six resolutions adopted by the UN Security Council Enter, In this section, attempts have been made to investigate Iranian sanctions with emphasis on the nuclear issue.

Most of Iran's sanctions were unilateral before 2006. After this year, with the consensus that the United States created against Iran over the risk of developing nuclear weapons, many countries, including the European Union, joined the United States in a crippling boycott against Iran. Many analysts believe that this has led the Islamic Republic of Iran to change with the arrival of Rouhani's government (1392) and to negotiate restricting nuclear activities. Of course, there is another theory, and Iranian officials also agree that Iran's scientific progress in the field of nuclear science has forced Western countries to ask Iran to negotiate. But it seems that the pressure exerted on Iran by sanctions, as well as Iran's rapid progress in nuclear activities (which has caused Western concern for nuclear weapons), are the two main reasons for this bilateral boycott of talks. To be One of the benefits of negotiations for Iran was that the sanctions had undergone many changes as a result of the end of the nuclear talks and achievements, with some of them fully abandoned in the first week (Security Council sanctions), another part After a year has been completely abolished (European Union sanctions), others have stopped like nuclear sanctions in the United States.

Although unilateral and multilateral sanctions left a lot of negative effects on Iran's economic growth and isolation, several factors led to less effective sanctions. Factors such as the oil revenues of the Islamic Republic of Iran, the adoption of a development strategy for import substitution, world competition in investing in Iran due to many profits (although this investment was risky), lack of cooperation with some emerging economies with sanctions against Iran and The existence of overseas banking led to a diminished effect of crippling sanctions, if not, the Iranian economy would be completely destroyed and the Iranian revolution would be at increased risk.[165]

On the contrary, there were several exacerbating factors that affected the sanctions: Unilateral sanctions of some:

Countries; Multilateral sanctions on the UN Security Council and the European Union;

The formation of a global consensus led by Western countries against Iran;

Internal dissatisfaction in Iran like 2009;

Sanctions on Iran's investment and purchasing oil;

Closing roads to circumvent sanctions;

Iran's dependence on the dollar and euro;

Raw materials in Iran, Iran's dependence on new technologies;

Iran's inability to manage public opinion in the countries of the world;[166]

Although some important nuclear sanctions, such as the UN Security Council, have been lifted, But at present, one of the most important threats to the Islamic Republic of Iran is sanctions that threaten the national security of the Islamic Republic of Iran. Sanctions imposed by some international institutions and countries on the Islamic Republic of Iran and its effects have been clearly outlined

---

[165] Thucydides ، *History of the Peloponnesian War" ،New York (translated by Warner R.),* Penguin Books, 1972, p. 116.

[166] Ibid, pp, 116-117.

in numerous articles and books[167]. The most obvious of these effects can be found in the reports of international economic institutions, such as the International Monetary Fund and the World Bank.

The main purpose of Iran's sanctions is to weaken, to create political and economic instability, and to prevent its political positions and revolutionary goals toward changing Iran's behaviour. This change in behaviour involves Israel's identification, a shroud of Iranian support for the resistance axis, non-intervention in Syria, the weakening of the Iranian defence system, nuclear issues and human rights. [168]

In addition to initial sanctions, the Islamic Republic of Iran has also imposed a second-hand sanction. Governments, in enforcing sanctions, naturally penalize their own agents, whether real or legal, against sanctions, the sanctions are called "initial sanctions". But in some cases, governments have stepped up and punished citizens of other states against violations of sanctions, which in the term is called "secondary sanctions". Although experts have spoken out in detail about the legitimacy of these sanctions, many attempts have been made to counter the expansion of these sanctions.[169]

UN Security Council Resolution 1929 contains a resolution on Iran's nuclear program, endorsed by 12 votes in favour, 2 against and 1 abstentions on June 9, 2010, and imposed severe economic sanctions on Iran. The resolution was issued by Iran in the wake of non-implementation of the provisions of resolutions 1696 (2006), 1737 (2006), 1747 (2007), 1803 (2008), 1835 (2008) and 1887 (2009).

Following the adoption of six United Nations Security Council resolutions in Iran's nuclear case, Western countries, by imposing economic sanctions under different

---

[167] Sahar Ahdiyyih, S. *The Impact of Economic Sanctions on Iran's Economy And Foreign Policy*, thesis submitted for degree of Master of Public Policy, Georgetown University ‹2011.

[168] Rodman, K, *"Sanctions beyond Borders: Multinational Corporations and U.S."* Economic Statecraft, Rowman & Littlefield, Oxford , 2001. Meyer, J "Second Thoughts on Secondary Sanctions", Journal of International Law, University of Pennsylvania, Vol. 30, Issue3, 2009.

[169] Ibid.

headings, have targeted the Iranian economy as a strategic analysis of sanctions imposed on the Islamic Republic of Iran. The most important efforts in this direction are seen by the United States through the adoption of sanctions legislation or the issuance of executive orders; One of the most important examples of these laws and regulations can be the sanctions law of Iran (1996), Iran's Comprehensive Sanctions and Accountability Act (2010), Executive Order 12925 (August 1994), and Executive Order 1390 (November 2011).[170] The European Union has, in conjunction with these sanctions, imposed restrictions on the rules, regulations and regulations of the Council of Europe, especially in 2012.

Sanctions on Production and Preservation of Nuclear Weapons

All pressures and sanctions in Iran are taking place in recent years, when the Atomic Energy Organization considers Iran's activities as peaceful, and senior Iranian officials have always emphasized the unmanageability of nuclear weapons.

Ayatollah Khamenei emphasized in various ways its opposition to weapons of mass destruction, nuclear and chemical weapons, and reciprocally the right of all countries to acquire and develop science in all fields, especially nuclear energy. Peaceful Purposes, They spoke in this regard on a very important point, which could be called the "nuclear weapons embargo".

For example, Ayatollah Khamenei said in February 2009: "We do not believe in atomic bombs, we have no atomic weapons; we will not pursue them. According to our religious beliefs, our religious foundations, using such weapons of mass destruction, Is forbidden, it's forbidden. "And in another lecture, "Nuclear Weapons have very important juridical and rational foundations." [171]

Somewhere else, they say: the controversy that they are launching is aimed at stopping us. They know that we are not looking for a nuclear weapon. It's not really our own nuclear weapon, in addition to being intellectually theoretically and

---

[170] Delaware Pourghadan, Mostafa and Jalil Mohebbi, *"Dimensions, Objectives, and Sanctions of the Islamic Republic of Iran*, Basij Lawyers Organization, 2012, p. 97.
[171] Statement by Ayatollah Khamenei, "Supreme Leader of the Islamic Revolution of Iran" in the lesson of jurisprudence, 27/12/2016 –

(http://farsi.khamenei.ir/speech-topic)

fiqh. We perceive this as a contradiction, and we consider this to be a false move, we consider the use of these weapons as "great sin," keeping us a "frivolous task" and never pursuing power. We do not consider authority in nuclear weapons. We can break the nuclear-weapon-based authority.[172]

Ayatollah Ali Khamenei states that Western countries know that Iran's goal is not nuclear weapons, but that the pretexts set out to stop Iran's progress. All this is a trick and blow to eliminate the components of the power of the Islamic Republic of Iran.

In addition to Iran's nuclear issue, there are other issues that have pushed Iran to sanctions against Iran, as follows:

1. Behaviours contrary to the international custom of Iran (such as the occupation of the American Embassy in Tehran);
2. Enemies and Iran with the existence of Israel have led to sanctions against Iran.
3. Iran's support for liberation and Islamic movements (such as Hamas and Hezbollah);
4. Iran's support from countries such as Yemen, Syria and Iraq;
5. Iran missile program;
6. Violation of civil liberties and human rights;
7. Iran's opposition to the Middle East peace process;
Any of the above can be a pretext for pressure and sanctions on Iran, but it does not seem to be the main reason for the embargo. Because around any of the above, other countries along with Iran should be sanctioned for the reasons, but this has not happened for those countries. So the question is why Western countries have only crippled sanctions against Iran? Does Iran have a mechanism to deal with economic sanctions? What should be done religiously, if a country is in such a situation?

The main reason for Iran's sanctions relates to the nature and objectives of the Iranian revolution, which is based on Islamic principles and values. And pursue the

---

[172] Statement by Ayatollah Khamenei, "Supreme Leader of the Islamic Revolution of Iran" in a meeting with nuclear scientists, 21/02/2012 –

(http://farsi.khamenei.ir/speech-topic)

ideals that jeopardized the interests of the United States and its allies. It would appear that the Islamic Republic of Iran would veto all the allegations raised by Western countries. In other words, if it does away with its opposition to Israel, it will completely shut down its nuclear activities, set aside Islamic human rights, and do what the West says, does not disturb the Middle East peace process, and even America and His allies are raising a new excuse to boycott Iran. What satisfies the United States is to change the nature and authority of the Islamic Republic of Iran. And it is not satisfied with this and it is impossible for Iran to do this.

The Washington Post, quoting a senior US official, admitted that Osama administration's goal of imposing sanctions against Iran was to undermine the country's system by provoking public dissatisfaction in Iran. The American newspaper acknowledged that the American effort to impose unilateral sanctions on Iran to cause general dissatisfaction and the abandonment of the Iranian regime. As a result, the goal of sanctions against Iran is to change its system, indicating that Washington has withdrawn from diplomacy and is taking steps towards economic warfare.

Given what has been said, the United States and its allies are not satisfied with the disappearance of Iran's current regime. It is natural for Iran to respond to this kind of behaviour and, as far as possible, counteract it. Some of Iran's political actions include:

• Protecting opposition countries to Israeli and US policies;

• Supporting the Axis of Resistance;

• Preventing the Middle East peace process;

• Challenging American interests in the Middle East;

• In economic terms, Iran also has capacities that can be countered by economic sanctions against the United States and the West through precise mechanisms. Mechanisms such as:

1. Use OPEC's capacity to raise oil prices;

2. Mutual sanctions of individuals and companies in Western countries;

3. Raise tariffs on goods from countries that have banned Iran.

4. Prohibition of import of goods from sanctioned countries (for example, the ban on import of Iranian goods by Iran to Iran, which means depriving the United States of the 80 million Iranian markets.) Creating investment incentives in Iran;

5. Reduce investment risk in Iran;

6. Use of energy tools against pressure on insurgent countries;

7. Strengthening the domestic economy (resistance economy);

8. Attract investors from emerging economies like India, Brazil and South Africa.

9. The threat of complete removal of economic relations with Western-sanctioned countries and the replacement of countries such as Russia, China, India, and Indonesia and...

Resistance Economics is one of the strategies to combat sanctions

It seems that the high capacity of the Islamic Republic of Iran in terms of manpower, primary resources, oil and gas, geographic location and, most importantly, the massive support of the people, makes it possible for this country to be able to stand against sanctions and surrender Do not go west. As previously stated, Iran has no choice but to put up with great powers until it is powerful. Of course, in the political dimension of Iran, Shi'a geopolitical formation has been able to become an influential power in the region, but at the same time is very blatant. Especially in the economic dimension, Iran will not be able to play a role in the economic equations of the world and secure its economy; others will play for it, and will make it weaker by sanctions and pressure.

In 2010, the term economic resistance was first introduced by Ayatollah Khamenei in order to organize the country's economic system in accordance with current domestic and international conditions, and based on the principles of the revolution. [173] They have three definitions:

1. Resistance economy, that is, a country that is under conditions of pressure, in conditions of sanctions, in conditions of hostility and hostility, can determine the country's growth and prosperity. "[174]

2. Resistance economy means the emergence of a situation in the country's economy, which will face internal and external obstacles and will advance its growth and progress towards its high goals.[175]

3. A resilient economy, that is, an economy that allows a nation to grow and flourish even under pressure.[176]

Given the capabilities and facilities available in Iran, the best way to secure Iran's economy is to implement resilient economy policies. In the past few years, the Supreme Leader of the Islamic Republic of Iran, the executive branch is required, with the assistance of the legislative and judicial authorities, to implement the policies of the resistance economy, as expressed by Ayatollah Ali Khamenei.

In the definition of resilient economy, it should be noted that resistance is a means of identifying areas of pressure or in the present situation, and subsequently attempting to control and neutralize, and in an ideal setting, to transform such pressures into opportunities, which are certainly believers and participatory partnerships and the actions of rational and disciplined management Precondition and requirement of such a subject. Resistance is a reduction of dependencies and an emphasis on the benefits of domestic production and self-sufficiency. [177]

---

[173] Statement by Ayatollah Khamenei, "Supreme Leader of the Islamic Revolution of Iran" in a meeting with a group of entrepreneurs across the country on 9/9/2010 - (http://farsi.khamenei.ir/speech-topic)

[174] Statement by Ayatollah Khamenei, "Supreme Leader of the Islamic Revolution of Iran" in a meeting with students on 6/8/2012 -(http://farsi.khamenei.ir/speech-topic)

[175] Statement by Ayatollah Khamenei, "Supreme Leader of the Islamic Revolution of Iran" among students: 6/8/2016 -(http://farsi.khamenei.ir/speech-topic)

[176] Statement by Ayatollah Khamenei, "Supreme Leader of the Islamic Revolution of Iran" among students: 6/8/2016 -(http://farsi.khamenei.ir/speech-topic)

[177] http://banki.ir/mellat/13827-

The movement of the Republic of Iran after the Islamic Revolution in the Iran-Iraq War, and then the United States and its allies, will boycott Iran with various titles and excuses.[178] This indicates that the nature of the Islamic Revolution of Iran is denied by large and influential governments in the world and has always tried to curb Iran.

The Iranian economy has many problems and weaknesses, which makes it vulnerable to sanctions. Regarding the policies of the Resistance Economy, there are some strategies for rebuilding the Iranian economy:

• Lack of reliance on oil revenues;

• Reducing dependence on foreign product;

• Prevent crude sales;

• pursuing resistance policies;

• Trust people in economic activities;

• Control of international economic interactions to prevent smuggling of goods;

• Privatization of the economy;

• replacing tax revenues instead of oil;

• Supporting domestic production;

• Supporting knowledge based companies;

• Promote incentives for exporters;

• Diversification to attract foreign investment;

• No permission to import consumer goods;

---

[178] Alikhani, Hossein, *Sanctioning Iran: Anatomy of a Failed Policy*, I.B.Tauris & Co Ltd, 2000, P. 71.

• Transparency of the economy;

• Management of resources and energy;

• Extract Iran from a single product;

• Supporting Exporters;

• Supporting vulnerable segments of the interior and accompanying people's thoughts with the government.[179]

Although sanctions against the Islamic Republic of Iran are obviously oppressive, the Islamic Republic of Iran, based on religious teachings, is not entitled to cease from the dangers of other countries under the pressure of other countries. You should not lose sight of revolutionary ideals and values under the domination and oppression of others. Of course, at some point in time and in accordance with the circumstances and preferences for expediency, it may be temporarily withdrawn from the right for a higher expedition.

Summing up

The Islamic Revolution of Iran was able to transform the international political equations by explaining the concept of evolution based on spirituality, Islam, and the revival of religion in the world, while challenging the material schools and the anti-value creation of the domination of the world powers. This cultural resurrection that emphasized Islamic convergence and the pursuit of the global pole of the Islamic world was able to take the flagship of the fight against the cultural invasion of the East and the West. The Islamic Revolution of Iran, by presenting a new image of religion as a set of beliefs, aspirations, actions and feelings that is organized around the concept of truth-centeredness, which has a regular relationship with the political, social and economic structures; it seeks to reconstruct Islamic civilization, and the Islamic Revolution At the same time, it was able to use the power of thought software as a platform for dynamic

---

[179] Nikoo goftar Safa, Hamid Reza; Radadi, Ali, "Strategic Analysis of Imposed Imposing on the Islamic Republic of Iran (Based on the Pattern of wardan)," *Journal of Strategic Studies of Basij(Iran),* Vol. 14, No. 66, 2015, p. 77.

interaction and constructive exchanges, and thus underpin the realization of the global cultural revolution.

The Islamic Republic of Iran has been able, through the use and reliance on software power, in particular values such as Shiite Islamic culture and components such as spirituality, God-centeredness, martyrdom, anti-Semitism, etc., to bring about transformation within, and morale Injecting self-belief in people, resisting arrogant powers and potential dangers. This has led the Islamic Republic of Iran to be recognized as an example for coping with arrogance and oppression outside the borders, Muslims and free nations of the world, and acknowledging its role as an important actor on the international scene. Today, the Islamic Republic of Iran has been able to illustrate the manifestation of the realization of soft power by means of the ability to influence the behaviour of others through the resurrection of the truth of Islam and the presentation of a new explanation and interpretation of the components of spiritual power.

In short, the general outline of the foreign policy principles of the Islamic Republic of Iran has emerged in the following two cases.

1. Challenging the West's hegemony:

The result of all the principles of foreign policy of the Islamic Republic of Iran, taken from Islam, has created the platform and capacity to fight Western domination. This spirit of self-belief created in the Muslims of Iran and the world has challenged the hegemony of the West, as they now fear and feel threatened by faith, religious beliefs, and political Islam as they seek to form an Islamic state.

2. Globalization of the struggle against domination, force and arrogance:

At the head of all this is the struggle against the United States and Israel. For example, after the victory of the Islamic Revolution of Iran, liberation movements in Palestine took on a new spirit and other nations around the world supported the Palestinian people against Israel, in other words, the fight against Israel became a universal symbol, especially in Islamic countries. Meanwhile, in the last three decades, no one dared to question Israel. Today, however, there are some pressures from the Zionist lobby to mitigate these movements or perhaps to silence these movements, but the situation will actually change, and the situation will get worse for both Israel and the United States, the recent revolutions in the Middle East and the loss of The key clauses in countries like Egypt and Tunisia, and the emergence of free convoys from the heart of Europe, all represent another reality, which undoubtedly loses to the West and Israel.

CHAPTER IV
Conclusion

Conclusion:

Given what was said in the previous three chapters, it is clear that Iran's foreign policy analysis is difficult and complex. And it is impossible to analyze the realities of foreign policy of the Islamic Republic of Iran with a factor and prescribe a single theory for it. Because the Islamic Republic of Iran, on the one hand, seeks national interests and strengthens power, as realists emphasize it. On the other hand, it is seeking ethics, interacting with the international community, and acting on international commitments and treaties that liberals emphasize. On the other hand, it emphasizes the culture, norms and norms that followers of constructivist theory seek it.

This section of the study, which in fact concludes the final, will address a few important issues that are as follows:

1. Paradigm shift in the theoretical foundations of foreign policy of the Islamic Republic of Iran;
2. Feature of Acting Foreign policy of Islamic Republic of Iran
3. Respect for dignity, wisdom and expediency in the foreign policy of the Islamic Republic of Iran;
4. Task oriented position in foreign policy
5. Foreign Policy Functions of the Islamic Republic of Iran

Paradigm shift in the theoretical foundations of foreign policy of the Islamic Republic of Iran;

With regard to what has been said in the previous three sections, we can say; The Islamic Revolution in Iran led to a particularly paradigmatic shift in Iranian politics in its general form and its foreign policy in a particular way. Following this revolution, the components, sources and resources, pillars, syndromes, structures, arrangements of priorities, contexts, processes, processes and current trends in Iran's foreign policy changed in a fundamental way.[1] The major shift of paradigm of the pre-revolution after the Islamic Revolution of Iran in 1979 was based on the principles of foreign policy of the Islamic Republic of Iran. Considering what will be expressed, a better understanding of foreign policy decisions of the Islamic Republic of Iran can be made. The following are some of the most important shifts. Understanding this paradigm shift helps a lot in understanding Iran's foreign policy.

1. Change theoretical approach to concepts such as anthropology, sovereignty, the centrality of monotheism and velayat-e faqih;
2. The paradigmatic shift from the proximity to the West and the struggle against communism into the policy of "no east or west";
3. The shift from the continuation of interests with the West to the struggle against the domination and imperialist system;
4. Shift from commitment to major powers to non-commitment to domination and arrogance;
5. Shift from militarism based on people and democracy;
6. Change the insight in reading from Islam to a universal, with the right to reform corruption and justice;

7. Shift from the central government to the core of the Islamic Ummah (the importance of the interests of the Muslim world)

8. Shift from dependence on independence;

---

[1] Amir Rezai Panah, Negin Nematollahi; "Principles of Paradigm Shift in Iranian Foreign Policy from the Pahlavi Age to the Islamic Republic", *A Quarterly Scientific Research Journal on Islamic Revolution* (Iran), Vol. 4, No. 15, summer 2015, pp. 119-122.

9. Theoretical shift from cooperation and interaction with Israel to its unreliability after the revolution;

10. Changing the approach with the strict adherence to the United Nations Charter and Western laws to accept and restrict criticism of some injustices and to ignore the rights of nations; (a change in the approach from the cooperation of Tom to countries and organizations with a critical approach to some Principles and Relationships Governing in International Organizations);

11. Shift from secular pseudo-Islam and quasi-liberal Islam to political Islam and Velayat-e Faqih;[2]

Feature of Acting Foreign policy of Islamic Republic of Iran:

The term activist here means a social and political actor whose sphere of activity is internalized in the internal and external arena. One of the most important points in foreign policy analysis of each country is to explain the position of its actors. The separation between actors should be seen in their different ontology's and anthropology. The theoretical political framework of Islam, from the perspective of anthropology, is not to look at humans, not pessimistic realism, and not optimistic liberalism; it considers the essence of man as a combination of instinct and instinct, and the theoretical basis in the Islamic approach is not based on power and Rationality, but on the basis of Shari's, and emphasizes the theory of The God-centered government.[3] According to what was said, the view of Islamic teachings on the nature of man is not an extreme look that considers him absolute evil or absolute good, but to look at the nature of man in Islamic teachings based on moderate, logical and moderate man. Belief in God-centeredness, the centrality of the law, leads to the rebellious instinct of man to be rational and rational to the extent that nature overcomes instinct.[4]

---

[2] Ibid, p. 127.

[3] Shahrooz Ebrahimi; Aliasghar Sotoodeh; Ehsan Sheykhoon, "Islamic Approach to International Relation; a Comparative Study with Realism and Liberalism," *political knowledge Quarterly (Iran)*, Vol. 6, No. 12 , winter and spring 2011, P. 5.

[4] Ibid, pp. 40-42

By overcoming the innate tendencies of instinct, which is talent in the essence of every human being,[5] divine and spiritual aspects prevail over other matters. The divine man is looking at the political, social and cultural phenomena on the basis of approaching God, and he is trying to reach perfection regardless of race, nationality, language or gender. Justice, oppression, freedom, and right to seek to communicate and interact, with others, However if an instinct overcomes one's temper, animal preference, such as oppression on others, injustice, self-interest, and self-interest, prevails over good tendencies.[6] According to what has been said, instinct and instinct are two times existential of man, one that is above and divine, and is at another level. Therefore, humans can be both good and evil, and one can choose one according to their freedom.[7]

Undoubtedly, the choice of his benevolent man leads him and the choice of the evil man (instinct) leads him to ruin.[8] Human being (individual activist) has an innate motive in the Islamic society because of the rule of Islamic teachings in decision-making and the existence of divine motives to approach Allah Almighty.

Islamic activist actions, the decisions of the foreign policy of the Islamic State (Islamic Republic of Iran) based on it, can be called task logic. The basis of the task logic is action directed toward the implementation of divine rules that determine the actor's legitimate behaviour in the realm of decision-making.[9]

---

[5] Morteza Motahhari, "*Human Social Evolution*," Tehran, Sadra Publication, edited, 1991, pp. 52-54.

[6] Seyyed Jalal Dehghani Firoozabadi, "Islamic Theory of Foreign Policy: A Framework for Foreign Policy Analysis of the Islamic Republic of Iran", Foreign Relations Quarterly (Iran), Vol. 3, No. 9, 2011, p. 14.

[7] Javadi Amoli, Abdullah, "*Velayat-e Faqih*", Qom, Center for the Publishing of Asra, 2000, pp. 115-135.

[8] Morteza Motahhari, "*Fitrat*", Tehran, Sadra Publication, 1997, pp. 162-165.

[9] Seyyed Jalal Dehghani Firoozabadi, "Islamic Theory of Foreign Policy: A Framework for Foreign Policy Analysis of the Islamic Republic of Iran", Foreign Relations Quarterly (Iran), Vol. 3, No. 9, 2011, pp. 20-21.

Respect for dignity, wisdom and expediency in the foreign policy of the Islamic Republic of Iran

To understand foreign policy of the Islamic Republic of Iran, understanding the three words of honour, wisdom and expediency is very important. The observance of the three main points stated in Article 11 of the Constitution of the Islamic Republic of Iran is referred to. Ayatollah Khamenei, the Supreme Leader of Iran, has also referred to these three principles in numerous speeches. Also all international relations and foreign policy chapters of the country's development plans and the "20-Year Perspective Document for Iran is based on these three principles,[10] The importance of these three concepts in this regard is essential and constituent of Iran's foreign policy.

First, the words of the Supreme Leader of Iran will be expressed in terms of the three principles of dignity, wisdom and expediency, after which the notification of the Islamic Republic's vision of the foreign policy will be examined and, in the final analysis, these three principles will be analyzed in detail.

A: The three keys to the word "esteem, wisdom and expediency" have been expressed more than 17 times in the messages and speeches of Ayatollah Khamenei, which shows the importance of these three principles in the foreign policy of the Islamic Republic of Iran. In the following three examples it is noted:

"It is wisdom that we said:" dignity, wisdom, and expediency. "The wisdom is that you can approach the opposing positions wisely to your own positions; these are not in conflict. Wisdom and dignity and goodness are complementary; It must be nationalistic; and in the first place, it must be accompanied by the preservation of national dignity and dignity of identity, that is to say, submission, enunciation, and submission, not at the stage of heart beliefs, nor in the stage of action and contract, should not exist; that is

---

[10] The 20-Year Perspective Document for Iran is an explanation for the development of Iran in various cultural, scientific, economic, political and social fields, which has been formulated by the Expediency Council. The implementation of this vision has been carried out since 2005 in the framework of four development plans of five years. The year 1404 solar (2025 AD) is the horizon of the landscape.

possible with wisdom. Fighting and hanging out the word of hatred can be painful once, but this is not a general method. The general method is wisdom. Wisdom means with logic, Matthew Engaging in diplomacy. If you go this way, God willing, we will never stop progress. " [11]

"Dignity, wisdom and expediency are an indispensable triangle for our international communications framework. Dignity:

"الاسلام يعلو و لا يعلى عليه"

Islam is higher and higher, and no school is superior to it.

"لن يجعل الله للكافرين على المؤمنين سبيلا"

And Allah has never ruled the disbelievers over the believers.

So we have every power that he wants. Suppress power, arrogance, and arrogance in relationships with other nations. If you are a race, you are for yourself. If you have the wealth or power and technology you are for yourself. It's yours; who is not for us; why are you proud of us?"[12]

"The Islamic Republic has proven that it is not in the wake of the seizure in its relations with the countries, and is interested in equal relations that are in line with the three principles of dignity and wisdom and expediency in foreign policy, and has proved that In these relations, the material and spiritual benefits of the country and the interest and dignity of the great nation of Iran and the maintenance of peace and security in the world's political atmosphere is its main indicator."[13]

---

[11] Statement by Ayatollah Khamenei, "Supreme Leader of the Islamic Revolution of Iran" during the visit of Ambassadors and heads of political departments of Iran abroad 29/09/2011(http://farsi.khamenei.ir/speech-topic)

[12] Statement by Ayatollah Khamenei, "Supreme Leader of the Islamic Revolution of Iran", in a meeting with State Department officials on 9 July 1991. (http://farsi.khamenei.ir/speech-topic)

[13] Statement by Ayatollah Khamenei, "Supreme Leader of the Islamic Revolution of Iran" to the Hajj Consolation, April 1, 1998. (http://farsi.khamenei.ir/speech-topic)

B. The general policies of the Islamic Republic of Iran in the 20-Year Perspective Document for Iran (1384-1404Sh) {(2005-2025 AD)} on political affairs and foreign relations are as follows:

Stability in foreign policy based on principles: dignity, wisdom and expediency and pursuit of the following objectives:

• Expansion of bilateral, regional and international cooperation;

• Continue to avoid seizure in relations with countries;

• Strengthening constructive relations with non-hostile countries;

• Using relationships to increase national capacity;

• Coping with the aggressive and aggressive action in foreign affairs;

• An attempt to rid the region of the military presence of foreigners;

• Coping with the unipolarity of the world;

• Supporting the Muslims and peoples of the oppressed and the oppressed, especially the Palestinian people;

• Striving for greater convergence between Islamic countries;

• Efforts to reform the United Nations structure; [14]

Other Announcement Policies in the 20-Year Perspective Document for Iran Regarding the Orientation of Political Relations and Foreign Relations of the Islamic Republic of Iran:

• The use of political relations with countries to institutionalize the economy, increase resource absorption and foreign investment and advanced technology. Expansion of Iran's export markets and increasing Iran's share of global trade and the fast-paced economic growth prospects;

---

[14] The Final Document of the 20-Year Perspective Document for Iran (General Policy for the Fourth Development Plan of the Islamic Republic of Iran) Article 28 – (http://en.farhangoelm.ir/)

• Strengthening relations with the Islamic world and providing a clear picture of the Islamic Revolution and explaining the achievements and experiences of the Islamic Republic of Iran's political, cultural and economic affairs, and the introduction of rich Iranian art and civilization and religious democracy.

• Efforts to transform a set of Islamic countries and neighbouring countries into a regional economic and technological science and technology economy;

• Enhance and facilitate the cultural presence of the Islamic Republic of Iran in international forums and international cultural organizations;

• Strengthening the Islamic and Iranian identity of Iranians abroad, helping promote Persian language among them, protecting their rights and facilitating their participation in national development.[15]

> A: Explaining the three terms of observance of dignity, wisdom and expediency referred to in article 11 of the constitution.

The purpose of honouring foreign policy, that is, type of decisions and orientations, is to prevent the conquering and defeat of rivals.[16] The purpose of the principle of dignity in foreign policy is contrary to that which is in the West. In the West, from the dignity of nationalism, national pride and materialism are interpreted,[17] but the purpose of this term in the foreign policy discourse of the Islamic Republic of Iran is to mean invincibility against oppression, rape and excess. In this regard, Ayatollah Khamenei says:

> "We do not want to prove our dignity by relying on race and nationalism, and words that, unfortunately, the whole world, by relying on them around them, fence around them. The European Union proves that my race is supreme. One says no, my race is the best ... No, for

---

[15] .The Final Document of the 20-Year Perspective Document for Iran (General Policy for the Fourth Development Plan of the Islamic Republic of Iran) Articles 29 to 33– (http://en.farhangoelm.ir/)

[16] Reza Hagapana, "Dignity from the Perspective of the Qur'an and Sunnah, Journal of Theology and Law", p. 54, summer and autumn 2002, p. 54.

[17] Interview with the Office of the Preservation and Publication of the Works of Ayatollah Khamenei with Dr. Manouchehr Mohammadi, *Kayhan Newspaper, No. 20295, 1/9/2012,* p. 12.

ourselves, our dignity is based on the belief in the monotheism that is the property of the Islamic thought and the heart of God and the love of the servants and divine gifts and the need to serve them. "[18]

Fear of the cruel and merciless is a pest of dignity; unfortunately, this fear has dominated Muslim states and nations. However, Islamic teachings disdained any kind of flexibility with fear, and one of the most important duties of Muslims is not to be submissive to the oppressed and enemies of Islam. [19]Principles 152 [20] and 153[21] of the Iranian Constitution refer to the principle of great dignity. Respect for the dignity of foreign policy decisions of the Islamic Republic of Iran is high. If we want to mention one of the cases in the early years of the Islamic Revolution, it is possible to point out the decision of the authorities of Iran after the conquest of Khorramshahr. The city that had been freed from the attacking Iraqi state for many months, and many believed that the conditions for peace with Iraq were available and regional and international organizations such as the NAM, the UN Security Council and the Organization of the Islamic Conference Defenders of Peace. However, Iran's diplomacy system did not go under such a peace and resist Iran because of its lack of national interests and dignity, and with the continuation of the war, impose its will on the introduction of Saddam Hussein (Iraqi President of the Republic of Iraq) as an aggressor, other areas under the control of the Iraqi government Was taken back.

---

[18] Statement by Ayatollah Khamenei, "Supreme Leader of the Islamic Revolution of Iran" during a meeting with officials of the Ministry of Foreign Affairs, July 18, 1991. (http://farsi.khamenei.ir/speech-topic)

[19] Interview with the Office of the Preservation and Publication of the Works of Ayatollah Khamenei with Dr. Manouchehr Mohammadi, *Kayhan Newspaper (Iran),* No. 20295, 1/9/2012, p. 12.

[20] The foreign policy of the Islamic Republic of Iran is based upon the rejection of all forms of domination, both the exertion of it and submission to it, the preservation of the independence of the country in all respects and its territorial integrity, the defense of the rights of all Muslims, non-alignment with respect to the hegemonic superpowers, and the maintenance of mutually peaceful relations with all non-belligerent States.

[21] Any form of agreement resulting in foreign control over the natural resources, economy, army, or culture of the country, as well as other aspects of the national life, is forbidden.

The meaning of wisdom in foreign policy means knowing in a decision that is accompanied by patience, justice, and verbal truth.[22] By observing wisdom, one can find the best way to decide on problems and identify the right path from the wrong one. Wisdom means deliberate action and wise decision making in accordance with the circumstances and circumstances we are in and always with wisdom, wisdom and courage. Deciding on wisdom can solve a lot of problems.[23] Ayatollah Khamenei spoke about wise and deliberate decision making in foreign policy:

"We should not move from the emotions and disregard to the benefits and conditions and the benefits that we have to make with the world ... We may now sit down and draw friendship with an enemy that we eventually face. This is wisdom. Do not imagine that these are not Islam. No, wherever it is, it is Islam, while the Prophet (pbuh) negotiated with many (including the Jews around Medina) from the three tribes, with a clan Fought and denied the other two tribes ... Therefore, when we speak of wisdom, namely ... considering all the uses that this system can relate to that state Him. We should move accordingly. "[24]

Diplomacy has the requisites for rationality and courage. Rationality and wisdom is that it fits well with ideals and realities, which means that we do not pursue the ideals that imply imagination. At the same time, we do not pursue our goals due to realism. Wisdom prescribes that actors and political decision makers seek realistic arrogance. In this regard, Ayatollah Khamenei says:

---

[22] The Encyclopedia of the Islamic World, the Islamic Encyclopedia Foundation, derived from the article "The Concept of Wisdom", Qom, No. 6380, 2008, P. 5.

[23] Interview with the Office of the Preservation and Publication of the Works of Ayatollah Khamenei with Dr. Manouchehr Mohammadi , *Kayhan Newspaper (Iran), No. 20295, 1/9/2012,* p. 12.

[24] Statement by Ayatollah Khamenei, "Supreme Leader of the Islamic Revolution of Iran" during the meeting of the officials and agents of the regime, 1990/1/29 - (http://farsi.khamenei.ir/speech-topic)

With realism on the road of idealism, you have to go through and, in the light of realism; you have to plan for the ideals. Wisdom and rationality is the key to doing this, and its proper diagnosis is a requirement of successful diplomacy.[25]

One of the examples of the use of wisdom in decision making by Iranian authorities is the Iranian diplomacy's orientation in the Persian Gulf War (January 16, 1991). In this war, which the United States attacked under the pretext of Saddam's attack on Kuwait, some argued that the need to combat arrogance ruled that Iran would enter the war along with Iraq. But decisions based on wisdom, tactics and reason prevented Iran from interfering. Because the Iranian revolution was very young and costly to Iraq, it was not at all easy to participate in this war. But he was condemned by taking deliberate positions on American involvement and attack on the Persian Gulf War. Iran also did not intervene in any way and only condemn it after the September 11 incidents in which the United States invaded two important neighbours, Iraq and Afghanistan, but tried to declare a policy of neutrality with an active diplomacy with the wisdom of To protect the interests of the republic and to eliminate the most expensiveness without spending any more because of the attack of Saddam and the Taliban who were the main enemies of Iran and that Iran, while communicating with the two countries, would enjoy the most economic and security benefits.

In addition to the two words of glory and wisdom, expediency has a special place. It is expedient to refer to the matter of peace and to say that it is a corruptor. Some scholars call it good and good, and anti-corruption, and some others consider it a practice that benefits human beings. The term expediency refers to any natural phenomenon or human action that is beneficial and beneficial.[26]

Expectation along with dignity and wisdom is one of the key and important issues in solving emerging issues. In order to properly understand the foreign policy

---

[25] Statement by Ayatollah Khamenei, "Supreme Leader of the Islamic Revolution of Iran" ,during a meeting with the State Department officials 13/8/2014 - (http://farsi.khamenei.ir/speech-topic)

[26] Hossein Rahmatollahi, "General Purpose or Religious Purpose: The Purpose of Exemptions in Jurisprudence, the West, and the Constitution," *Monthly Mehrname (Iran)*, No. 9, March 2010, P. 85.

issues of the Islamic Republic of Iran, the term "expediency in foreign policy" should be explained. There should be no contradiction between dignity and expediency in foreign policy, because they both become meaningful together. If reason cannot be achieved by observing the principle of dignity, the wisdom decides through the other, which is the same measure of expedition, should pursue the goal. Expediency does not mean retreat from revolutionary ideals and Islamic principles, but it seeks to take the best decisions with priority in terms of reaching Islamic and revolutionary goals with regard to the possibilities, conditions and assets of corruption.

Although the three principles of dignity, wisdom and expediency form the basis of the foreign policy of the Islamic Republic of Iran, and the unification of all three principles that makes sense to this framework. But observance of dignity is more important in making decisions about wisdom and expediency and is preceded by two other principles. But if there can be no place for profit on the basis of dignity, it must be wisdom and wisdom, therefore, wisdom becomes decisive after dignity. Ultimately, if it is impossible to move and orientate diplomacy on the basis of dignity and wisdom, then it must be done with a pragmatic assessment of the decision that has the greatest benefit for political actors and governments.

Task oriented position in foreign policy:

One of the main motivations of Islamic State actors (Islamic Republic of Iran) in foreign policy is the practice of divine duty. It seems that understanding the foreign policy of the Islamic Republic of Iran is difficult without understanding the theory of home-affairs. Subjectivism is a work done with thought, optional and with an internal motive engine (human conscience). Objectivism does not aim at contradiction and loss due to thinking, such as tackiness. Also, due to the intrinsic motive force, and not being tied to the result, the actor is not disappointed and does not feel at risk.

The focus of self- Task oriented on conscience is based on divine nature. The sense of homework means the responsibility of the person against others, and in the field of foreign policy, the social aspect of responsibility is revealed. Human social responsibility is defined as the observance of divine rules in relation to one another and the human society in general, and Muslims and the Islamic society in particular, defined in terms of legal and moral duties. The responsibility of man to nature is also derived from his obligation to use the best of divine blessings in personal and social life.[27]

The task involves rationality and observance of expediency, and there is a logical relationship between the two. Because performing a task and assigning an assignment requires its recognition before acting in foreign policy decision making, to know the assignment, it was necessary to know the divine commandments. Understanding the interest, recognizing the subject matter and the meaning of the verdict is very important in understanding the right to practice divine duty. Hence, not only controversy, rationality, and expediency, but are necessary and necessary,[28] the interest in deducing the religious law and the determination of the divine duty plays a key role. The rationale of forging

---

[27] Mohammad Hussein, Jamshidi, "Imam Khomeini and assignments at the Iran _ Iraq war," *Negin Iran, Quarterly Journal of Iranian-Iraq War Studies, (Iran)*, Vol. 1, No. 4, 2002, pp. 14-15.

[28] Seyyed Jalal Dehghani Firoozabadi, "Islamic Theory of Foreign Policy: A Framework for Foreign Policy Analysis of the Islamic Republic of Iran", *Foreign Relations Quarterly (Iran)*, Vol. 3, No. 9, 2011, p. 20.

government orders plays a fundamental role, so that the criterion of issuing a ruling is the expediency of society. [29]

With regard to what has been said, the concept of Task oriented becomes clear. Subjectivism means to pay attention to action and move towards it to motivate God to obey the commandments and to satisfy him. Therefore, self-actualization is not a particular act, but a specific method of action; it may be a two-dimensional orientation and decision-making process. Individuals with different motives, but the person-oriented in taking all their actions and decisions, first and foremost, and above all, the attention to the popularity and motility of action in the eyes of God and its place in the field of obedience and religious desecration And that is the reason to act or leave his action. This kind of look for a foreign policy actor has always fuelled the invincibility, because in the event of a defeat, he also finds himself victorious.

Protecting the disenfranchised and free-runners of the world, fighting against the oppressed, the intolerance of foreign powers and the struggle to form a peace-based international community, cooperation and acceptance of divine sovereignty, including the duties of an Islamic state, However, it would not be beneficial for the Islamic State (for example, the Islamic Republic of Iran) to act as a home worker. Imam Khomeini, in this regard, states:

"Protecting the oppressed and fighting the oppressed and oppressors is a divine duty that must be pursued, there is no financial gain and profit, because we (the Islamic Republic of Iran) defend the oppressed and fight against the tyrant." This is an Islamic duty Is.[30]

The government of Islam (Islamic Republic of Iran) may be deprived of some material interests by performing divine duties, but it is important to obtain God's consent for moral, human and divine duty. With such an idea of protecting the oppressed, the confrontation with the arrogant and the priority of the Islamic world's issues is placed on the national interests of the countries in the priority of foreign policy.

---

[29] Ibid, p. 26.

[30] Rouhollah, Khomeini (Imam), *"Sahifeh Noor,"* vol.16, Tehran, Ministry of Culture and Islamic Guidance, 1992 , p. 259.

One of the important principles Imam Khomeini emphasized in domestic and foreign politics was self-sufficiency (Task oriented), regardless of the outcome that may have been incomprehensible at first glance, but the performance of Imam Khomeini and its analysis can largely be this issue. The question is whether, in any situation and in any context, the practice of duty, regardless of its profit or loss, is considered. It seems that according to Imam's performance, this question cannot be answered positively.

Imam Khomeini, in the field of preserving Islam and preventing any aggression against its values, acted in Islamic duty without any result, profit or loss, but this was not the case in all aspects of foreign policy.

The basis of foreign policy of the Islamic Republic of Iran is based on the guidance of Imam Khomeini. They believed that they repeatedly stated that we (the Islamic Republic of Iran) are obliged to work, not the result of[31] "triumph in all fields, but if we act because of the failure of our duty and duty, we should not worry because It is a victory for God to perform his duty to himself, and they say: "We have a duty to act, and we are obliged to confront oppression. We are obliged by the God of the Almighty and the Exalted with oppression we will deal with these creepers and confront these bloodthirsty people. "[32]

The conquest of the US embassy in Iran, hostile relations with the United States, the legitimacy of not knowing Israel, supporting the liberation movements, the death sentence of Salman Rushdie, and the explicit and historical message to the last President of the Soviet Union, either directly or indirectly, on the basis of home affairs Who was Imam Khomeini? Obviously, home affairs in this sense do not take into account "national interests". If our assignment is to be done, we must act, albeit at the expense of our national interests.
The sensitivity of the foreign policy actors of the Islamic Republic of Iran, especially Imam Khomeini, to the situation in the Muslim world and his interdisciplinary efforts to perform divine duty and to restore the greatness of the lost Muslims to them, reveals the role of the duty of duty in examining his views. Imam Khomeini's emphasis on the fact that "Muslims should be awakened, Today

---

[31] Ibid, vol. 12, p. 259.
[32] Ibid, vol. 1, pp. 321-322.

is not a day when Muslims each have a lonely life and they themselves have a particular life in their own countries in every country, Muslims must take care of themselves.[33]

Therefore, Imam Khomeini (RA) addressed the Islamic states and, in numerous statements to the heads of the Islamic countries, they were invited to preserve the purposes of Islam, and they were distressed by their negligence and their weakness in not enforcing the Islamic law in these countries. "Islamic states have made us like that, Islamic states, the poor have been neglected, they have shown us this day, they introduce Islam to this day." Islam was once the one who had taken half the world and had it He went ahead ... These are the backwardness of the heads of Islam; these are not Islam. The leaders of Islam, which are under the dominant position, have shown us this day; we handed over our supplies to others, and we were miserable, poor and hungry.[34] "

 Divine duty does not always coincide with the recognition of the political duty of a politician. Because the criteria of the divine duty are the criterion of the politicians, according to a set of important criteria in the view of a self-oriented person, sometimes a practice that is politically unproblematic and not definitely victorious is desirable and necessary.[35]

Imam points out in the difference between these two kinds of views, referring to acts that belong to the divine duty: "In all matters that man does, one way is that one aspect of the problem is that, one must consider. What is the result of this action that does not result? Does not it come to this destination? If he is sure that he will arrive at that destination, he will do nothing if he is not sure. One of the issues is this. There is also an oddity of issues that a person has a duty to do with God, which is the main point of a task. And the results are likely to be achieved, and probability is not going to be achieved. In these issues, which one has an obligation to act, we no longer have to be knowledgeable in those problems of science, as a result of what we want, that does not need to be learned; which is to him, to act on it.

---

[33] Ibid , p. 10.

[34] Rouhollah, Khomeini (Imam), *"Sahifeh Noor,"* vol. 1, Tehran, Ministry of Culture and Islamic Guidance, 1992, p. 282.

[35] http://www.imam-khomeini.ir/fa/n21304

And, in the same vein, they say: "We should not worry that losing luck, we need to worry that we will not be doing our duty; it is our concern.[36]

If we act on the assignments that the God of Almighty and Excellency has set for us, we will not fail to fail, whether from the East or the West, or from inside and outside, and if we do not do our homework, we have failed; ourselves, we defeated ourselves. "[37]

Political doctrines in Islam have drawn two lines for action on grafting: gravity and repulsion. Existence of gravity and repulsion is the sign of the growth and perfection of human personality. Whose advent is in friendship with God and hostility and hatred of God's enemies? Governance and political management should also embody two types of attributes, one that embodies morality and the other in oppression. If we look at the attributes of God, we see that some traits are the hallmark of the image, and some of the manifestations of the divine, in other words, are seen in some of the attributes of God's mercy, and in others, arrogant and arrogant. These two traits are seen together in God.[38]

The Holy Qur'an makes good reference to this issue and states:

"«مُحَمَّدٌ رَسُولُ اللهِ وَ الَّذِينَ مَعَهُ أَشِدَّاءُ عَلَى الْكُفَّارِ رُحَماءُ بَيْنَهُمْ تَراهُمْ ...؛»[39] "

Muhammad is the Messenger of Allah and those who are with Him are against the stubborn unbelievers, but merciful with each other and among themselves. "From this verse you can get two results:

A) From the first part of the verse, "أَشِدَّاءُ عَلَى الْكُفَّارِ" ", anti-Semitism, oppression, rejection of the oppression and negation of the domineering dominance over Muslims, but human beings are understood.

B) And from the second part of the verse "رُحَماءُ بَيْنَهُمْ" ammunition "Engagement, cooperation and kindness are understood among Muslims.

---

[36] Rouhollah, Khomeini (Imam), "*Sahifeh Noor*," vol. 5, Tehran, Ministry of Culture and Islamic Guidance, 1992, p. 18.

[37] Ibid, vol. 15, p. 70.

[38] Mehdi Jafari Panah, "*Soft Power, Functions and Components in Islam and the Islamic Republic of Iran*," Qom, Asre Javan Publishers, 2014, p. 84.

[39] Surah Fatah, Verse 29.

C) From the perspective of Islam, a person has a strong repugnance and grievance that stands firmly against the oppressed, injustice and injustice, and meets the weaknesses of the oppressed and the believers. The Islamic Republic of Iran is strong in its policies towards friends and enemies with gravity and repulsion. The main basis of gravity and repulsion of the Islamic Revolution and the system of the Islamic Republic of Iran is following the principles of pure Islam, peace be upon him and accepting the sovereignty of God. Another important point in attracting and disposing of people is the Iranian politics. The policy of arrogant arrogance of the Islamic Republic of Iran. Imam Khomeini, and then Ayatollah Khamenei, has not had the slightest justification from the first period of the revolution to this day, and this made some people who did not tolerate this matter to gradually find the angle of the system.

Another feature that has caused gravity and repulsion in the Islamic Republic of Iran is the discussion of firmness in the vote and thoughtfulness of the behaviour of the Iranian regime's rulers on the basis of Islamic principles that are committed to friends and enemies, and in no circumstances give up Islamic principles and beliefs, and have shown sacrifices against false beliefs, innovations and distortions.

Every ideology and ideology that comes across globally has attraction and repulsion; one should not expect the ideals of the Islamic Republic to be in line with it. However, these ideals endanger the interests of some, and naturally they will do their best to destroy the face of Iran, and this is obvious. What is seen in the world is sensitivities to Iran. This is a sign of the role and importance of the Islamic Republic in international equations that has been able to attract some, and stand against some who have not accepted the rule of Allah. Undoubtedly, if Iran did not have its own gravity and repulsion, and played an indifferent role in international equations, this was not so sensitive to our country.

Task-oriented ability can extend the individual from his level of ability and focus his perspective on cross-sectional goals and concrete and tangible results towards the realization of long-term goals; to achieve the goals, develop resources and provide facilities beyond apparent life Available to human beings to strengthen his social behaviour. This view naturally leads to the development of social, cultural and political capacity of the individual and society.[40]

Foreign Policy Function of the Islamic Republic of Iran:

The foreign policy of the Islamic Republic of Iran has unique characteristics that are made up of different theoretical models. These patterns include:

A. Principles of foreign policy based on Islamic teachings;
B. foreign policy based on elementals;
C. Orientation of foreign policy based on dignity, wisdom and expediency;
D. The special characteristics of the Islamic State actors, whose views ontology and anthropology are based on the mixing of nature and instinct. And religion and religion are at the center of the theory of foreign policy. According to the proposed models, the following functions can be developed for foreign policy of the Islamic Republic of Iran.

This section tries to analyze the foreign policy functions of the Islamic Republic of Iran in accordance with the models presented.

Strengthening the place of religion in international equations:

With the establishment of the Islamic Republic of Iran, religion found its place in the international equation. On this basis, the foreign policy of the Islamic Republic of Iran was based on the principle of "Nine East and the West", which, in addition to breaking the mercy of global arrogance and interrupting the interference of foreigners in the affairs of the affluent countries of the poor, offered a message and a third way to the world. Which emphasizes the following?

• Establishment and implementation of justice;

• Relying on freedom with human responsibility before God;

• Creating a favorable environment for the growth of moral virtues;

• Fighting all manifestations of corruption and ruin;

---

[40] http://www.magiran.com/npview.asp?ID=3570278.

• Ensuring the full rights of the oppressed;

• Denial of foreign domination in the political, economic, social and cultural spheres;

• Supporting the Muslims and the Oppressed;

• Strengthening the power of Islam and Muslims;

• The expansion of Islamic culture and spiritual beliefs around the world;

• Strengthening the unity of the Islamic Ummah towards the establishment of justice;

• Denying the domination of arrogant powers;[41]

The advent of software power of Iran:

The distinction of the Iranian Republic from other revolutions in the world is the Islamic, religious, and popular nature of this system. At the beginning of the formation of this government and the system, Islam as a principle in this upheaval and revolutionary movement provided the people's mobility and was the main factor in the victory of this revolution. It seems that with the advent of the Islamic Revolution of Iran, under the guidance of a clear-minded reference, Imam Khomeini, the familiar disappearance occurred, and the inner demand of Imam Khomeini came to a universal and existential demand for the revolution, in the community, which was the cause of unity and in Meanwhile, people were mobile. These movements centered around a common desire, namely, Islam, and these components of Islam were among the people creating power, and no superpower could escape it.[42]

---

[41] Mehdi Jafari Panah, Hosseinpour Ahmadi, Soft Power from the Viewpoints of Islam and Application of its Components in the Islamic Republic of Iran, *Quarterly soft power studies, (Iran),* Vol. 3, No. 8, 2013, p. 110.

[42] Mehdi Jafari Panah, *"Soft Power, Functions and Components in Islam and the Islamic Republic of Iran"*, Qom, Asre Javan Publishers, 2014, pp. 111-113.

Today, contrary to the past, culture and identity form the core of the spirit of international relations. If in the past the focus was on material and economic factors. But today, in the new ideas of international relations, the position and position of culture in the formation of political behaviour and the decision of foreign and domestic politics are the first.[43]

A look at power in the system of the Islamic Republic of Iran, and in the view of its founder, Imam Khomeini, was influenced by the principles and teachings of Islamic discourse, which has a software nature. The Islamic Revolution of Iran is essentially a cultural one whose culture is influenced by the teachings of Islam. The experience of the Islamic Republic of Iran has shown that enjoying the power of software is capable of repelling large threats such as imposed war, economic sanctions, and so on.[44]

As stated, the Islamic Republic of Iran has had its components and cultural and Islamic components since its inception, and this has led the Islamic Republic of Iran, in the light of its culture, to seek to exercise cultural power over global politics. Today, we see that the strongest resistance in the Islamic world is from the cultural area, which has made the culture and civilization of the West feel at risk. Huntington acknowledged Western renowned theorists that economies and weapons in our Islamic countries did not challenge us, but that their culture was standing in front of us and threatening our civilization. [45] Also, Joseph Nye, a well-known theorist of soft power, states: A country like the Islamic Republic of Iran, with its cultural context, which is based on Islam and Shi'ism, cannot be broken by hard power.[46]

---

[43] Hossein Pour Ahmadi, *"Soft Power in the Islamic Republic of Iran"*, Qom, Bostan Book Publishing, 2010, p. 319.

[44] Joseph, Nay, Soft Power Tools for Succeeding in International Politics, Translated by Rouhani, Seyyed Mohsen, Tehran, Imam Sadiq Publishing, 2012, p. 15.

[45] John, Bilissa and Smith, "Globalization of Politics: International Relations in a New Age," Translated by Qasem Rahchamani and others, Tehran, Abrar Contemporary Publishing, 2004, p. 135.

[46] Joseph Nay, (Joseph Nye Speech at the Council of England), Soft Power and Public Diplomacy in the 21st Century - Mohsen, Mohammadi Fomeni, Comes with Soft Power with Cultural Diplomacy in the Soft power (.http://www.farhangenab.ir)

The Islamic Republic of Iran has established a relationship between religion, politics and spirituality, which has been shown in terms of virtue, morality and justice. Based on these beliefs, the Islamic Republic of Iran presented peace, interactivity and friendship among nations, and also led to the creation of a new approach and attitude to the issue of human and divine knowledge and has a significant role for religion and ethical values in the direction of human learning and evolved the religion.

The Islamic Revolution of Iran was able to transform the international political equations by explaining the concept of evolution based on spirituality, Islam, and the revival of religion in the world, while challenging the material schools and the anti-value creation of the domination of the world powers. This cultural resurrection that emphasized Islamic convergence and the pursuit of the global pole of the Islamic world was able to take the flagship of the fight against the cultural invasion of the East and the West. The Islamic Revolution of Iran, by presenting a new image of religion as a set of beliefs, aspirations, actions and feelings that is organized around the concept of truth-centeredness, which has a regular relationship with the political, social and economic structures; it seeks to reconstruct Islamic civilization, and the Islamic Revolution At the same time, it was able to use the power of thought software as a platform for dynamic interaction and constructive exchanges, and thus underpin the realization of the global cultural revolution.

The Islamic Republic of Iran has been able, through the use and reliance on software power, in particular values such as Shiite Islamic culture and components such as spirituality, God-centeredness, martyrdom, anti-Semitism, etc., to bring about transformation within, and morale Injecting self-belief in people, resisting arrogant powers and potential dangers. This has led the Islamic Republic of Iran to be recognized as an example for coping with arrogance and oppression outside the borders, Muslims and free nations of the world, and acknowledging its role as an important actor on the international scene. Nowadays, the Islamic Republic of Iran has been able to show the manifestation of the realization of soft power in terms of the ability to influence the behaviour of others by enlivening the truth of Islam and presenting a new explanation and interpretation of the components of spiritual power.

Islamic awakening;

The Islamic Revolution of Iran revived self-confidence, culture and identity of Muslim nations, and revived the principles of religious beliefs based on the pure nature of humanity (including justice, independence, justice, liberation, anti-statelessness, and support for the oppressed) The Islamic world. Following this revolution, the hope for the rule of Islamic ideals doubled. The Islamic Republic of Iran, through raising awareness and waking widespread among the Muslim people, the deprived and deprived of the Islamic world, was able to create the spirit of courage and courage necessary for them to fight, and by creating self-control over the power and resources of the inner world and encouraging the need for recognition as much as possible. In contrast to the historical and practical experience of the liberation movement, it has increased the ventures of popular movements to fight on the basis of the revolutionary ideas of Islam.

Resistance to arrogance and Zionism and challenged their hegemony;

The Islamic Revolution of Iran, with the aim of transforming the international environment, through the transformation of thoughts and minds and the provision of mental conditions for changing international rules and norms, has succeeded in challenging the domination of the system itself, and the political message of the idea of statelessness, independence, and strategy It reveals neither the east nor the west for the world. The Islamic Revolution of Iran, while creating an intellectual and political challenge to the West, was able to draw a new pattern by relying on its software power and redefining the new relationship of spirituality and politics.

The Islamic Republic of Iran, from the beginning of the formation of the state, has a policy based on Islamic principles, and by providing clear and firm stance, strong attraction and repulsion towards friends and enemies in line with Islamic principles. One of the existential philosophies of the Islamic Republic of Iran is supporting the liberation movements around the world. The importance of this duty and mission is to a point that is even considered as a principle in the constitution and foreign policy of the Islamic Republic of Iran. Of the obvious examples, it is possible to support the Palestinian resistance movement. Also, after the victory of the Islamic

Revolution, by declaring the last summit of the holy month of Ramadan as the "Quds Day of the World" by Imam Khomeini, opposition to arrogance, especially the Zionist regime and the United States became public. This illustrates the depth of Iran's attention to the issue of Palestine and the belief in supporting the struggles of its people. The Islamic Revolution of Iran, through the promotion of the Islamic Awakening and awareness of the Islamic world, could reveal the oppression of the Palestinian people and support the Palestinians against the crimes of the Zionist regime.[47]

Revival of political Islam discourse;

The Islamic system of Iran, with its own revolution, has shown that religion can be considered as an effective element in the global decision-making system, and that the Islamic world, based on indigenous beliefs and norms, has the power and strength to formulate social and political structures. The Islamic Revolution gave this self-belief to Muslim nations, which can be understood through the exact recognition of Islamic culture and the redefinition of ideals such as independence, freedom, dignity and justice, and based on the pattern of thinking, awareness, decision-making and information on Islamic creativity. Opened the door, The Islamic revolution has been able to invoke the Islamic world to link the manifestations of modernity with religious traditions and invite man to select the positive points of modernity and its conformity with the components of religion and tradition. The Islamic Revolution of Iran presented the third place in the field of political equations internationally, which, while taking into account the western experience in political, cultural and social development, can be based on the development of religion and cultural components.

---

[47] Mehdi Jafari Panah, *"Soft Power, Functions and Components in Islam and the Islamic Republic of Iran"*, Qom, Asre Javan Publishers, 2014, pp. 205-207.

The positions and political decisions of the Islamic Republic in the international arena further illustrate the existence of diverse identities in the political and social structure of Iran, which affects the foreign policy of the Islamic Republic of Iran directly.

The Islamic Republic of Iran believes in the existence of an Islamic theory for analyzing foreign policy, and sees this theory as a general actor theory that has a generalist approach to foreign policy actor. In such a way that the Islamic State is viewed as an integrated actor whose foreign policy is derived from the decisions of the agents who are acting on it, and the Islamic State actors have the same funds and the same magnitude despite differences in views[48]. All actors in the Islamic State act in their own decisions based on a particular procedure, and the Islamic Republic of Iran is one example, so any government based on Islamic teachings will be treated in the same way.

In other words, despite the change of actress and the emergence of a new actor, the nature and principles of foreign policy are irreversible, although they may differ in the adoption of strategies and strategies, but in practice, to the unchangeable principles of Islam, all actors co-exist To make Hence, if there are many discursive periodicals for analyzing the foreign policy of the Islamic Republic of Iran, it does not mean the absence of genuine Islamic discourse, but it means the approach and strategic difference of governments to various issues in order to achieve the goals set forth in Islam. Therefore, we see that some governments have an idealistic, somewhat realistic or constructive approach to the foreign policy of the Islamic Republic of Iran and evaluate the foreign policy analysis of the Islamic Republic of Iran based on that model.

By examining theories of international relations to study and analyze the foreign policy of the Islamic Republic of Iran, it can be said that the foreign policy of the Islamic Republic of Iran is not in the direction of rejecting or accepting the dominant theories in international relations to analyze the foreign policy of the Islamic Republic of Iran. One might imagine that the policies and positions of the actors were dual after the Islamic Revolution of Iran, this claim is not correct, since the Islamic Republic of Iran has chosen a third way of directing its foreign policy,

---

[48] Seyyed Jalal Dehghani Firoozabadi, "Islamic Theory of Foreign Policy: A Framework for Foreign Policy Analysis of the Islamic Republic of Iran", *Foreign Relations Quarterly (Iran)*, Vol. 3, No. 9, 2011, p. 11.

which has a basis, ontology and a different nature from all systems. , Revolutions and governments around the world. Moreover, in foreign policy of the Islamic Republic of Iran, there are many influential factors, such as religion and jurisprudence, as the law and the basis for decision making, national interests, ancient history, geopolitical factors, and idealist goals. It's complicated and difficult to understand foreign policy. The Islamic Republic of Iran, with the choice of the slogan "neither west nor east," revealed its line with two western blocs under the leadership of the United States and Western European and Western-led countries of the Soviet Union. This position was not in the direction of confrontation and non-cooperation with them, nor in the sense of declaring war with them. But the announcement of this policy meant the rejection of their domination, the lack of dependence and the approval of their policies in pursuit of a policy independent of the great powers and the practice of Islamic teachings and principles.

The analysis of the foreign policy of the Islamic Republic is based on a special nature that separates it from all analyzes, in such a way that none of the rational and non-rationalist theories and analyzes allow the ability to understand the external behavior of an Islamic state (the Islamic Republic of Iran) Does not. Because it's theoretical framework is based on Islamic teachings. There is a fundamental issue for the decision of an Islamic state (Islamic Republic of Iran), and it is influenced by the principles of political and social jurisprudence based on Islamic teachings. This view looks at the universe differently from the framework of Western theories.[49]

Within the framework of the Islamic State's intellectual system, based on jurisprudential frameworks, there is a kind of hierarchical system and divisions of the world, states, actors, and nations, which are based on the remoteness and proximity to monotheism, faith, and divine beliefs Gets This creates a clear distinction in positions based on the Islamic state and faith with non-existent, and, as stated, this view is not seen within the framework of Western theories and is not

---

[49] Davood Feirhi, *"Power, Knowledge and Legitimacy in Islam"*, Tehran, Ney Publication, 2009, pp. 229-231.

understood in this framework. The result of this look is the orientation of the foreign policy of the Islamic Republic of Iran.

Principles and rules of jurisprudence, such as the negation of foreign domination, the lack of cooperation with the enemies of religion, the help of Muslims (oppressed), the rule of law and ordinance on all international treaties and obligations, all indicate the different approach and the decision making of an Islamic state) It is considered that the violation of the jurisprudential principles mentioned in the sacred Islamic law of Islam is a sinful act.